THE LORDS OF B

IMAGE AND REALIT
THE *COMITATUS*
IN DARK-AGE BRITAIN

THE LORDS OF BATTLE

IMAGE AND REALITY OF
THE *COMITATUS*
IN DARK-AGE BRITAIN

STEPHEN S. EVANS

THE BOYDELL PRESS

First published 1997
The Boydell Press, Woodbridge
Reprinted in paperback 1998, 2000

ISBN 0 85115 678 9 hardback
ISBN 0 85115 662 2 paperback

The Boydell Press is an imprint of Boydell & Brewer Ltd
PO Box 9, Woodbridge, Suffolk IP12 3DF, UK
and of Boydell & Brewer Inc.
PO Box 41026, Rochester NY 14604–4126, USA
website: http://www.boydell.co.uk

A catalogue record for this book is available
from the British Library

Library of Congress Catalog Card Number: 96–35358

This publication is printed on acid-free paper

Printed in Great Britain by
Athenæum Press Ltd, Gateshead, Tyne & Wear

CONTENTS

For my wife, Melody

ACKNOWLEDGEMENTS

Though it has undergone extensive revisions and a change of emphasis, since this book is derived in large part from my dissertation, I'll begin with an acknowledgement of my dissertation committee – Dr. Russell Weigley (Chair), Dr. Ruth Mazo Karras, and Dr. Robert Schwoebal, all from the History Department at Temple University – whose efforts certainly made that work (and by extension, the present book) a far better one than would have been possible had I been left to rely solely on my own expertise. My particular thanks are extended to Dr. Weigley, who managed to keep the dissertation on schedule, despite changes in my committee due to retirements and ill health. Further, I am deeply indebted to Dr. Karras, whose comments and suggestions were invaluable in the completion of the dissertation.

Though not actively involved in the dissertation, I also would like to acknowledge the debt owed to Dr. Ann Matonis of the English Department at Temple, both for her tireless efforts to teach me Old English and Medieval Welsh, and for her herculean assistance in improving the effectiveness and clarity of my writing, as well as its style. Any evidence of good writing that might be seen in the following pages is attributable in very large part to her sage advice and mentoring.

I would also like to thank Kathryn Schueler for her work in placing the data/graphics used to compile the map found in this book onto a computer disk in order to facilitate its production by the Boydell Press.

Further, I would like to take this opportunity to give my sincerest thanks to Dr. John Tachovsky, of the Department of Planning and Government at West Chester University, for his support and counsel at several critical junctures of my academic career.

Most importantly, I wish to thank Melody, my wife, for her longstanding and unequivocal support, without which neither the dissertation nor the present work would have been possible.

ABBREVIATIONS

AHR	*American Historical Review*
AI	*Annals of Insfallen*
ASE	*Anglo-Saxon England*
ASPR	*Anglo-Saxon Poetic Records: A Collective Edition*
AT	*Annales of Tigernach*
AU	*Annals of Ulster*
BBCS	*Bulletin of the Board of Celtic Studies*
Beowulf	*Beowulf and the Fight at Finnsburg* (Fr. Klaeber's edition)
CA	*Canu Aneirin*
CMCS	*Cambridge Medieval Celtic Studies*
CSSH	*Comparative Studies in Society and History*
Cuthbert	*Life of Saint Cuthbert*
DE	*De Excidio et Conquestu Britanniae*
EHR	*English Historical Review*
EWP	*Early Welsh Poetry: Studies in the Book of Aneirin*
Fortunes	*The Fortunes of Men* (in *ASPR*)
Germania	*De Origine et situ Germanorum*
Gifts	*The Gifts of Men* (in *ASPR*)
Gododdin	*Aneirin: Y Gododdin, Britain's Oldest Heroic Poem* (A.O.H. Jarmon's edition)
GOSP	*The Gododdin: The Oldest Scottish Poem*
Guthlac	*Felix's Life of Saint Guthlac*
HB	*Historia Brittonum*
HE	*Historia Ecclesiastica Gentis Anglorum*
PT	*Poems of Taliesin* (Ifor Williams' English edition)
SC	*Studia Celtica*
Senchus	*Senchus Fer n Alban*
WHR	*Welsh History Review*
Widsith	*Widsith* (in *ASPR*)
Wilfrid	*The Life of Bishop Wilfrid*

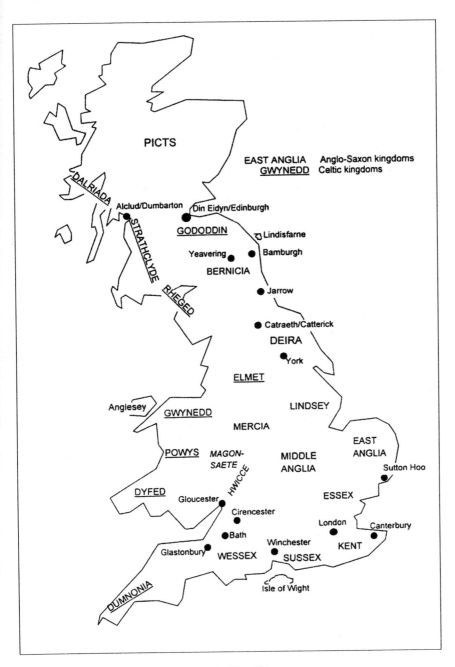

PICTS

EAST ANGLIA   Anglo-Saxon kingdoms
GWYNEDD   Celtic kingdoms

DALRIADA

Alclud/Dumbarton

Din Eidyn/Edinburgh

STRATHCLYDE

GODODDIN

Lindisfarne

Yeavering

Bamburgh

RHEGED

BERNICIA

Jarrow

Catraeth/Catterick

DEIRA

York

ELMET

Anglesey

LINDSEY

GWYNEDD

MERCIA

POWYS   MAGON-
SAETE

EAST
ANGLIA

Sutton Hoo

HWICCE

DYFED   Gloucester

MIDDLE
ANGLIA

ESSEX

Cirencester

London   Canterbury

Bath

Winchester

KENT

Glastonbury   WESSEX   SUSSEX

DUMNONIA

Isle of Wight

BRITAIN c.600

CHAPTER ONE

INTRODUCTION

The "heroic" or "Dark" Age in Britain spans nearly three centuries. The period opens during the final decades of the fifth century both with the rise of native military governments in the former Roman province and with a widespread Germanic migration to the island. It closes with the waning importance of the *comitatus*, or warband, in the third quarter of the eighth century.

Defining the years that constitute this period of Britain's history with any degree of precision is difficult at best. The period is known in broad terms: the foundation and proliferation of Germanic kingdoms, the conversion of the Germanic tribes to Christianity, the struggle for military supremacy throughout England (with the subsequent collapse of the British realms), the triumph of the Roman Church over a Celtic one, and the division of the island into two broad regions – a Celtic highland zone and a Germanic lowland zone. Above all, these centuries witnessed a great deal of movement by, and interaction between, the various peoples who inhabited the island. The rise and fall of these Celtic and Germanic kingdoms brought many changes to Britain's political and cultural landscape during this formative period.

Through all these social and political changes, the diverse cultures of the native Britons and the Germanic invaders came to share one dominant feature – the institution of the *comitatus*, or warband. Whether the culture was Celtic or Germanic, Christian or pagan, Roman or barbaric, literate or oral, the institution of the *comitatus* can be seen as the common thread that, according to our Dark-Age sources, ran through and bound together the very fabric of Dark-Age Britain. Because of its pervasive influence on the warrior-aristocracies that dominated the Germanic and Celtic cultures of Britain during this period, a better understanding of the overall period can be achieved through a detailed examination of the *comitatus*.

The present work is a social and cultural history, and one whose emphasis is on an ideal – the warband – that is pervasive in the period's heroic literature. The image of the *comitatus* is also one that found frequent expression in other written sources of Dark-Age Britain. This study attempts to impose some type of order on the chaos and disorder of this turbulent age through

1

its study of the warband by using the institution of the *comitatus* as the lens through which the history and society of Dark-Age Britain should be seen.

There are several reasons that recommend this course of action. First, the material and social requirements of the *comitatus* helped to determine the structure and economy of the society at large. Second, the ideals and the social context of the warband provided the conceptual framework in which political and military decisions were made, and also influenced the methods and means by which they would be accomplished. Consequently, an analysis of this framework should provide a better understanding of this period. It is this conceptual framework that is the province of the following chapters.

Most studies have tended to equate the *comitatus* with a lord's personal retainers or bodyguard; that is, with a lord's personal warband. This view equates the Latin term *comitatus* with the Anglo-Saxon *heorðgeneatas* (hearth-companions) and with the Welsh *teulu* (family). Instead, this book prefers a wider, more inclusive view of the *comitatus*, seeing it as including the warriors who typically resided at the hall of the king or chieftain, as well as those lesser lords (along with their own warriors) who were expected to be in frequent attendance. Thus, the *comitatus* can be equated with that body of armed men which a lord, whether king or chieftain, could muster from his own (often tribal) local resources. The *comitatus* does not include the mustering of distinct warbands from subject peoples for the purpose of creating large-scale armies.

The following pages examine the formal structure of the *comitatus* and its supporting cultural, social, and economic institutions as they are seen in the written sources – both historical and literary – that derive from this period. Also addressed is the manner and extent to which the image, or ideal, of the *comitatus* manifested itself in the historical record among the Celtic and Germanic cultures found in Dark-Age Britain. The Celtic cultures include those of "The Men of the North" (*Y Gwyr y Gogledd*), the Dalriadic Scots, and the British kingdoms that were found in present-day Wales. The Germanic cultures are those of the Saxon, Anglian, Jutish, and other groups that were active in Britain. It is against the backdrop of all these cultures that the structure of the *comitatus* can be seen and highlighted. When taken together, the following chapters present a full, rich, and detailed picture of the *comitatus* as it is seen in the written sources for this period, and offer an analysis as to how it may have functioned within the larger context of Dark-Age Britain.

This study differs from earlier, more general works in several key respects. First and foremost, it views the *comitatus* as a formal institution that possessed a definite structure and organization, and one that made use of underlying cultural and social *apparatus* to sustain its existence. This distinction of a formal structure for Dark-Age warbands is not found elsewhere, with the exception of Charles-Edwards, who saw the *comitatus* as a "central institution" of heroic aristocratic society, whose "functioning . . . required a particular adaptation of certain moral values".[1] Second, the *comitatus* itself provided the framework and parameters in which the study was organized and conducted, again in sharp contrast to earlier studies that treat the *comitatus* in a peripheral manner, in a piecemeal fashion, or not at all.[2] A third difference is the study's disregard for the common practice of treating the Celtic and Germanic peoples separately, preferring instead to view these peoples within a broadly comparative context.[3] Given the similarities in the overall social structure, economy, and material culture of the societies in-

---

1 T.M. Charles-Edwards, "The Authenticity of the *Gododdin*: An Historian's View", in *Astudiaethau ar yr Hengerdd: Studies in Old Welsh Poetry*, edited by Rachel Bromwich and R. Brinley Jones, pp. 44–71 (Cardiff: University of Wales Press, 1978), pp. 47 and 45. There have been studies which ascribe a similar importance to the concepts found in Chapters 6–9 of this study. These include: Ann Matonis, "Traditions of Panegyric in Welsh Poetry: The Heroic and the Chivalric", *Speculum* 53 (1978), pp. 667–87; Kathryn Hume, "The Concept of the Hall in Old English Poetry", *Anglo-Saxon England* III (1978), pp. 63–74; and especially Michael Cherniss, *Ingeld and Christ: Heroic Concepts and Values in Old English Christian Poetry* (The Hague: Mouton, 1972).

2 This is not to say that the features of the *comitatus* have been neglected entirely by scholars. Jackson, for example, in his introduction to his translation of the *Gododdin* (*The Gododdin: The Oldest Scottish Poem*. Edinburgh: Edinburgh University Press, 1969), examined several aspects of the *comitatus* and the concepts that helped to sustain it. Still, since his focus was on the poem itself, Jackson's handling of the *comitatus* is piecemeal and far from definitive. Similarly, the structure of the warband is lost in Nora K. Chadwicks, *The British Heroic Age: The Welsh and the Men of the North* (Cardiff: University of Wales Press, 1976). The warband suffered the same fate in two seminal works by H.M. Chadwick: *The Heroic Age* (Cambridge: Cambridge University Press, 1912; repr., Cambridge University Press, 1967), and *Early Scotland: The Picts, the Scots, and the Welsh of Southern Scotland* (Cambridge: Cambridge University Press, 1949).

3 Like the present study, Leslie Alcock treats the Celtic and Germanic warbands together in his *Economy, Society, and Warfare Among the Britons and Saxons* (Cardiff: University of Wales Press, 1987). Still, such treatment remains an exception. This almost total lack of a comparative viewpoint is unfortunate. In view of the extreme paucity of sources for the fifth, sixth, and seventh centuries, the study and application of comparative theory and methodology in the fields of history and literature, can be instrumental in shedding more light on this period of Britain's history.

For the theory and methodology of comparative analysis, see: Theda Skocpol and Margaret Somers, "The Uses of Comparative History in Macrosocial Inquiry" and Victoria E. Bonnell, "The Uses of Theory, Concepts, and Comparison in Historical Sociology", both found in *CSSH* (April 1980), at pp. 174–97 and 156–73; Raymond Grew, "The Case for Comparing Histories", *AHR* 84 (1980), pp. 763–78; and William H. Sewell Jr., "Marc Bloch and the Logic of Comparative History", *History and Theory* VI (1967), pp. 208–18. See also: Robert T. Holt and John E. Turner (edd.), *The Methodology of Comparative Research* (Los Angeles, University of California Press, 1971); and Amatai Etzioni and Frederick L. Dubow (edd.), *Comparative Perspectives: Theories and Methods* (Boston: Little, Brown, and Co., 1970).

volved, a comparative context is warranted.[4] While archaeologists have consistently emphasized social structure and material culture in their studies of this period's cultures, historians for the most part continue to neglect these subjects. In any event, the study seeks to provide a thorough analysis of both the formal structure and the supporting institutions of the *comitatus* as it is portrayed in the written sources for the period, and as it manifested itself (to whatever degree and in whatever specific forms) among the kingdoms of Dark-Age Britain.

Before reviewing the sources at our disposal in studying the *comitatus*, it should be noted, clearly and unequivocally, that the picture of warbands that is presented by this study necessarily is that of the *image* of the *comitatus* as it is found in the literary and historical sources. Further, it is admitted that the view of the *comitatus* that our sources present is a static one, and one that may not reflect changes in the economy or landholding, nor account for differing rates of development among the various Celtic and Germanic groups and chiefdoms. In essence, though the written sources are consistent in their portrayal of the *comitatus* and archaeology has supported many aspects of this portrayal, the structure of the *comitatus* presented in these pages is not meant to provide an overarching model that can be employed to understand the military structures of Dark-Age kingdoms. Given the dearth of sources for this period as well as the differing rates of development of the various kingdoms, it is impossible to determine the precise degree to which the image of the *comitatus* manifested itself in the historical record at any given time or place. Still, the overall picture is a consistent one, and one that may have been instrumental to the functioning of Dark-Age cultures.

References to the *comitatus* are found in a wide and varied array of historical and literary sources, ranging from saints' lives and epistles to law codes, annals, chronicles, narrative histories, genealogies, and heroic literature. Further information also can be derived from the findings and conclusions of archaeology, which not only supplement the written sources and provide a richer, more detailed picture of material culture, but also detect any anachronisms that might be contained in written sources, especially in the heroic literature. Essentially, archaeology becomes the yardstick against which the veracity and accuracy of the written sources can be measured.

Heroic literature – primarily *Beowulf*, *Y Gododdin*, and the historical poems of Taliesin – is used as a source in the areas of material culture, social

---

4   For the relationship between social structure and material culture, see C.J. Arnold's *An Archaeology of the Anglo-Saxon Kingdoms* (London: Routledge, 1988) or his *Roman Britain to Saxon England: An Archaeological Study* (London: Croom Helm, 1984). For the period's Anglo-Saxon and Celtic cultures, see Stephen T. Driscoll and Margaret R. Nieke (edd.), *Power and Politics in Early Medieval Britain and Ireland* (Edinburgh: Edinburgh University Press, 1988), and their *Early Historical Archaeology* (Edinburgh: Edinburgh University Press, 1981).

structure, and societal values; that is, in the areas where oral-formulaic texts can be used with a degree of safety.[5] Given that the period's other sources rarely focus on these subjects, the information regarding them found in works such as *Beowulf* and the poetry of the *Cynfeirdd* ("Earliest [Welsh] Poets") becomes all the more important. The rapidly expanding field of oral-formulaic studies[6] has found that, for the most part, these are subjects about which this genre of literature can provide surprisingly accurate information, especially in regard to material culture.[7] Since there is little to effectively

---

5 Oral-formulaic literature carries some inherent disadvantages. In fact, Albert Lord cautioned historians (such as M.I. Finley and Dennis Page) against using Homer's works as a source for historical fact, at least as historians understand the phrase. In "Homer, the Trojan War, and History", *Journal of the Folklore Institute* 8 (1971), Lord stated (pp. 90–1) that "Fact is present in the epic, but relative chronology in the catalogue is confused. Time is telescoped. The past of various times is all assembled into the present performance . . . Oral epic presents a composite picture of the past." In fact, the biggest drawback of an oral tradition is its lack of a reliable chronology. On this, see David Henige, "Oral Tradition and Chronology", *Journal of African History* XII (1971), pp. 371–89 or his *The Chronology of Oral Tradition: Quest for a Chimera* (Oxford: Oxford University Press, 1974). This statement would apply more to *Beowulf's* epic style than to panegyric Welsh poetry. Still, while "historical" items of interest, such as an accurate chronology of events and the names of people, may suffer by the oral-formulaic process, there is little reason to suspect that descriptions of material culture would undergo a similar fate. The conservative tradition and diction of this type of poetry would tend to retain such descriptions, especially in the "celebration poetry" of the Welsh. Fortunately, because of its emphasis on material culture, archaeology can serve to confirm this type of information.

6 The advent of oral-formulaic studies began with Milman Parry, based upon his field work on the Balkan Peninsula in the 1930s. For his writings, see Adam Parry (ed.), *The Making of Homeric Verse: The Collected Papers of Milman Parry* (New York: Oxford University Press, 1971). The discipline was advanced by the writings of one of Parry's students, Albert Lord, the most important of which is his *The Singer of Tales* (Cambridge, Mass.: Harvard University Press, 1960). For an overview on the theory, methodology, and early history of Oral Theory, see John Miles Foley, *The Theory of Oral Composition: History and Methodology* (Bloomington and Indianapolis: Indiana University Press, 1988), and his "The Oral Theory in Context", in *Oral Traditional Literature: A Festschrift for Albert Bates Lord*, edited by John Miles Foley (Columbus, Ohio: Slavica Publishers, 1981). Also see Ruth Finnegan's *Oral Poetry: Its Nature, Significance, and Social Context* (Cambridge: Cambridge University Press, 1977) and Jan Vansina's *Oral Tradition as History* (London: James Currey, 1985) and *Oral Tradition: A Study in Historical Methodology* (Oxford: Oxford University Press, 1965).

7 The remarkable similarities between the weapons, treasures and other items of material culture that have been unearthed at Sutton Hoo (in particular) as well as other sites in Britain and Scandinavia and those described in *Beowulf* are well known, and has been remarked upon many times.

   Within a Celtic context, Kenneth Jackson has argued forcefully that the *Tain Bo Cualinge* and other stories of the Ulster Cycle accurately portray the social structure, material culture, and ideals of the pre-Christian Irish; stories that had been transmitted orally over the course of several centuries before being written down in the eighth or

oppose the view that the heroic literature used by this work was orally composed and transmitted, the use of such sources for these purposes is justified.

Beyond heroic poetry, there are other sources that shed some much-needed light on the structure of the Dark-Age warband. Several narrative histories touch upon the subject at hand with varying degrees of success. For the mid-sixth century, an invaluable, contemporary source is Gildas' *De excidio et conquestu Britanniae* (*The Destruction and Conquest of Britain*). While there are some minor differences of opinion regarding the *floruit* of this sixth-century British ecclesiastic, no one questions the potential utility of his work in matters pertaining to the sixth century. Most of the scholarship on *De Excidio* has centered on the question of how accurately Gildas has presented the island's history during its Roman and sub-Roman periods. Gildas appears to have possessed a decent knowledge of his own period, though this information often is submerged in the lakes of venom from which Gildas evidently wetted his quill when writing his epistle. Once it is seen that a good portion of *De Excidio* is devoted to attacking the secular lords and important churchmen of his time, it is possible, with due care, to extract some useful information from even his most strident tirades.[8]

Bede's *Historia Ecclesiastica Gentis Anglorum* (*Ecclesiastical History of the English People*) is another indispensable history, especially for the latter portion of this period. Unlike Gildas, Bede performed his job as a historian in an exemplary manner, and it is not surprising that (with few exceptions) his work – a model of meticulous scholarship – is a remarkably accurate one. Besides the insights that are presented by that work into the political and ecclesiastical history of the island (especially during the seventh- and early eighth-century period), there are passages in Bede's *Historia* that offer rare glimpses into the aristocratic life and ideals of the *comitatus* of this turbulent

ninth century. See his *The Oldest Irish Tradition: A Window on the Iron Age* (Cambridge: Cambridge University Press, 1964). Also see Proinsias Mac Cana, "Conservation and Innovation in Early Celtic Literature", *Etudes Celtiques* 13 (1972–73) and David Dumville, "Beowulf and the Celtic World: The Uses of Evidence", *Traditio* 37 (1982), pp. 109–60. Regarding the tales of the Ulster Cycle, Dumville (*ibid.*) has concluded that: "Whichever way one looks at the problem, it seems clear that there has been an accurate literary transmission of the ethos and material culture of a society distant in time (and perhaps place) from the eighth- or ninth-century Irish author. That we have to due merely with an imaginative reconstruction of a non-existent society is ruled out by the continental evidence."

8 For the historiography of *De Excidio* (*DE*), see Thomas O'Sullivan, *The De Excidio of Gildas: Its Authenticity and Date*, Volume VII of the *Columbia Studies in the Classical Tradition* (Leiden: E.J. Brill, 1978); Michael Lapidge and David Dumville (edd.), *Gildas: New Approaches*, Volume 5 in Studies in Celtic History (Woodbridge, England: The Boydell Press, 1985); Molly Miller, "Bede's Use of Gildas", *EHR* CCCLV (1975), pp. 241–61; E.A. Thompson, "Gildas and the History of Britain", *Britannia* 10 (1978), pp. 203–26; Patrick Sims-Williams, "Gildas and the Anglo-Saxons", *CMCS* 6 (Winter 1983), pp. 1–30; and Kenneth Jackson, "Gildas and the Names of the British Princes", *CMCS* 3 (Summer 1982), pp. 30–40.

age. Another vital narrative for the period is found in the *Historia Brittonum*, whose compilation (c.829–30) traditionally has been assigned (incorrectly) to Nennius.[9]

In addition to these histories, information on the *comitatus* is found in a wide array of source material. These would include annalistic compilations such as the *Anglo-Saxon Chronicle*, the *Annales Cambriae*, and the related Irish chronicles – the *Annals of Ulster*, the *Annals of Tigernach*, and the *Annals of Insfallen* – which were derived from the now lost (but reconstructable) text that has been named the "Chronicle of Ireland".[10] Another useful source would be the earlier saints' lives. While the utility of most Welsh lives is problematic, those of the Anglo-Saxon saints – in particular those of Wilfrid, Guthlac, and Cuthbert – were written down not too long after their deaths, and should prove to be of benefit for the subject at hand.[11]

Lastly, the extant Welsh and Anglo-Saxon law codes[12] provide much information regarding the Germanic and Celtic societies in a general context, the

9 Much has been written on the utility of the *Historia Brittonum* (*HB*), and on its purported compiler. For its utility and historiography, see: David Dumvilles, " 'Nennius' and the *Historia Brittonum*", *SC* X/XI (1975/76), pp. 78–95; or his "The Historical Value of the *Historia Brittonum*", in *Arthurian Literature VI*, edited by Richard Barber (Cambridge, England: D.S. Brewer, 1986), pp. 1–26; Kenneth Jackson, "On the Northern British Section in Nennius", in *Celt and Saxon: Studies in the Early British Border*, edited by Nora Chadwick (Cambridge: Cambridge University Press, 1963), pp. 20–62; and David Dumville, "On the North British Section of the *Historia Brittonum*", *WHR* 3 (June 1977), pp. 345–54.

10 The scholarship regarding these analistic texts and their textual history/interrelationships is too complex to present here. I refer readers to the notable works in the field, and let them sort through the arguments and evidence presented there.

    For the *Annales Cambriae*, see Chapters V and VI in Kathleen Hughes, *Celtic Britain in the Early Middle Ages: Studies in Scottish and Welsh Sources*, Volume II of Studies in Celtic History (Woodbridge, England: The Boydell Press, 1980).

    For the Irish chronicles, see in particular Kathryn Grabowski and David Dumville, *Chronicles and Annals of Medieval Ireland and Wales: The Clonmacnoise-group Texts*, Volume IV of Studies in Celtic History (Woodbridge: The Boydell Press, 1984). The final chapter of the work deals with the *Annales Cambriae*. Also see the introduction in Joan Newlon Radnor, *Fragmentary Annals of Ireland* (Dublin: Dublin Institute for Advanced Studies, 1978).

    A new edition of the *Anglo-Saxon Chronicle* is being published by D.S. Brewer with the venacular texts A–G being volumes 3–8 in the series. The A, B and D texts have been published, edited by Janet Bately, Simon Taylor and Geoffrey Cubbin respectively.

11 The best works on the Anglo-Saxon saints remain those by Bertram Colgrave, all published by Cambridge University Press. These are: *The Life of Bishop Wilfrid by Eddius Stephanus* (1927), *Felix's Life of Saint Guthlac* (1956), *The Earliest Life of Gregory the Great* (1968), and *Two Lives of Saint Cuthbert* (1940). For those of the Welsh, see G.H. Doble, *Lives of the Welsh Saints* (Cardiff: University of Wales Press, 1971).

12 These law codes include those of Aethelberht of Kent, Ine of Wessex, and Ethelberht of Hwicce. For these, see F.L. Attenborough, *The Laws of the Earliest English Kings* (Cambridge: Cambridge University Press, 1922). Further evidence might be derived by comparing these Anglo-Saxon law codes with those of their Germanic brethren on the

place of the *comitatus* within that context, and the amount and types of interaction that occurred between these warbands and the agrarian societies over which they presided. As with their saints' lives, the Welsh took their time in committing their laws to writing. However, even given the lateness of the manuscripts in which it is contained, the Welsh tribal law found in the tenth-century law code of Hywel Dda may reflect some aspects of earlier periods.[13] The Anglo-Saxons, on the other hand, codified several of their tribal laws during this period. In any event, the literary and historical sources for the *comitatus* reflect a wide and varied tradition, both written and oral, that encompassed Latin, Welsh, and Anglo-Saxon.[14]

continent. Katherine Fisher Drew's translations of three of these, published by the University of Pennsylvania Press, are: *The Burgundian Code* (1949); *The Lombard Laws* (1973); and *The Laws of the Salian Franks* (1991).

13 For specifics on the Welsh laws, see Chapter 4 (fn. 15).

14 Even given the difficulties of working in three languages, the study has effected its own translations. For poetry, dual-language editions certainly are available, most notably A.O.H. Jarman's *Aneirin: Y Gododdin* (Llandysul, Wales: The Gomer Press, 1988) and Chickering's *Beowulf: A Dual-Language Edition* (New York: Anchor Press/Doubleday, 1977). No dual-language edition is available for Taliesin's poetry. Foreign language citations for the poems are drawn from: Klaeber's edition of *Beowulf* (Lexington: D.C. Heath, 1950), Ifor Williams' *The Poems of Taliesin* (Dublin: Dublin Institute for Advanced Studies, 1975) and, because of its more sensible organization, Jarmon's edition of the *Gododdin* (rather than Ifor Williams' edition of the poem: *Canu Aneirin* (Cardiff: University of Wales Press, 1978)).

Foreign language citations of prose works are drawn from: Michael Winterbottom, *Gildas: The Ruin of Britain and Other Works* (London, Phillimore, 1978); J.E. King's *Historia Ecclesiastica Gentis Anglorum* (Cambridge, Mass.: Harvard University Press, 1930); John Morris, *Nennius: British History and the Welsh Annals* (London: Philli-more, 1980); A.B.E. Hood, *St. Patrick: His Writings and Muirchu's Life* (London: Phillimore, 1978), while those of the lives of the Anglo-Saxon saints are from Col-grave's editions (cited already).

For the editions of the various chronicles and law codes, see fnn. 10, 12, and 13 above.

CHAPTER TWO

HISTORICAL BACKGROUND
OF DARK-AGE BRITAIN

Any attempt to define precisely the years that constitute Britain's "heroic" or "dark" ages[1] is problematic. For present purposes, the boundaries that mark the limits for Britain's heroic period are the final decades of the fifth century and the third quarter of the eighth. The selection of this period can be justified on several counts. First, the study views the *comitatus* as an unequivocal hallmark of heroic culture. Consequently, this period was selected because it can be equated with the years in which the strength of both the Germanic and Celtic *comitatus* appears to have been at its greatest. A second premise assumes that the *comitatus* structure will function best in an unsettled and chaotic political and social environment, the antithesis of the more settled and stable situation that was found in later periods under more established patterns of kingship. For the Anglo-Saxon kingdoms of this period, in a statement that holds true for the Celtic kingdoms as well, it is seen that:

In socio-economic terms these kingdoms can be characterized less as states than as chiefdoms, that is, they were not so much centralized regimes, the

---

[1] There are many works that offer a good overview of the period's historical background or an analysis of specific kingdoms. See: Chapters 2–5 in James Campbell, Eric John, and Patrick Wormald (edd.), *The Anglo-Saxons* (Ithaca, New York: Cornell University Press, 1982); the overviews in Steven Bassett's (ed.) introduction to *The Origins of Anglo-Saxon Kingdoms* (Leicester: Leicester University Press, 1989); Barbara Yorke, *Kings and Kingdoms in Early Anglo-Saxon England* (London: B.A. Seaby, 1990); and Chapter II in Nora K. Chadwick's *The British Heroic Age* (Cardiff: University of Wales Press, 1976).

Works written about specific geographic regions or tribes include: Alfred Smyth, *Warlords and Holy Men: Scotland AD 80–1000* (Edinburgh: Edinburgh University Press, 1984); Peter Brandon (ed.), *The South Saxons* (London: Phillimore, 1978); K. Rutherford Davies, *Britons and Saxons: The Chiltern Region 400–700* (London: Phillimore, 1982); Peter Hunter Blair's articles, edited by Michael Lapidge and Pauline Hunter Blair, in *Anglo-Saxon Northumbria* (London: Variorum Reprints, 1984); David Kirby, *The Earliest English Kings* (London: Unwin Hyman, 1991); or the essays found in *The Origins of Anglo-Saxon Kingdoms*, *Kings and Kingdoms in Early Anglo-Saxon England*, and *The Earliest English Kings*.

economic base of which was a thriving market economy, as noncentralized communities with a relatively weak market economy and fissaparous (separatist) tendencies which precluded any overlord, however powerful, from establishing anything other than a merely personal hegemony in the absence of a sound enough economic base.[2]

Politically and militarily fragmented, the early foundation and proliferation of many small Celtic and Germanic kingdoms, compounded both by weak institutions of kingship and by the era's incessant warfare, allowed the *comitatus* to become a defining principle for these years of drastic and fundamental change. As is illustrated by numerous examples in the following chapters, the ties that bound together the social fabric of this turbulent age, and that afforded some sense of continuity, were those that were based upon personal relationships, and not upon any clear set of governmental institutions.

However, after the seventh century, the institutional power of the *comitatus* began to decline as its social structure became based on territorial considerations with the political movement of the fragmented states toward nationally integrated states. Seeing this development as a widespread and fundamental one, a societal evolution that the kingdoms in Britain shared with those on the continent, Swanton has declared that:

> The eighth century, and in particular its second half . . . witnessed a significant transition in the governmental concepts of the western European kingdoms, which at this time were in the process of changing from the more open, amorphous pattern of ancient pagan Germanic society, to a new, closed, feudal form, under the influence of the Roman church. To put matters more simply: during the course of the Anglo-Saxon period, a social structure based on personal relationships transferred to one with a territorial base . . . In political terms, the fragmented, amorphous society of Migration times, with a restricted local lordship founded on an open contract with the *folc*, alters rapidly under the influence of antithetical authoritarian notions . . . towards the nationally integrated state with regnal direction from a strong administrative center.[3]

This transition toward nationally integrated kingdoms would have held true for the Celtic territories that managed to survive into the seventh and eighth centuries. It appears that these surviving kingdoms had undergone a period of consolidation as larger units of political organization became more prevalent. Given the often transitory nature of power during this unsettled period, this is not to say that the processes of political and geographic consolidation and amalgamation were steady and unbroken ones, but only that there

---

[2] Kirby, *The Earliest English Kings*, p. 3.
[3] M.J. Swanton, *Crisis and Development in Germanic Society 700–800: Beowulf and the Burden of Kingship* (Goppinger: Kurmmerle Verlag, 1982), p. 12.

were far fewer chiefdoms and kingdoms by the latter part of this period than had been seen earlier. Part and parcel with these processes was the continued stratification of Celtic and Germanic society.[4]

It seems clear that the advent and growth of the *comitatus* as an institution was an early development on the island. During the course of the early sixth century, Britain witnessed the rise of a series of native military states among the Britons within the boundaries of the former Roman province. These newly-established states were fashioned in the tradition of other British kingdoms that had been founded during the late- and sub-Roman periods in regions outside of Roman control. With few exceptions, especially after the disastrous *barbarica conspiratio* in 367, the British tribes between Hadrian's Wall and the Antonine Wall had maintained a status that was essentially independent of Roman control. After the events in 367, Theodosius and the Roman authorities decided (out of military necessity) to enlist the cooperation of these native tribes in securing the northern, highland portion of the island (*Brittania Inferior*) in order to prevent further Pict attacks against the wealthier, more Romanized, southern lowlands (*Brittania Superior*). Given the situation in Roman Britain after 367, though most of these British chiefdoms cooperated with Rome and proved to be effective allies, there is little reason to relegate them to the status of "client states" or to question their independence. After all, the Picts were the enemies of the Britons as well as of Rome. Similarly, there is evidence for independent British warlords during the sub-Roman period, who filled the power vacuumcreated by Rome's withdrawal from the province. Saint Patrick condemns Coroticus (Ceretic), lord of the Strathclyde Britons, for allowing the warriors of his *comitatus* to raid a Christian Irish settlement. Patrick's "letter"[5] is addressed to the warlord himself, and not to any type of civil authority. Furthermore, if the migration story in the *Historia Brittonum* (*HB* 62) about Cunedda and his sons (and other warriors from the Votadini tribe) from Manaw Gododdin to northern Wales has any basis in truth, it also would reinforce the argument that military threats in the west and north were countered not by foreign *foederati*, but rather by native warlords.

Early, detailed references to the newly-established British kingdoms of the sixth century (and to their warbands) are found in Gildas' *De excidio et conquestu Britanniae*. Gildas, in a wide condemnation of the ruling lords of his day and the nascent *comitatus* structure over which they presided, declared (*DE* 27) that "Britain has kings, but they are tyrants . . . [whose] blood-thirsty, haughty, and murderous military companions are adulterers and

---

4 This stratification is reflected in the grave-goods evidence. The establishment of these hierarchical structures is addressed in Chapter 4. For a discussion of this development, see *Arnold's Archaeology of Early Anglo-Saxon Kingdoms*, at pp. 142–93.

5 A.B.E. Hood, *St. Patrick: His Writings and Life* (London: Phillimore, 1978), pp. 35–8.

enemies of God" (*Reges habet Britannia, sed tyrannos . . . sanguinari super-
bos parricidas commanipulares et adulteros dei inimicos*). Gildas condemned
five kings in particular, all of whom ruled in western Britain: Constantine, Aure-
lius Caninus (Kynan), Vortiper, Cuneglasus, and Maglocunus (Maelgwn).[6]

Despite its limitations, Gildas' *De Excidio* (c.540) is important for several
reasons. First, it offers a rare contemporary glimpse of Britain's geopolitical
landscape during the early and mid-sixth century. Second, beyond providing
the names of contemporary rulers and attaching some of these names to
Dark-Age chiefdoms, Gildas' testimony is important because it indicates that
the long-term processes of political and military consolidation and amalgamation may already have begun during these decades. Maelgwn, whom Gildas
called the "Dragon of the Island" (*insularis draco*), evidently had waged a
series of military campaigns (*DE* 33.1) that had caused many rulers of other
British kingdoms to be deposed or killed (*insularis draco, multorum tyran-
norum depulsor tam regno quam etiam vita*), perhaps in part to allow for the
continued expansion of his own kingdom. Further evidence for Gwynedd's
expansion might be seen in Gildas' remark (33.2) to Maelgwn that "The king
of all kings has made you mightier than nearly all the generals in Britain, in
both your kingdom and the features of your stature" (*regum omnium regi, qui
te cunctis paene Britanniae ducibus tam regno fecit quam status liniamento
editiorem*). Finally, *De Excidio* is useful because it provides information about
the British kingdoms in Wales and Dumnonia that can be compared with that
found in the heroic poetry of Taliesin and Aneirin regarding the British
kingdoms of "The Men of the North" (*Y Gwyr y Gogledd*).

It is certain that the governments that had been established by these British
lords were of recent origin[7] and that, at least in Gildas' eyes, their legitimacy
was far from unquestioned. It is clear that Gildas preferred the orderly government that he claimed the victors at Badon Hill had managed to maintain for the
brief span of a generation. Nowhere in his chapters about these five warlords
does Gildas refer to them as kings (*reges*), in sharp contrast to his earlier,
approving treatment of Ambrosius Aurelianus, upon whom he appears to have
conferred (*DE* 25.3) some type of Roman, imperial status. Instead, Maelgwn
and his fellow princes are called tyrants (*tyranni*), generals (*duces*), or other

---

6 The section on these British lords is found in *DE* 28–36. For more on the names, see the
notes in Winterbottom (pp. 152–53). For greater detail, see Jacksons, "Gildas and the
Names of the British Princes", *CMCS* No. 3 (Summer, 1982), pp. 30–40, or Chapter 5
in O'Sullivans, *The De Excidio of Gildas*, pp. 87–133.

7 Gildas' claim that these chiefdoms were of recent origin is substantiated by the findings
of archaeologists. Alcock in particular has argued that the resettlement of the Iron Age
hill-forts during this period indicates that they were used as power centers for the
warrior-chieftains of the new Celtic kingdoms in the western portion of the island. For
more on this proposal, see Alcock, *Economy, Society, and Warfare*, at pp. 153–71.

terms of a more personal and less flattering nature, during the course of Gildas' attack. Nowhere is Gildas' utter and total condemnation of these lords and their governments more evident than when he declares (*DE* 27) that:

> Britain has kings, but they are tyrants; she has judges, but they are wicked. Often they pillage and trouble the innocent, but they defend and protect the guilty and bandits; they have many wives, but they are whores and adulteresses; they swear oaths, but they are perjuries; they make vows, but almost at once tell lies; they wage wars, but they are civil and unjust wars; they pursue greatly thieves furiously throughout the country, but love and reward the thieves who sit with them at table; they give alms abundantly, but heap up a huge mountain of crime in their district; they take their seat as judges, but rarely seek out the rules of proper judgement; they despise the harmless and humble, but exalt . . . their military companions, bloody-thirsty, proud, and murderous, adulterers and enemies of God . . . They confine many in their prisons, who are more often oppressed with onerous chains because of intrigue than because they deserve punishment. Around the altars they swear oaths, then a short time after scorn them as if they were dirty stones.

In Gildas' view, these governments were fundamentally flawed, not by the functions they performed, but by the manner in which, and against whom, these functions were carried out. Gildas would have had no philosophical problems with lords who rendered proper judgments at judicial proceedings, who chased down thieves, who provided for law and order, who imprisoned those who ought to be jailed, who gave alms to the poor, and who fought "just" wars.

The type of warfare mentioned by Gildas is of interest here. Unlike the military campaigns against the Saxons that had been waged by the Britons under Ambrosius' leadership during the final decades of the fifth century, the wars of Gildas' period were "civil and unjust" (*civilia et iniusta*). The rulers of the British kingdoms in Gildas' own time evidently needed little provocation to attack their neighbors whenever they felt it neccessary, even given the Germanic threat which, in hindsight, should have been the focus of a united military response.

Gildas mentions no form of a British military coalition, or even of a campaign, against the Germanic tribes during his own era. Certainly, the British kingdoms were capable of coordinated military actions against the Anglo-Saxon tribes when they saw the threat to be large enough. Examples of coordinated, military campaigns and strategy throughout this period would include the campaign and counter-offensive of the Britons under Ambrosius leading up to their victory at Badon Hill (c.495), the British coalition under Urien resulting in the besieging of Hussa and his sons at Lindisfarne, and Mynyddawg Mwynfawr's ill-fated expedition, comprised of warriors from various British kingdoms, which met with total and utter destruction at Catraeth. Unfortunately for the British cause, coalitions during this period were short-lived affairs in an age when the politics of nationhood, or even of religion, held little sway. The distinct impression that can be derived from the entire range of sources is that, for the period's British and Anglo-Saxon kingdoms, their relations with other kingdoms and chiefdoms were predatory and opportunistic in the extreme. In fact, this situation is best illustrated by the *Chronicle* entry for 597, which recounts that, after his reign in Wessex began, Ceolwulf "always fought and strove against either the Angles, or the Welsh, or the Picts, or the Scots" (*Her ongan Ceolwulf ricsian on Wesseaxum ⁊ simle he feaht ⁊ won, oþþe wiþ Angelcyn, oþþe uuiþ Walas, oþþe wiþ Peohtas, oþþe wiþ Scottas*).

According to Gildas,[8] during the second quarter of the fifth century Germanic lords and their warriors had been "invited" to Britain by Vortigern and the civil authorities in the official capacity of *foederati*. As is addressed in the next chapter, the Germanic tribes coming to Britain during the migrations of the fifth and sixth centuries brought with them the institution of the *comitatus* as their principal method of military organization. In Gildas' account, the task assigned to these *foederati* was to counter Pictish raids, launched from north of the Antonine Wall, which struck all along the North Sea coast of the former Roman province. After all, the employment of barbarians as *foederati* had been common Roman practice during its days of imperial rule, and it should cause little surprise that the Britons, who also faced Irish encroachments and raids in the west and Saxon raids along their southeastern shoreline, should have selected this often-used option as a means to husband their own, limited military resources.[9] Given the early and widespread archaeological evidence,

---

8 Gildas' account of Vortigern's decision to use the Saxons as *foederati*, their rebellion and its subsequent destruction, the British counteroffensive under Ambrosius, and the long period of relative peace between these two groups is found *DE* 22–27. Bede's account of the same story, with some additional details (such as naming two brothers – Horsa and Hengest – as the leaders of the first group) and from an Anglo-Saxon perspective, is drawn almost entirely from Gildas. For Bede's use of *DE*, see: Patrick Sims-Williams, "The Settlement of England in Bede and the *Chronicle*", *ASE* 12 (1983), pp. 1–41; Molly Miller, "Bede's Use of Gildas", *EHR* 90 (1975), pp. 241–61.

   Yorke has noted that Bede's information regarding Hengest and Horsa "presumably came from Abbot Albinus of Canterbury, who was Bede's chief Kentish informant" (*Kings and Kingdoms*, p. 3). Furthermore, she sees this information as coming from an oral tradition, stating that "Bede introduced his information about Hengest and Horsa with the phrase 'they are said . . .' (*perhibentur*), a formula he used elsewhere in his history when he was drawing on unverifiable oral tradition" (*ibid.*).

9 How the Britons managed their military situation in the west is not known with certainty. The *Historia Brittonum* claimed (*HB* 62) that a certain Cunedda had effected a migration – with his eight sons and some of the Votadini – from the Manaw Gododdin region in Scotland to north Wales, where he drove out "with great slaughter" the Irish settlers who had made encroachments there, and where he subsequently established the kingdom of Gwynedd. According to the same passage, this migration had been effected some 140 years before Maelgwn's era. In the later genealogies, some of the British dynasties in northern Wales claimed descent from him. Still, that such a migration occurred is problematic, and even if such a migration did occur, it certainly was not

the introduction of barbarian troops to counter military threats against Britain must have been an early and common development.[10] Armed with hindsight, Gildas bitterly condemned Vortigern and his counselors for deciding to bring in the first units of Germanic *foederati*,[11] recounting (*DE* 22.1) that:

> Then all the counselors, together with the haughty tyrant [Vortigern], were blinded; the defence – nay rather the destruction – they devised for our land was that the most ferocious Saxons, name not to be spoken!, hated by God and man, should be introduced into the island like wolves into the fold, to keep back the peoples of the north. Certainly nothing more destructive, nothing more bitter has ever happened anywhere.[12]

Gildas continues with his story (*DE* 22.3), saying that, upon receiving the British offer, "a pack of cubs burst forth from the den of the barbarian lioness, coming in three, as they say in their language, *keels*, warships in our language" (*erumpens grex catulorum de cubuli leaenae barbarae, tribus, ut lingua eius exprimitur, cyulis, nostra longis navibus*). Gildas further relates (*DE* 23.4) that, upon learning that the first contingent was prospering, this initial *comitatus* was joined by a second, larger group of "satellite dogs" sent by the "mother lioness" under the guise of *foederati* (*Cui supradicta genetrix, comperiens primo agmini fuisse proseratum, item mittet satellitum canumque prolixiorem catastam quae ratibus advecta adunator cum manipularibus spuriis*). These two entries provide clear evidence that the lead elements for the initial stages of Germanic migration to the island were small groups of warriors who had arrived prior to the later settlement of the non-

---

effected under the auspices of some type of centralized, sub-Roman government, which is the inference that some historians (John Morris, Leslie Alcock, *et al.*) have drawn from this passage. If Cunedda and his sons subdued northern Wales, they did so for their own purposes, and not under the guise of *foederati*. For objections to the migration story see David Dumville, "Sub-Roman Britain: History and Legend", *History* LXII (1977), pp. 173–92.

10 For the archaeological evidence, see James Campbell, "The Lost Centuries: 400–600", in *The Anglo-Saxons*, at pp. 27–37. It is this early, geographically widepread, archaeological evidence that led Campbell (*ibid.*, p. 34) to state that "the very diversity of the archaeological evidence suggests that the settlement of Germans for defence must have been by a variety of arrangements made by various authorities".

11 Gildas gave no date for this invitation. Bede, in a valiant though unsuccessful effort, assigned the initial *adventus Saxonum* to the year 449. Based upon the archaeological evidence, the common consensus is that a date in the late 420s, or the 430s, would be much more likely.

12 *Tum omnes consiliarii una cum superbo tyranno caecantur, adinvientes tale praesidium, immo excidium patriae ut ferocissimi illi nefandi nominis Saxones deo hominibusque invisi, quasi in caulas lupi, in insulam ad retundendas aquilonales gentes intromitterentur. Quo utique nihil ei usquam perniciosius nihilque amarius factum est.*

military segments of their tribes.[13] Even after the rebellion of the Saxon *foederati* in the mid-fifth century, this pattern of settlement – the introduction of the civilian elements of a tribe after the *comitatus* had first seized and secured an area – remained a constant.[14] The *Anglo-Saxon Chronicle* records the arrival of warbands under the command of various chieftains and lords. Among the examples cited in the A-text: Hengest and Horsa, with three keels (449), Ælle and his sons in three ships (477), Cerdic and his son Cynric, with five ships (495), and Port and his sons in two ships (501). Given the archaeological evidence, both insular and continental, there is little reason to doubt the *Chronicle* entries, at least in regard to the number of ships, and the size of their crews, that were involved in this migration.[15]

·It is through this process – initial military activity to secure a particular region followed by civilian settlement – that Germanic settlement patterns

---

[13] This certainly is true for the warriors who arrived in three keels. Alcock proposed (p. 301, *Economy, Society, and Warfare*), about fifty men per warship for estimating the size of the fifth and sixth-century Germanic warbands arriving in Britain. Similarly, Sonia Chadwick Hawkes ("Weapons and Warfare in Anglo-Saxon England: An Introduction", in *Weapons and Warfare in Anglo-Saxon England*. Oxford: Oxford University Committee for Archaeology, 1989, p. 3), has estimated that the early invasion craft were comprised of "crews of about forty apiece, such as had manned the ship at Sutton Hoo". The number of warriors in the initial contingent would be on the order of 120 to 150 men. The number involved for the second contingent, while larger, probably was on the same scale. This subject is addressed in the following chapter.

[14] In this regard, these initial processes of settlement and state-formation are similar to the second of two ideal mechanisms that, according to Steven Bassett, were involved in the creation of Anglo-Saxon kingdoms. On the question of how the first Anglo-Saxon kingdoms came into being, Bassett, in his "In Search of the Origins of Anglo-Saxon Kingdoms" (in his *The Origins of the Anglo-Saxon Kingdoms*), proposed (p. 22) that: "Two ideal types of formation can be proposed (though they are not necessarily the only two types). The first involves the steady coalescence of adjacent settlement areas, a process accompanied by the translation of the leaders of the dominant tribes into kings. This would have been well advanced long before the end of the Migration Period, though at different rates of speed in different areas; and it could no doubt have begun long before there were Anglo-Saxons in the area. The second type involves the takeover, by an outside group, of an existing territory in the early post-Roman period."

[15] While the *Anglo-Saxon Chronicle*'s figures for the number of men and ships involved in these landings are accurate in their essentials, the dates assigned to the landings sometimes are not. Relying on Bede's mistaken dating of the *adventus Saxonum* and on royal genealogies that had been manipulated to reflect better the foundation legends of which the ruling families were proud, the dates in the *Chronicle* for this early period leave much to be desired. For example, if Hengest and Horsa were indeed the first Germanic *foederati* in Britain, then their arrival, based upon the available archaeological evidence, must be placed in the 420s or 430s rather than in 449. Further, Dumville has shown ("The West Saxon Genealogical List and the Chronology of Wessex", *Peritia* 4 (1985), at pp. 50–56) that the landing of Cynric and Cerdic should be placed in 532, and not in 495 as the *Chronicle*'s entry would lead us to believe. For more on the *Chronicle*'s shortcomings, see Yorke, *Kings and Kingdoms* (pp. 3–4, and the works cited there).

should be viewed. Far from being an organized, long-range campaign of conquest initiated and directed by a "mother lioness" (as Gildas would have us believe), the seizure of territory was an informal, almost haphazard affair, whose success or failure depended on the unique personalities and the polit-ico-military situation of a particular region at a specific period of time. The overall patterns of Anglo-Saxon settlement were shaped in their specifics by the boldness, initiative, and military prowess that were exhibited by the lords of small warbands acting independently, far from the direction and support systems of their tribal chieftains and homelands. Through their own initiative and daring, these warlords would become the kings of the new Anglo-Saxon kingdoms that were founded, and that subsequently proliferated, in the former Roman province throughout this period. Given this fluid and unstable back-ground, and given that there are no references to Germanic kings or to any sort of civilian component, the initial stages of Germanic migration should be viewed primarily in a military context. It seems clear that, for the most part, the men who led these warriors were not tribal chieftains, leading their peoples across the North Sea.

Bede (*HE* I.15) names the specific tribes – primarily the Jutes, Angles, and Saxons – that formed the wave of Germanic migration to Britain during these years, their geographic regions of origin (on the continent), and their settle-ment patterns on the island itself. Bede claimed that the Germanic peoples in Kent and the Isle of Wight (called the *Victuarii*) were decended from the Jutes, as were the people of that name who were located in the kingdom of the West Saxons. According to Bede, from the Saxons came the East Saxons, the South Saxons, and the West Saxons. From the Angles – whose homeland (*Angulus*) was located between the lands of the Jutes and the Saxons, and which Bede claimed "is said to have remained deserted from that time to the present" – come the East Angles, the Middle Angles, the Mercians, and all of the Northumbrians and the other Anglian peoples.

While Bede's source for this paragraph remains unknown, it was evidently an accurate one, whose information regarding the tribes, their origins, and their settlement patterns, has been validated by archaeologists working in Britain and on the continent.[16] Even Bede's claim about the abandonment of *Angulus*, long dismissed as literary fiction, has been shown to be correct by recent archaeological work.[17] Bede relates (*HE* V.9) that these major tribes were joined by others from the various Germanic homelands – the Frisians, the *Rugini*, the Danes, the Huns, the Old Saxons, and the *Boructari* – at least some of whom reached Britain's shores during the same period. All this makes clear that Germanic settlement had been effected by different tribes

---

[16] *Ibid.*, pp. 27–31. A notable lapse by Bede was his failure to note the migration to East Anglia of Scandinavian tribes.

[17] *Ibid.*, p. 30.

from a variety of homelands, with varying levels of interaction between them, and for a variety of reasons, all of which resulted in a complex pattern of settlement within Britain.

While some of these immigrants had been in Britain since the early sub-Roman period, probably under the status of *foederati*, Germanic migration probably began in earnest after the rebellion of these mercenaries somewhere around the mid-fifth century. If the *Anglo-Saxon Chronicle*'s entries for these early years are reliable, this increased tempo of migration continued even during the successful British resurgence and counteroffensive, led by Ambrosius, that culminated in the Britons' victory at Badon. According to Gildas (*DE* 26.1, 2), the victory at the siege at Badon Hill (*obsessionis Badonici montis*) led to a long period of relative peace between Briton and Saxon that lasted almost five decades, in which "was permitted the cessation of external wars, but not civil ones" (*cessantibus licet externis bellis, sed non civilibus*). It also would seem (*DE* 10.2) that the settlement acknowledged the "mournful partition with the barbarians" (*lugubri divortio barbarorum*) of the island – a partition that is evidenced in the archaeological record[18] – with the Germanic tribes consigned to those areas (mostly in the southern and eastern portions of the island) in which they had settled already. During these years of uneasy peace, it is likely that the pace of Germanic migration continued unabated as the Angles, Saxons, Frisians, Jutes, *et alia*, seeking to reinforce their geo-military situation on the island, continued to be joined by other contingents from their homelands. In fact, the foundation of many Anglo-Saxon kingdoms probably took place during this specific period.[19] The maintainence of this uneasy status quo, established in the year of Gildas' birth by the battle at Badon Hill, would collapse soon after he completed *De Excidio*.

The second half of the sixth century saw the balance of power between the Britons and the Germanic tribes tilt precariously against the British cause, resulting in the destruction of most of the British chiefdoms that had maintained their existence in the lowland regions of England during the first half of the sixth century. The *Anglo-Saxon Chronicle* records a number of signal victories of the Anglo-Saxons (primarily those of Wessex) against their British adversaries. In particular, the [A] *Chronicle* records that: in 552, "Cynric fought with the Britons in a place called Salisbury, and put to flight the Brito-Welsh" (*Her Cynric gefeaht wiþ Brettas in þære stowe þe is genemmed [æt] Searobyrg 7 þa Bretwalas gefliemde*); in 556 "Cynric and Cealwin fought with the Britons at Barbury" (*Her Cynric 7 Ceawlin fuhton wiþ Brettas æt Beranbyrg*); in 571 "Cuthwulf fought against the Brito-Welsh at Biedcanford, and took four villages . . ." (*Her Cuþwulf feaht wiþ Bretwalas*

18 Yorke, *Kings and Kingdoms*, p. 7.
19 As Yorke has noted (*ibid.*, p. 4), recent work on the regnal lists and genealogies of the Anglo-Saxon ruling families has tended to suggest dates for the foundation of these early kingdoms that must be placed within the sixth century.

æt Bedcanford 7 *.iiii. tunas genom . . .*); in 577 "Cuthwine and Cealwin fought the Britons, and killed three kings . . . in a place called Dyrham, and took three cities: Gloucester, Cirencester, and Bath" (*Her Cuþwine* 7 *Cealwin fuhton wiþ Brettas* 7 *hie .iii. kyningas ofslogon . . . in þære stowe þe is* ge[cueden Deorham], 7 *genamon .iii. ceastr[o], Gleawanceaster* 7 *Cirenceaster* 7 *Baþanceaster*); in 584 "Cealwin and Cutha fought with the Britons at a place men call Fethanleag, and Cutha was slain; Cealwin took many towns and countless spoils of war" (*Her Cealwin* 7 *Cuþa fuhton wiþ Brettas in þam stede þe mon nemneþ Feþanleag,* 7 *Cuþan mon ofslog;* 7 *Ceaulin monige tunas genom* 7 *unarimedlice herereaf*). These entries attest a series of unmitigated military disasters for the British kingdoms as Wessex extended its power to the shores of the Severn estuary. These campaigns resulted in the destruction of the British chiefdoms in the south of England, with the subsequent confinement of British authority to the Dumnonian peninsula and to Wales. As in the other frontier kingdoms (Mercia and Northumbria), the seizure of territory through warfare (and the tribute that followed) allowed Wessex to maintain a military advantage over the other Anglo-Saxon kingdoms south of the Humber river.

In the north, the situation and course of events differed markedly. Here the expansion of Germanic power and territory was contested by the British kingdoms – chief among them: Manaw Gododdin, Rheged, and Strathclyde – and by the *Scotti* (an Irish tribe) of Dalriada with far more effectiveness than had been shown by their compatriots in Britain's southern regions. In part, this British success might be attributable to demographics; archaeology has shown that there were far fewer Germanic settlers north of the Humber than there were in the kingdoms to its south. This is not to say that the British never suffered any military setbacks at the hands of the Angles in the north. Like the much earlier campaigns under Ambrosius, the military situation in the north favored one or the other side at different times. In fact, the mid-sixth century saw the utter destruction of Manaw Gododdin's expedition against the Deirians in a battle at Catraeth (Catterick). It is possible that the Deiran defeat of this British force in itself may have allowed for the expansion of Bernicia.[20] The battle at Catraeth was recorded in *Y Gododdin* by Aneirin, one of

---

20 Dumville, "Early Welsh Poetry: Problems of Historicity", in *EWP*, p. 3. Given its close geographic proximity, it is impossible to believe that Manaw Gododdin would not have targeted Bernicia for destruction had the Bernician settlements represented any type of military threat in the mid-sixth century. Instead, the Gododdin expedition bypassed the nascent kingdom to strike at the demographically larger, and militarily stronger, Deiran kingdom. In this regard, we should credit Mynyddog Mwynfawr, the Votadini chieftain, with some semblance of prudent military strategy. After all, who would have known better their own military situation and their principal military threat than the Votadini themselves? Furthermore, the archaeological evidence would indicate that the Angle presence in Deira was earlier (since the mid-fifth century), more widespread (from York to Catterick/Catraeth), and in a greater concentration than that which

the *Cynfeirdd* whose *floruit* the *Historia Brittonum* viewed (*HB* 61 and 62) as being contemporary with the reign of Ida (547–59), Bernicia's founder.

The military disaster at Catraeth served to awaken the *Gwyr y Gogledd* to the Germanic threat. These rulers initiated varying levels of military action against both Deira and Bernicia. This is certainly the response of Urien's Rheged. Clear references in two of Taliesin's poems (*PT* II and *PT* VIII) call Urien and his *comitatus* "lord of Catraeth" (*lyw katraeth*) and "men of Catraeth" (*gwyr katraeth*), indicating that Urien had seized the Catterick area from the Deirans at an early stage. Given its stategic location, it seems likely that the seizure of this area, perhaps as a forward staging area, was part of a larger campaign against the two Germanic kingdoms. Urien's son Owain was sent to raid the coastal settlements of Bernicia or Deira (or both), for which he earned (*PT* VI.9) the epithet "scourge of the eastlands" (*dwyrein ffossawt*). While the Deiran response is unknown, these raids evidently provoked a full-scale military response from Bernicia: its king, Theodric, at the head of "a four-fold host" (*petwar llu*), campaigned against Rheged, but was defeated by Urien and Owain at Argoed Llwyfain. The Britons, responding to Theodric's failed expedition against Rheged, resolved to crush Bernicia. To this end they formed an alliance and, after a series of campaigns, besieged Lindisfarne. The *Historia Brittonum* recounts (*HB* 62) the events leading up to the siege, and its final result:

> Against him fought four kings, Urien, and Rhydderch Hen [or Hael], and Gwallawg, and Morcant. Theodric fought bravely with his sons against that Urien. During that time, sometimes now the enemy, then the citizens [i.e. the Britons] were overcome, and [Urien] himself enclosed them for three days and three nights upon the island of Medcaut [Lindisfarne]. Then it was that [Urien] was butchered during this undertaking, on the instigation of Morcant out of envy. . . .[21]

It is ironic that, at the very moment of triumph, Urien, the overall commander of the British hosts and the period's greatest warlord, was murdered at the instigation of an allied chieftain. After Urien's murder, the British coalition dissolved, giving the Bernicians a much-needed respite. It was a respite that was to be put to good use by the Bernician kingdom, and one that the *Gwyr y Gogledd* would soon regret giving. For the British kingdoms, the

---

is in evidence for Bernicia during this early period. In sum, Deira posed a greater military threat than did Bernicia, a fact that I am confident was not lost on the warriors of Manaw Gododdin. For additional information, see Dumville, "The Origins of Northumbria" (p. 215) and Campbell, "The Lost Centuries" (p. 41).

[21] *Contra illum quarttuor reges, Urbgen, et Riderchhen, et Guallauc, et Morcant, dimicaverunt. Deodric contra illum Urbgen cum filiis dimicabant fortier. In illo autem tempore aliquando hostes, nunc cives vincebantur, et ipse conclusit eos tribus diebus et tribus noctibus in insula Metcaud et, dum erat in expedtione, jugulatus est, Morcanto destinante pro invidia.*

window of opportunity that had been opened by the armed might of Urien's short-lived coalition soon would be closed forever.

The seventh century saw a fundamental change in the balance of power between the Celtic and Germanic kingdoms. In the north, the Bernician kingdom saw a great expansion of its military might under Æthelfrith (592–616). In 603, responding to this Bernician expansion, the *Anglo-Saxon Chronicle* records that "Aedan, King of the Scots, fought with the Daelriodi [against] Aethelferth, king of Northumbria, at Daegsanstan; almost all his army was killed" (*Her [wæs gefeoht æt Egesanstane] Ægþan Scotta cyng feaht wið Dælreoda ⁊ wið Æðelferþe Norþhymra cynge æt Dægstane, ⁊ man ofsloh mæst ealne his here*), with the result, as Bede (*HE* I.34) relates, that "never from that time to the present day has any Scottish king in Britain dared to come to give battle against the English people" (*Neque ex eo tempore quisquam regum Scottorum in Brittaniae adversus gentum Anglorum usque ad hanc diem in proelium venire audebat*). Bernicia followed up this victory against Dalriada with an invasion of Deira in 604. During this campaign, the Deiran king (Æthelric) was slain and his heir (Edwin) fled into exile. The addition of Deira, whose rival warlords often had opposed Bernician aims during the sixth century,[22] allowed the rulers of a unified Northumbria to focus on a policy of expansion. The year 613 finds Æthelfrith fighting the Britons as far away as Chester; 638 saw the siege of Edinburgh (*Obsessio Etin*), perhaps marking the end of Manaw Gododdin; the latter half of the seventh century saw the expansion of Northumbrian power to the north of the Firth of Forth (fighting the Picts) and to the west of the Pennines (fighting Rheged). Given the grave-goods evidence, the result of these conquests was that a small Anglian warrior-élite came to govern a large and powerful kingdom whose population was largely Celtic.[23] The seventh century also saw continued strife with Mercia over territorial claims and over attempts by both kingdoms to establish hegemony over the other Anglo-Saxon kingdoms. However, after the reign of Aldfrith (685–705), Northumbrian rulers preferred to avoid the military costs associated with dealings with the Anglo-Saxon kingdoms south of the Humber.[24]

To the southwest, Mercia's territorial expansion, as well as its political and military aims, made it Northumbria's chief rival in its quest for dominance over the other Anglo-Saxon kingdoms throughout the seventh century. To thwart Northumbrian aims, Mercian rulers often allied themselves with the

---

[22] Yorke, *Kings and Kingdoms*, p. 77. This is not to say that hostility between the Deiran and Bernician nobilities ceased at this time. Edwin, supported by the Deirans, returned from exile in 616; Æthelfrith met his death in the battle between his and Edwin's forces. Throughout the seventh century, Deira continued to pose problems to a united Northumbria. A lasting union of the two provinces would be accomplished in 679 by Ecgfrith.

[23] Campbell, "The Lost Centuries", pp. 41–42.

[24] Yorke, *Kings and Kingdoms*, p. 83.

lords of British kingdoms. The most notable of these alliances was the one established between Penda of Mercia and Cadwallon of Gwynedd which, as the *Anglo-Saxon Chronicle* (633) relates, effected the death of Edwin and the defeat of his Northumbrian forces at Hatfield Chase (*Her Edwine wæs of-slægen*). Bede further relates (*HE* II.20) that, after the battle, Penda and Cadwallon ravaged all the churches and land of Northumbria (*maxima est facta strages ecclesia vel gente Northanhymbria*). With the battlefield death of Cadwallon in the following year at Heavenfield at the hands of Oswald, Penda continued to ally himself with other British lords, a practice he was to continue until his death at Winwidfeld in 655. After Winwidfeld, the military advantage went to Northumbria for a short time, but the Mercians were to repay their longstanding enemies for this loss with another major victory in 679 at Trent, which ended Northumbrian overlordship south of the Humber. Warfare between these two major kingdoms would continue well into the next century, with Mercian rulers (whose fortunes generally were on the rise) attempting to gain recognition of their claims of supremacy from their northern neighbor (though without much success). In the eighth century, competition for overlordship over the southern kingdoms would involve Wessex for the most part. Regarding its internal organization during the eighth century, Mercia appears to have fully incorporated many of the sub-kingdoms (whose peoples are shown in the "Tribal Hidage") that previously had been permitted some degree of independence as "buffer states". Mercian power also was strengthened through its hegemony, by the end of Offa's reign, over the lands between the Humber and Thames rivers.

For the most part, the emphasis of the written sources was placed on military, religious, and political events that involved the major kingdoms of the Heptarchy, and in particular the three frontier kingdoms of Northumbria, Mercia, and Wessex. Lost beneath the epic sweep of events – of battles won, kings slain, alliances made and broken, and *bretwaldas* establishing overlordship far and wide – recounted by the *Anglo-Saxon Chronicle* and Bede's *Historia Ecclesiastica*, are two related trends, whose processes helped shape the face of Britain. The first of these is a pattern of migration that saw many smaller tribes settle in the interior and western regions of Britain. The second was the subsequent establishment of many smaller kingdoms by these peoples that would eventually come to be absorbed, through a long period of amalgamation[25] and consolidation, by other, more successful kingdoms. In essence,

---

[25] For this process of amalgamation, both at this and lower levels, and its role within the overall process of state formation, see Bassett, "Origins of Anglo-Saxon Kingdoms", at pp. 17–27 (and the references cited there). By no means was this process of amalgamation uniformly smooth or incapable of reversal. In the north, the example of Deira (which managed to detach itself from Bernician control on several occasions in the seventh century) comes immediately to mind. Yorke has noted the same situation for other parts of Britain, relating (*Kings and Kingdoms*, p. 13) that "The existence of

the entries in the *Anglo-Saxon Chronicle* and in Bede's writings mask the wide diversity of peoples and kingdoms that must have been the hallmark of Anglo-Saxon settlement and social organization during the sixth and seventh centuries.[26]

Evidence for this diversity is found in a seventh-century document known as the "Tribal Hidage"[27] and in Bede. The *Tribal Hidage* lists many of the smaller, formerly independent tribes of England's interior region after they had been partly incorporated within the expanding Mercian kingdom. The diverse settlement patterns and early proliferation of a wide array of Germanic kingdoms of differing size, strength, wealth, and status that are inferred by the evidence in the *Tribal Hidage* likely can be extended to other parts of England as well. The impression of a wide variety of kingdoms, both in complexity and geographic size, is reinforced by Bede who, through incidental references found throughout the *Historia*, provides a description of the geopolitical situation as it was found in his own day. It is instructive that Bede continued to treat various peoples – the Wihtware, the Hwicce, the Middle Angles, the Lindesfara, and the Magonsaete – and their territories as distinct social entities.[28] Further, Bede's terminology[29] in regard to the rulers and to

these numerous small provinces suggests that southern and eastern Britain may have lost any political cohesion in the fifth and sixth centuries and fragmented into many small autonomous units."

[26] Various models and theoretical constructs, regarding the underlying social and economic processes which were instrumental in the formation and development of these kingdoms, have been proposed. Because this chapter has presented a rather cursory political history of the period, theories of state-formation have been ignored for the most part. They are, however, of the utmost importance in providing a better understanding of the underlying causal agents that helped to shape the course of events in Britain during the sixth and seventh centuries.

Principal among these works are: C.J. Arnold, "Wealth and Social Structure" and "Stress as a Factor in Social and Economic Change" (already cited), his "Territories and Leadership: Frameworks for the Study of Emergent Polities in Early Anglo-Saxon Southern England", in *Early Historical Archaeology*, edited by Stephen Driscoll and Margaret Nieke, pp. 111–27 (Edinburgh: Edinburgh University Press, 1981), and his *Archaeology of Early Anglo-Saxon Kingdoms*. See also R. Hodges, "State Formation and the Role of Trade in Middle Saxon England" (in *Social Organization and Settlement*, edited by D. Green, C. Haselgrove, and M. Spriggs), "The Evolution of Gateway Communities: Their Socio-Economic Implications" (in *Ranking, Resource, and Exchange*, edited by C. Renfrew and S. Sherman).

[27] For more on the dating, contents, interpretation, and importance of this document, see: Bassett, "In Search of the Origins of Anglo-Saxon Kingdoms", pp. 26–7; Kirby, *The Earliest English Kings*, pp. 9–12 and map on p. xv; Yorke, *Kings and Kingdoms*, pp. 10–14, and David Dumville, "The Tribal Hidage: An Introduction to its Texts and their History", in Bassett, *Origins of the Anglo-Saxon Kingdoms*, pp. 225–30.

[28] A brief discussion of this point is provided by D.P. Kirby on pp. 5–8 in his *The Earliest English Kings*.

[29] Bassett has observed that Bede used the terms *regiones* and *provinciae* in referring to early kingdoms and their equivalents of greatly varying size and importance (*ibid.*,

the regions over which they presided also serves to illuminate both the complex and diverse array of relationships and the varying gradations of power and authority that were possible (and were taken for granted by Bede and our other sources) within the overall command-structures of the Anglo-Saxon Heptarchy.

p. 26). His terms for the rulers of these territories – *totius Britanniae imperator, subreguli duces, regii ducibus nobilissimus* – show the diversity of rule that was possible among the Anglo-Saxons. See also Kirby, *The Earliest English Kings*, pp. 14–20.

CHAPTER THREE

MILITARY ORGANIZATION

Given that the fortunes of Dark-Age kingdoms often were bound together with the fortunes of their warbands, the military organization of their war-bands – their roles and functions, relative size, internal "task organization", tactics and strategy, and weapons and equipment – was a matter of great importance. The principal function of the *comitatus* of a Dark-Age kingdom was the conduct of warfare. The period's heroic poetry and historical sources testify that the conduct of warfare was a function of government that was pursued with a great deal of enthusiasm by British and Anglo-Saxon rulers. As the previous chapter showed, both the *Anglo-Saxon Chronicle* and the Welsh and Irish annals are replete with entries regarding battles fought, lords and warriors slain, towns and villages pillaged, strongholds besieged, and regions ravaged and burned. In no uncertain terms, these entries attest to the pervasive, incessant nature of warfare throughout the period. Chapter 2 also showed that a similar picture was drawn from Gildas' testimony, from the works of Nennius and Bede, and from other sources. Furthermore, the period's heroic poetry paints a picture, a scarred and bloody portrait, of this turbulent age, which comes from the same canvas. As the following chapters show, this poetry is replete with references to warfare and violence. Taliesin recounts the military exploits of the lords for whom he sang – Gwallawg, Urien, Owain, and Cynan Garwyn – with unbridled, unabashed enthusiasm. Aneirin's *Gododdin* makes it clear that many of the warriors of Mynyddawg's expedition were established warriors and warlords, veterans of other campaigns, prior to Catraeth. *Beowulf*, with its frequent references to feuds, battles, and wars, indicates that warfare and violence were endemic[1] among Germanic tribes even before they landed on British soil. In fact, it is likely that the martial ideals found in heroic poetry helped to promote the high level of violence noted in our sources. The causes of war during this period were

---

[1] For a comparative overview of the endemic warfare in Anglo-Saxon and other pre-industrial societies, see Guy Halsall, "Anthropology and the Study of Pre-Conquest Warfare and Society: The Ritual War in Anglo-Saxon England", in *Weapons and Warfare in Anglo-Saxon England*, edited by Sonia Chadwick Hawkes, pp. 155–78 (Oxford: Oxford University Committee for Archaeology, 1989).

integral to British and Anglo-Saxon society and its economy and to the processes of territorial and political amalgamation and consolidation. Regarding this, Arnold has stated that:

> Such aggression is almost inevitable in societies with primitive exchange systems; warfare, trade and marriage meant external relationships of hostility and alliance, relations of antagonism and dependence . . . Warfare, raiding, revenge, and feud were probably major preoccupations entailing the extermination of lineages, capturing women and children, and slavery. This level of aggression gradually gave way to the political incorporation of the defeated. The nature of the aggression was not so regular and institutionalized to have encouraged the construction of defensive structures . . .[2]

The warbands responsible for much of the endemic chaos and high levels of violence that are evidenced in the period's sources were not large. This is true for Celtic and Germanic kingdoms alike, which faced essentially the same economic and logistical constraints which were inherent in the agrarian, subsistance-type economies over which they presided. These economic and logistical constraints, along with other factors – the hierarchical social structure, for example – precluded the establishment of large armies among these kingdoms. Alcock used this argument in his discussion of the controls that limited the size and military capabilities of Dark-Age warbands, noting that since "the best calculation for the field army for Roman Britain in about AD 400 puts it at not more than 6,000 troops" it is almost "impossible to believe that any of the dozen or so successor-kingdoms could have raised a force of a thousand men".[3]

Even a force that numbered anything near a thousand warriors would have far exceeded the abilities of all but the most powerful and wealthy of these kingdoms to support them. It is possible that armies of this size could have existed in the latter portion of the period, when the ongoing processes of amalgamation and consolidation would have allowed the fewer surviving kingdoms – both Celtic and Germanic – the economic wherewithal to support larger forces. This is not to say that these ongoing processes precluded the use of smaller companies of warriors even as late as the mid-eighth century, as the *Anglo-Saxon Chronicle*'s entries about Cynewulf and Cyneheard make clear. The entries (for 755 and 784) recount that a certain Cynewulf had seized control of Wessex from Sigeberht, who was killed shortly thereafter while in exile. Thirty-one years later, Cynewulf and his bodyguard were slain and his kingdom nearly overthrown by Cyneheard, Sigeberht's brother, with an armed following of only eighty-five men. The story shows that, even late in this period, when the processes of political and territorial amalgamation and consolidation would have made the use of such a small force unlikely, one

[2] Arnold, *Archaeology of Early Anglo-Saxon Kingdoms*, p. 169.
[3] *Economy, Society, and Warfare*, p. 301.

sees the continued use of small-scale forces in order to achieve specific political and military objectives. In any event, in the fifth and sixth centuries, a kingdom's army rarely exceeded several hundred at the most, and in most cases were far smaller.

Early sources are misleading regarding the size of Dark-Age military forces, with their frequent references to armies wreaking widespread havoc and destruction while slaughtering their foes by the thousands. In part, the problem is due to overzealous exaggeration, and in part due to an imprecise, or at least a misleading, definition of terms. The long-standing and time-honored military practice of inflating casualty figures for an enemy should of course surprise no one; unconfirmed casualty figures for the enemy of any war must be taken with a very large grain of salt. Regarding the latter feature, the law code of Ine of Wessex[4] (688–726) provides a particularly relevant example. The law code (13.1) gives specific definitions to three types of armed force: any party of armed men numbering less than seven were considered to be thieves, between seven and thirty-five men was a band, and anything above this figure was a *here*, or army (*Đeofas we hataδ oδ VII men; from VII hloδ oδ XXXV; siδδan biδ here*). The term *here* should therefore be used with caution.

The early sources contain other information that can be used to estimate the size of Dark-Age armies and warbands. For the size of Anglo-Saxon warbands, the *Anglo-Saxon Chronicle* entries about the early Germanic landings and Gildas' *De Excidio* are particularly instructive. As the previous chapter showed, there is every reason to believe that Gildas' claim that the original Germanic *foederati* arrived in three keels (*cyulis*), with an inferred landing force of 120–150 men, is accurate. Similarly, given the archaeological evidence,[5] the *Chronicle*'s "much maligned record of land-takings by two, three, or five ship-loads of men, far from being merely formulaic, must represent something approximating the truth".[6] Assigning a crew of about 40–50 men for each ship, we can estimate that the size of these landing forces during the initial stages of settlement would be on the order of 80–200 or 100–250 men, depending on which figures are used for the crews. Additionally, some of these entries name more than one leader, which might mean that these small figures can be broken down into yet smaller units of organization. In short, Anglo-Saxon military organization during their migration to the island was on a very small-scale and personal basis.

---

4 F.L. Attenborough (ed. and tr.), *The Laws of the Earliest English Kings* (Cambridge: Cambridge University Press), at p. 41.

5 This archaeological evidence is covered in this and the following chapter. In sum, it can be said that the archaeological evidence available – regarding the period's ships and halls, the reoccupation of only small areas of Iron Age hillforts by the Britons, the absence of weapons among the grave-goods of most Anglo-Saxon graves – shows in no uncertain terms the small numbers of warriors who formed Dark-Age warbands.

6 Hawkes, "Weapons and Warfare", p. 3.

These numbers would continue to be valid for the dozens of Anglo-Saxon kingdoms that were founded and that subsequently proliferated throughout the sixth century. This proliferation was caused both by the establishment of new kingdoms as the various Germanic tribes settled the new territories that had been wrested from Celtic control, and by the loss of political cohesion during the fifth and sixth centuries within the older Anglo-Saxon kingdoms of the southern and eastern regions of the island, which had fragmented into many small autonomous units[7] during these same years. Especially for many of the smaller groups that are listed in the *Tribal Hidage*, the number of warriors in a warband could not have approached a hundred, and likely was far less. While these small forces could not defend their chiefdoms and kingdoms from outright conquest and annexation by larger, more determined kingdoms – the eventual fate for most of these tribes – they were large enough to accomplish the routine, day-to-day tasks (such as raids against neighboring tribes) that are associated with Dark-Age warbands.

The story of Guthlac's warband (*Guthlac* XVI–XVIII), which he led for nine years (c.690–99) as a young warrior, demonstrates the ease with which such a force could be assembled, the types of expedition in which it could be engaged, the "immense booty" (*immensas praedas*) that military success could bring, and the further recruitment of warriors, coming from "various races" (*diversarum gentium*), who joined the warband because of its military prowess and wealth. Lastly, the *Chronicle* entries about Cynewulf and Cyneheard show that the small-scale, highly personal basis of leadership and organization of warbands continued even during the last half of the eighth century.

Literary and archaeological evidence show that the size of the British and Celtic warbands was about the same as those of the Anglo-Saxons. The Britons shared the same economic, social, and logistical constraints that had effectively precluded Anglo-Saxon employment of large military forces. Furthermore, two other factors pertaining only to the British kingdoms almost certainly ensured that these constraints would have had a greater impact on the size of the Britons' *comitatus* structure than on the warbands of their adversaries. These factors are: (1) the Britons' use of the horse, at least in a logistical capacity, and (2) after the early seventh century, the location of the surviving British kingdoms in the agriculturally poorest regions of the island (in Wales, on the Dumnonian peninsula, and in the southern Scotland/ northern England region). Obviously, the logistical requirements for a warrior and

---

[7] Yorke, *Kings and Kingdoms*, p. 13. Already reviewed in Chapter 2 were the patterns of migration and fragmentaion that had caused a proliferation of many small Germanic chiefdoms and territories in Britain's Germanic-controlled regions. Also covered was the validity of the evidence for this proliferation – primarily the *Tribal Hidage* and references in Bede's *HE*.

his horse were greater than for a warrior only. All variables being weighed evenly, one would expect British warbands to have been smaller than Germanic ones on this basis alone. The poorer regions occupied by the Britons could not, on a per unit basis, support the same number of warriors as the richer agricultural lands controlled by the Anglo-Saxons. On a theoretical basis, one should expect to see the size of a British warband as smaller than its Anglo-Saxon counterpart as a result of these factors. Of course, the Britons may have been able to mitigate these factors by having fewer, but geographically and demographically larger, kingdoms.[8]

The period's sources confirm the impression that the size of Celtic warbands, with a few notable exceptions, was indeed small. The best known references on the size of British warbands are found in the *Gododdin*. The poem puts the size of the ill-fated expedition, with slight variations,[9] at around three hundred men. This figure has provoked a great deal of debate, primarily by those who refuse to believe that such a small force would have been sent to fight at Catraeth. In particular, Jackson's insistence on increasing the size of the expedition ten-fold and on numbering their enemies in the thousands[10] has no basis whatsoever in the archaeological evidence nor in the text itself. Simply, to use an old adage, the poem "says what it means, and means what it says" in giving the size of the Gododdin force. In view of the composite nature of the expedition, with warriors drawn from throughout the Celtic lands, a warband the size of the one seen in the *Gododdin* might have been a source of envy and awe on the part of other British rulers. Though they should be used with caution, one of the Welsh triads numbers the warriors of three especially fierce and successful warbands at three hundred each, relating that:

> The three hundred swords of the tribe of Cynfarch and the three hundred shields of the tribe of Cynwyd and the three hundred spears of the tribe of Coel, on whatever expedition they might go in unison, they would not fail.

---

[8] There is little to suggest that the British kingdoms underwent the degree of fragmentation that is evidenced for the Germanic kingdoms by the *Tribal Hidage*. Of course, many small British chiefdoms existed, especially in the period's earlier years. Taliesin praises (*PT* I) Cynan, the lord of Powys, for his attacks on Anglesey, Gwent, Dyfed, and Cernyw. As were their Anglo-Saxon counterparts, some of these chiefdoms were absorbed by larger kingdoms. Nonetheless, the extreme level of fragmentation that is surmised for the Anglo-Saxons is not found among the Britons. Also, tribute and booty (see Chapter 9) was a source of wealth but was not factored into this construct since it was available to both sides.

[9] As Jackson has stated, the poem usually calls the expedition "the army" or "host of the three hundred", or simply "the three hundred". The variants of 303 and 363 (the latter representing the poetic three hundred and three score and three ones) are also found. See Jackson, *GOSP*, pp. 25–27.

[10] In advancing this proposal (*ibid.*, pp. 13–18), Jackson ignored the logistical, economic, and social factors that would have precluded such large-scale forces. For other objections, see Alcock (*Economy, Society, and Warfare*, pp. 264 and 301).

Trychan cledyf Kynuerchyn. a thrychan ysgvyt Kynnv(y)dyon. A thrycha(n) wayv Coeling pa neges bynhac yd elynt iddi yn duun. nyt amethei hon honno.[11]

Other figures on the size of British warbands are hard to find. In this regard, Taliesin's poems are notoriously unhelpful – in no place does the poet bother to provide numbers for the warbands of any of the lords by whom he was employed. One gets the overall impression that the numbers involved were small. One of Taliesin's poems (*PT* V) is useful in illustrating the routine and small-scale fighting that must have comprised the bulk of the warfare during this period. Taliesin relates (*PT* V.8) that Urien took his warriors on a raid against Manaw Gododdin for the purpose of stealing "eight-score cattle of the same color" (*wyth vgein vn lliw; o loi a biw*). It seems unlikely that such an operation would have involved hundreds of battle-hardened warriors. The *Historia Brittonum* similarly fails to provide any figures for the number of warriors in Urien's coalition.

The only other firm figures – and these relate to the Irish kingdom of the Dalriadic Scots – are found in the problematic *Senchus Fer n Alban* (*History of the Men of Scotland*).[12] While the *Senchus'* extant manuscripts are of a late date, they evidently derive from a tenth-century compilation, which in turn might have been based on a seventh-century document.[13] If valid, the figures in the *Senchus* would put the total strength of the armed muster required of the three principal districts of Dalriada at around twelve hundred men,[14] figures that seem to call for a Dalriadan military capability that would have greatly

---

[11] The Triad and translation are found in Rachel Bromwich (ed. and tr.), *Trioedd Ynys Prydein: The Welsh Triads* (Cardiff: University of Wales Press, 1978), p. 238. The consistent use of 300 in *The Gododdin* and the triads prompted Williams (*CA*, p. lvii) to propose that the figure represented the standard number of warriors that were to be found in the *teulu/gosgordd* of a Dark-Age chieftain or lord. This view was countered by Jackson (*GOSP*, p. 16).

I would propose that the Triad's use of 300 to reflect the size of a warband was meant to instill a sense of awe of its military prowess and size. Considering the amount of mythological material in the triads, this is a reasonable assumption. In short, rather than representing the actual size of some type of standardized warband (as Williams would have it), the mustering of 300 warriors by a British lord represented such an unusual event that such an accomplishment acquired near-mythic proportions in the Triads.

[12] For text and commentary, see J. Bannerman, *Studies in the History of Dalriada* (Edinburgh: Edinburgh University Press, 1974), pp. 26–156.

[13] See Alcock, *Economy, Society, and Warfare*, p. 216 and the references cited there.

[14] Alcock, *ibid.*, p. 301. However, Alcock noted (*ibid.*, p. 219) the figures as they stand would have meant a crushing military "burden on the *tech* (house) of Dalriada [that] was twenty times as great as that on the *hide* of late Saxon England". Alcock's discussion of these figures, and the problems they present, is found on pp. 216–19. Despite the difficulties surrounding the use of the *Senchus*, Alcock concluded (*ibid.*, p. 216) that "it is possible to discern something of seventh-century military arrangements, provided that the detailed figures are not pressed".

exceeded those of the British chiefdoms already discussed. Even if we were to dismiss the figures in *Senchus*, there is other evidence that reveals Dalriada's marked ability to field relatively large-scale armies. Adomnan's *Life of Columba* relates that the battlefield losses of the Dalriadic Scots, when they fought and defeated the Miathi (a Pictish tribe) in c.590, numbered 303 men.[15] The number of casualties incurred by this victory indicates that Aedan mac Gabran, king of Dalriada, had gone there with a much larger force. Another indication for Dalriada's military pre-eminence can be seen in Aedan's decision to oppose the growing Bernician military threat, a decision that led to the destruction of his forces in 603 by Æthelfrith's army at Degsastan. These references seem to indicate that Dalriada may have been unique in its ability to muster a military force that greatly exceeded several hundred men.

Despite some problems of interpretation and analysis,[16] the archaeological evidence also supports the contention that the numbers of a Dark-Age warband were small. On a comparative basis, the deposits of weapons and other military equipment that have been found in the bogs and lakes of Jutland, the Danish islands, and southern Sweden are particularly instructive. These weapon-deposits have been shown to be, in all probability, the weapons of defeated warbands that were deposited at ceremonial locations by the victors as an offering to their war gods.[17] As such, these deposits offer a unique opportunity

---

[15] A.O. and M.O. Anderson (edd. and tr.), *Adomnan's Life of Columba* (Edinburgh: University of Edinburgh Press, 1961). It should be noted that Columba was on good terms with Aedan, and there is therefore no reason to suspect the general level of casualties that is implied by his figures. The exact figure itself (303) should be regarded as a literary convention.

[16] Most of these problems relate to the question of how accurately the types of weapons, as well as their distribution patterns among pagan Germanic cemeteries, actually reflect the military realities of the day, rather than reflecting a host of other factors, such as an individual's wealth and/or status, the differing burial practices among the diverse groups of Germanic tribes and peoples who settled in Britain, or if the weapons were selected on a symbolic or practical basis. On these problems, see Heinrich Härke's "Early Saxon Weapons Burials: Frequencies, Distributions, and Weapon Combinations", in *Weapons and Warfare in Anglo-Saxon England*, edited by Sonia Chadwick Hawkes, pp. 49–62 (Oxford: Oxford University Committee for Archaeology, 1989). Also, as Hines ("The Military Context of the *Adventus Saxonum*", p. 26 in Hawkes, *op. cit.*) has related, these manifold problems are compounded by the fact that the warriors who met their deaths far from home would not have been brought home for burial, a fact (I might add) that is applicable to victor and vanquished alike. Hines also noted that none of these battlefield gravesites, which must have existed for the proper burial of the fallen of at least the winning side, has yet been discovered (*ibid.*). Hines notes (*ibid.*) as does Härke (*ibid.*, p. 52) that the result is that: "the deceased in weapon-graves in early Anglo-Saxon England and in northern *Germania* in the relevant periods would appear to be those who did not die on the battlefield, and their weapons, to judge by the criterion of cuts, seem normally to have been unused."

[17] See Hines, *ibid.*, pp. 34–35 and the references cited there. These bog sites, while less problematic than the evidence found at Anglo-Saxon cemeteries, are not without some associated difficuties of their own. For these, see *ibid.* at p. 27.

to gauge the size of these defeated warbands with some degree of precision. Using the data of these deposits from thirty or so sites, Hines estimated the size of these warbands from slightly over two hundred men down to forces that numbered in tens instead of hundreds.[18] For the pre-Christian Anglo-Saxons, studies of the distribution of weapons found among the grave-goods in Germanic cemeteries have shown that the percentage of graves in which there are weapons – both in Britain and on the continent – is relatively small. For inhumation burials in Britain, the percentage of adult males buried with a least one weapon ranges from 36% to 62%, depending on the geographic region, figures that consistently are higher than those seen on the continent.[19] However, these figures are artificially high; if cremation burials had been included in the sample, the percentages of weapon-graves for all of these cemeteries – on both sides of the North Sea – would have to be reduced by varying degrees to less than 30% of all male adult burials.[20] The archaeological evidence relating to Dark-Age halls also supports the idea of small warbands during this period. Only the massive timber-framed halls postulated for Yeavering and Cowdrey's Down come close to *Beowulf's* description of Hrothgar's hall at Heorot. In line with the small size of most Dark-Age warbands, most of the British and Anglo-Saxon halls were much smaller affairs.

It is difficult to discern any consistent type of internal "task organization" (that is, organization for combat) within the structure of many of the smaller warbands, or to determine a clear and definite pattern regarding their usual composition. While it is patently obvious that the organization and composition of no two warbands were the same, a few common trends can be noted.

---

[18] *Ibid.*, p. 39. The actual figures for several representative deposits are found at pp. 38–39.

[19] Härke's "Early Saxon Weapons Burials" contains tables, maps, and charts showing relative proportions and absolute numbers of weapon burials in inhumation graves by geographic region, and over time. He also provides an analysis of weapons combinations by region and tribal group, and also compares the types and number of weapons found in Britain with those on the continent. See text and figure on p. 50 for proportion of weapon-graves by region and p. 54 for a comparison of weapon-grave frequencies (by weapon-type) in Britain with those on the continent.

[20] For both Britain and the Germanic homelands, the percentage of cremation burials containing weapon deposits cannot exceed 2 or 3%. Weapon finds in cremation burials are very rare: out of 2,300 or so cremation burials at Spong Hill, perhaps 10 contained weapons (Hines, "Military Context", p. 43). Härke noted ("Early Saxon Weapon Burials", p. 51) that regional disparities of weapon-graves in Britain were in large part due to regional variations in the use of these burial rites (i.e., cremation and inhumation). Specifically, he stated that "the high percentage of weapon burials among inhumations coincides with a high overall proportion of cremations, whereas . . . the virtual absence of cremations coincides with a low percentage of weapon burials among inhumations". Accordingly, if cremations were factored into the sample they would produce overall percentages that would not exceed 30–35% or so of adult male burials.

For more on weapon burials, see Arnold, *Archaeology of Early Anglo-Saxon Kingdoms*, pp. 118–20 and Alcock, *Economy, Society, and Warfare* (pp. 255–81).

The first of these is the marked ability of Celtic and Anglo-Saxon warbands to recruit warriors from outside their own tribal areas. Among the Britons, the most notable example is the composite force, composed of warriors drawn from many British chiefdoms and regions – from Gwynedd, Strathclyde, Elmet, Rheged, and other regions[21] – that had been assembled by Mynyddog Mwynfawr to form the expedition to Catraeth. Similarly, there is at least one clear reference (*PT* XI) in Taliesin's poems that points to this practice of recruiting warriors from outside a kingdom. The poem relates (XI.36) that one of the most valued warriors of Gwallawg's *comitatus* was a certain *Owein mon* (Owain of Anglesey) Also, the *Annals of Ulster* make it clear that British warbands, probably comprising dispossessed warriors from Rheged, were fighting for Irish chieftains along the east coast of Ireland from 682 to 709.[22] Finally, Bede's (*HE* III.14) and Eddius' (*Wilfrid* XLII) stories regarding the success of Ceadwalla in attracting enough warriors to his service to seize the throne of Wessex in 686 demonstrate the marked ability of Dark-Age lords to muster a fighting force for whatever purpose.

Germanic chieftains were equally adept at attracting warriors from outside their tribal areas to serve in their warbands. The story about Guthlac's *comitatus*, which had attracted warriors from "various races" (*diversarum gentium*), was seen earlier in this chapter. To this should be added Bede's story about Oswine, the ruler of Deira. Bede attributed to Oswine many of the virtues of a just and noble ruler while noting (*HE* III.14) that many men from other provinces had come to join his warband (*ad eius ministerium de cunctis prope provinciis viri etiam nobilissimi concurrerent*). Examples in *Beowulf* reinforce the impression that the recruitment of warriors from other kingdoms was not an uncommon practice. Hrothgar's court attracted foreign warriors. Beowulf and his men are one obvious example. Another would be Wulfgar, a prominent member of Hrothgar's retinue, who is described (line 348) as a Vendel chief (*Wendla leod*). Lastly, Beowulf declares (lines 2493–96) that he had always given good service to Hygelac, his Geatish lord, so that "He had not any need to seek the Gifthas, or the Spear-Danes, or the Swedes, for some worse battle-fighter to buy with gifts" (*Næs him ænig þearf, þæt he to Gifðum, oððe to Gar-Denum oððe in Swio-rice secean þurfe wyrsan wigfrecan, weorðe gecypan*). Given the high status of warfare in heroic poetry, the manifold rewards that a successful lord could bestow upon his followers, the frequency of exile, and the geographic dislocation of warriors caused by the ongoing proc-

---

21 See Jarmon's *Aneirin: Y Gododdin*, pp. xxxvi–xxxvii and Jackson's *GOSP*, pp. 18–22 and 27–28.

22 Smyth (*Warlords and Holy Men*, pp. 23–27) makes a good case that Rheged managed to survive until the reign of Aldfrith. Among several of his arguments, he stated that the collapse of Rheged at this time would help explain the sudden appearance of these British warbands into the Irish record and onto Ireland's fragmented military landscape.

esses of amalgamation and consolidation, the use of warriors by Dark-Age kingdoms from outside their own tribal areas should surprise no one.

Another common thread that is woven through our evidence is the consistent use of a chieftain's kin in positions of authority within the structure of the *comitatus*, and as a component of the warband itself. Thus, in Taliesin's poem *Gwaith Argoed Llwyfain* (*PT* VI), despite Urien's presence at the battlefield, we see his son Owain as the principal antagonist to Theodric; it is Owain and not his father who is at the vanguard of Rheged's forces. It is evident that Owain had led the warband during some earlier raids against the coastal regions of Northumbria, where he had earned (*PT* VI.9) the epithet "scourge of the eastlands" (*dwyrein ffossawt*). Among the Dalriadic Scots we find the same thing. For the year 595, the *Annals of Tigernach* record the deaths of three of Aedan's sons at the Battle of Circhenn (*cath Chirchind*), in which the Dalriadan forces were victorious.[23] Since Aedan clearly survived the battle, either he had not been present (having sent his sons to command the army in his stead), or his sons had been assigned to the lead elements of the army. Lastly, if the evidence from the law code of Hywel Dda can be applied to this period (which is problematic), one finds that the placement of relatives in key positions in the warband had taken the force of law, declaring that the chief of the *comitatus* (*penteylu*) was to be a son of the prince (*mab y'r brenhyn*) or his nephew.[24] The Anglo-Saxon kings also used their kinship ties to good advantage, most prominently at the battle of Degsastan in 603, which saw Æthelfrith's army defeat Aedan's army. The *Anglo-Saxon Chronicle* relates that Hering, the son of Hussa, was the leader of the army. Moreover, as Bede relates (*HE* I.34), Æthelfrith was represented in the battle by his brother Theodbald, who was "slain with all those whom he had led of the army" (*cum omni illo quem ipse ducebat exercitu, peremptus est*).

While the internal divisions of a small-scale *comitatus* are difficult to discern, the task becomes somewhat easier when discussing the larger military forces that could be marshalled, at least periodically, by the more powerful kingdoms of this period. The formation of these large armies was, in effect, accomplished by mustering the warbands of a powerful kingdom's subject and/or allied tribes or territories. In other words, the basic unit of organization, or the "building block", for these large-scale armies was the *comitatus*. Commanded by its own lord – whether king or chieftain, Celtic or Germanic – each warband was assigned a particular mission or task for the battle, and each was committed to the fray as an integral fighting unit.

[23] See Stokes, *The Annals of Tigernach* (*AT*), p. 120. The battle is also noted by the *Annals of Ulster* (*AU*) and the *Annals of Insfallen* (*AI*), for the years 595 and 590 repectively.
[24] Aled Rhys Wiliam (ed.), *Llyfr Iowerth: A Critical Text of the Venedotian Code of Medieval Welsh Law* (Cardiff: University of Wales Press, 1960), p. 4.

The period's sources are replete with information that would indicate that this was the manner in which large-scale armies were formed, organized, and committed to battle. Some examples already have been seen: the British coalition forces of Urien, Rhydderch Hen, Morcant, and Gwallawg; the mustering of large Dalriadan forces, according to the *Senchus Fer nAlban*, by combining the musters of its principal provinces and districts; the "four-fold host" (*petwar llu*) that was led against Urien at the battle of *Argoet Llwyfein*, and the *Anglo-Saxon Chronicle* entry regarding the "three kings" (*iii. kyningas*) who were killed at Durham by Cuthwine and Cealwin in 577. Other examples can be added: the mustering of warriors from distinct regions of Rheged; the "compact and clearly sketched little party from Gwynedd", forming one of the contingents of the Catraeth expedition; Edwin's retaliatory strike into Wessex, where he "struck down five kings"; and the thirty *duces regii* who were slain with Penda at Winwidfeld.[25] A final example might be Bede's story (*HE* II.12) about Rædwald's overthrow of Æthelfrith, though Bede does not give the particulars of how these forces were mustered. Given Æthelfrith's inability to muster his all his forces in a timely manner, it might be inferred that distinct warbands missed the rendezvous with the other warbands constituting the Northumbrian army.

The assumption that these large-scale armies comprised allied or subordinate warbands, each of which was assigned a particular mission or region on the battlefield, also helps to explain how important lords and their men, fighting on the winning side, were nevertheless destroyed during the course of these battles. Bede's information about Theobald at Degsastan and the entry from the *Annals of Tigernach* about the death of three of Aedan's sons during Dalriada's victory at *cath Chirchind*, are explained more satisfactorily by assuming that these unlucky princes (and their equally unlucky men) had been assigned a particularly dangerous task in a hazardous portion of the battlefield. In any case, when it did occur, the mustering of diverse warbands to form larger armies must have been a notable event, recalling the "Mustering of the Companies" scenes found in the *Tain Bo Cualinge* and other mythological tales and sagas of the Ulster cycle.[26]

An equally difficult topic is the question involving the tactics and overall strategy (if any) that the warbands employed to accomplish their military objectives. In particular, the task of defining, with any degree of clarity,

---

25 See, respectively: Alcock, *Economy, Society, and Warfare*, p. 291; Jackson, *GOSP*, pp. 27–28; and the *Chronicle* entries for the years 626 and 655.

26 On the historical validity and use of this material, see Jackson, *The Oldest Irish Tradition*. Typically, these scenes depict company after company of fierce warriors as they arrive at a designated mustering site; often the story gives details about the companies themselves as well as about the lords who led them. Such scenes represent a stock literary device used in many of the Irish sagas and myths. At least for the Irish, it would seem that military units were organized on the basis of these companies.

strategic considerations that might have played a role in the decision-making processes of the chieftains and kings of this turbulent age is a difficult, if not an impossible, one. In part, this is due simply to the non-applicability of strategic considerations to most of the endemic warfare and high levels of violence that characterized this period.[27] Another factor that hampers an understanding of strategic goals during the period is our virtual lack of knowledge regarding the political boundaries of Dark-Age kingdoms and the location of many key battles.[28] Consequently, we cannot determine whether the defense of kingdoms was effected at their boundaries, or which terrain was considered to be vital during the course of a campaign. While it stands to reason that chieftains would have preferred to engage a raiding force at the borders of their territories, before any damage or theft could occur to people or property, how often this preferred course of action actually was translated into historical reality is unknown. The only clear instances of a force than can be viewed as a "border patrol" are found in one of Taliesin's poems and in *Beowulf*. In the former, Taliesin relates (*PT* VIII.36–8) that warriors from Rheged guarded her borders from the advent of summer "until winter" (*y dan araf*). In *Beowulf* (lines 229–30) the hero and his men are spotted at the shore while securing their ship by a warrior who had been assigned to guard the shoreline. In any case, without such fundamental and rudimentary knowledge, an analysis of the underlying strategy that may have helped to shape the conduct of warfare is futile.

Regarding the overall conduct of warfare, about the only thing that can be

[27] Endemic warfare refers to small-scale activities: feuds, banditry, raids, and counter-raids. In anthropological terms, it is referred to as "ritual" warfare. While the *Chronicle*, Bede, and the Irish and Welsh annals focus on the large-scale "Non-Ritual" warfare (called "Wars of Conquest"), it is clear that the former type must have been the norm for this period's warfare. For the differences between these two levels of warfare (in definition, purpose, and result), see Halsall's "Anthropology . . . Warfare and Society". In light of this, it is obvious that strategic considerations are inappropriate for the level of warfare in which Dark-Age warriors were engaged.

[28] It is with good reason that maps fail to provide boundary lines for Dark-Age kingdoms and peoples: they are unknown. This is not to say that the "core areas" of kingdoms cannot be plotted spatially; trend surface maps of Anglo-Saxon cemeteries have been used to define population nodes, or aggregates, which then can be used to locate a kingdom's core area. (For an example, see the map on p. 165 in Arnold's *Archaeology of Early Anglo-Saxon Kingdoms*).

Of potential use in this regard are the theoretical models created by the use of unweighted Theissen Polygons in order to delineate Anglo-Saxon frontiers (see Arnold, *op. cit.*, pp. 184–87 for methodology and results, and map on p. 186). While such constructs may prove useful, my chief objection to them, as they are designed at present, is their lack of weighting for the different sizes of the populations involved in the models. This methodology is at odds with the more accurate and reliable gravity-modeling techniques used by the field of economic geography to explain, in spatial terms, various modes of human interaction. Despite this shortcoming, the models do have much potential.

said with confidence is that armies during the period's later years were larger and had a greater degree of mobility than did earlier ones. The presence of larger military units can be seen as a natural result of the ongoing processes of territorial amalgamation and political consolidation. The increased mobility of these armies, reflected in the longer distances that can be surmised for seventh-century campaigns than those seen for the fifth or sixth, is due in large part to an increasing use of the horse on the part of the Anglo-Saxons during the course of the seventh century.[29] Furthermore, forts and other fortified sites – such as Scottish *crannogs* and the British *llys*, or defended stronghold – do not seem to have played a major role in warfare. In fact, with the exception of Bamburgh, there is no archaeological evidence that the Anglo-Saxons even used fortified places.[30] Finally, this discussion about Dark-Age strategy might itself be unnecessary. Strategic considerations, at least as we know the term, simply may not have existed in the minds of these kings and chieftains. The usual geopolitical and economic causes of war – the typical "reasons of state" – do not appear to have figured prominently in the deliberative process of Germanic and Celtic rulers in deciding when, where, and against whom to wage war. Instead, we find that, "with the few exceptions where land is mentioned, the majority of the recorded causes of wars stress human grievances or insults".[31]

An accurate portrayal of Dark-Age tactics presents a challenge that is only slightly less formidable than that offered by Dark-Age strategy. As was the case for the training of British and Anglo-Saxon warriors, the chief difficulty is that the annals, chronicles, and major histories for the period (by Bede, Gildas, Nennius, *et alia*) offer little or no insight into the battlefield tactics that were practiced by their contemporaries. Heroic literature offers a few clues about contemporary tactics, though the information is obscured at times in the chaos of the poetry's battle scenes, and even this information is subject to a variety of interpretations.[32]

---

[29] For these campaigns, see p. 303 (map) in Alcock, *Economy, Society, and Warfare*. For Anglo-Saxon use of the horse, see Campbell (p. 59), "The First Christian Kings", in *The Anglo-Saxons*, edited by James Campbell, Eric John, and Patrick Wormald, pp. 45–69 (Ithaca, New York: Cornell University Press, 1982).

[30] Alcock, *Economy, Warfare, and Society*, pp. 307, 214–16, 307–10.

[31] Halsall, "Anthropology . . . Warfare, and Society", p. 168. These recorded causes relate to the causes of these wars as the people involved in them perceived them. For more on this point, see J.E. Cross, "The Ethic of War in Old English", in *England Before the Conquest: Studies in Primary Sources Presented to Dorothy Whitelock*, edited by Peter Clemoes and Kathleen Hughes, pp. 269–82 (Cambridge: Cambridge University Press, 1971).

[32] For example, Jackson proposed various tactics for the Britons based on passages and terms in the *Gododdin*, though the results of his analysis (*GOSP*, pp. 28–33) are mixed. For the difficulties of using heroic poetry for this purpose, see Alcock, *Economy, Society, and Warfare*, pp. 306–07; for a different analysis of the *Gododdin* data, see Alcock, *ibid.*, pp. 234–54.

Despite these problems, a few tactics do stand out. First, the *Gododdin* contains enough references to infantry being drawn up into ranks or squares for the purpose of forming shield walls to allow the conclusion that this was a common tactic used by the Britons at least.[33] Equally clear is British use of the horse, in contrast (at least during the fifth and sixth centuries) to the Anglo-Saxons; there is a virtual absence of equipment associated with horses – horse bits, spurs, and the like – among Anglo-Saxon pagan grave-goods.[34] References in the *Gododdin* and in Taliesin's poetry[35] show that, apart from some very limited value for the harassment of enemy lines by individual warriors, the horse was used only to carry warriors to the site of a battle, where they would dismount prior to the start of real hostilities. Given the surprisingly small size of horses of this period,[36] no other scenario is credible. Another possible tactic used by both sides is the dawn attack.[37] Because most warfare was conducted during the summer months, the cooler temperatures found during dawn attacks would have been less draining on the warriors' stamina, and allowed them to sustain a higher level of physical activity than would have been the case had the battles taken place in the relative heat of the afternoon. Beyond these proposals, no other tactics for this period can be discerned with any confidence.

Because of archaeology, we can discuss the weapons and equipment of Celtic and Germanic warriors[38] with a higher degree of confidence. The principal weapons were the double-edged sword, the spear, and the shield. Other weapons included the single-edged military knife (or *seax*), and the axe. Grave-goods evidence reveals that the sword was the least common of the

---

[33] For the *Gododdin's* examples, see Jackson, *GOSP*, p. 30. The evidence for Anglo-Saxon use of this tactic is more problematic; the terms *bord-weal* and *scyld-burh* are found only in tenth-century heroic poetry (in *The Battle of Maldon* and *The Battle of Brunanburh*). However, if these "shield walls" proved to be effective, it is likely that the Anglo-Saxons would have been quick to incorporate the tactic.

[34] For example, only one grave out of 702 burials in Britain that were examined by Härke were found to contain horse bits or spurs. See Table 4.1 (p. 54), in "Early Saxon Weapons Burials". See also Alcock, *Economy, Society, and Warfare*, p. 300.

[35] For examples, see Jackson, *GOSP*, pp. 28–30.

[36] According to R.H.C. Davis (p. 141 in "Did the Anglo-Saxons Have Warhorses?", in *Weapons and Warfare in Anglo-Saxon England*, edited by Sonia Chadwick Hawkes, pp. 141–44) "the indigenous horse of N. W. Europe and Britain was no larger than a Shetland pony (8–10 hands)".

[37] See Alcock, *Economy, Society, and Warfare*, p. 307 for some examples.

[38] A summary of the weapons and equipment of the Britons, Irish, and Anglo-Saxons is found in *ibid.*, pp. 295–300. Figures 19.3 and 19.4 (on pp. 296–7) are particularly useful for comparing weapon characteristics of the three groups. Alcock's analysis regarding the archaeological and literary evidence is convincing. For a further overview of weapons, see Arnold, *Archaeology of Early Anglo-Saxon Kingdoms*, pp. 118–20 and pp. 100–04.

principal weapons, found in only about 11% of Anglo-Saxon graves;[39] various weapon-deposits in Jutland and southern Sweden suggest that between 10 and 30% of warriors carried swords.[40] While there is no archaeological evidence as to the distribution and characteristics of swords among the Britons, numerous references to swords in the *Gododdin* and in Taliesin's poems make it clear that they existed. Given their similar social structure and degree of economic development, the distribution of swords among British warriors probably was comparable to that seen for the Anglo-Saxons. In sum, the sword should be seen as the weapon that can be associated with the wealthier or more successful[41] members of a warband. Still, it should be noted that, at least in heroic poetry, swords could be given to any member of a warband, regardless of his standing within the *comitatus'* social structure, as a reward for particularly notable service.

The spear and shield appear to have formed the basic weapon set for most of the warriors of a Celtic or Germanic warband. The spear was far easier to construct and consequently was far less expensive than the sword, yet must have been a greatly effective weapon. Numerous references in battle poetry clearly show that spears could be used either as hand-held infantry pikes or as thrown javelins, to be hurled at enemy lines. In view of the improbable use of the horse in a cavalry context, it is highly unlikely that spears were used as cavalry lances.[42] If the two-spear set often found in Anglo-Saxon graves offers any accurate reflection of an actual warrior's gear, then one can infer

---

[39] See figures 4.1 and 4.3, in Härke's "Early Saxon Weapon Burials", pp. 54 and 56. Out of 534 burials examined, only 62 contained swords. Figure 4.4 on p. 57 shows the regional differences in sword burials. See also graphs on p. 119 in Arnold (*ibid.*).

[40] Hines, "Military Context", pp. 38–9.

[41] There has been much work on Anglo-Saxon swords, most notably H.R.E. Davidson's *The Sword in Anglo-Saxon England: Its Archaeology and Literature* (Oxford: The Clarendon Press, 1962; repr. Woodbridge, England: The Boydell Press, 1994). For an overview of the subject see Peter Bone, "The Development of Anglo-Saxon Swords from the Fifth to the Eleventh Century", in *Weapons and Warfare in Anglo-Saxon England*, edited by Sonia Chadwick Hawkes, pp. 63–70 (Oxford: Oxford University Committee for Archaeology, 1989). For the construction of swords, and for the importance of the "pattern-welding" process in the manufacture of stronger, more flexible blades, see Janet Lang and Barry Ager, "Swords of the Anglo-Saxon and Viking Periods in the British Museum: A Radiographic Study", in Hawkes, *ibid.*, pp. 85–122. For Irish swords, with which British swords of this period might be compared, see: J.P. Mallory, "The Sword of the Ulster Cycle", and E. Rynne, "A Classification of Pre-Viking Iron Swords" in *Studies in Early Ireland*, edited by B.G. Scott, pp. 99–114 and pp. 93–97.

[42] Both Jackson (*GOSP*, p. 32) and Alcock (*Economy, Warfare, and Society*, p. 298) envision the use of the spear as a cavalry lance, in addition to its use as an infantry pike and a javelin. Given the objections to the existence of cavalry during this period, such a use is not credible. For references to spears in the *Gododdin*, see Jackson, *ibid.* For references to spears (*par*) in the poems of Taliesin, see Williams' *PT*, at *PT* V.29 and VIII.13 (*pren on*: ash wood, meaning a spear).

that one of the spears was thrown as a javelin, while the other was retained for use as a pike once the opposing sides had closed on each other. In any case, based on the heroic literature and the archaeological evidence,[43] it is evident that the spear was the most common weapon on the battlefield. Other potential weapons, such as the single-edged sword (i.e., military knife, or *seax*), axe, bow and arrow, and other, more exotic weapons, appear to have been used only rarely, if at all.[44]

Against this array of offensive weaponry, the Dark-Age warrior entrusted his safety first and foremost to his shield. Given the grave-goods evidence and the numerous references in heroic poetry to shattered and splintered shields, one should conclude that all warriors carried one into battle. The shields were small and circular, made of wood, and sometimes covered with leather or (in a few, rare instances) embossed with metalwork. It seems that the Britons preferred to whitewash their shields.[45] The central hole through which the handle was fixed was protected by a metal boss, which could be used as an offensive weapon.[46] Further, as Alcock has argued,[47] with the exception of all but a few of the wealthiest individuals, body armor should be seen in the form of protective leather jerkins, and not as chain mail. Finally, the existence and use of helmets among Britons and Anglo-Saxons is as rare as that evidenced for chain mail. For the most part, the only things that prevented a warrior's death or serious injury[48] were a small wooden shield, his own military prowess, and his physical strength and agility.

[43] For the distribution of spears in Anglo-Saxon graves and in continental weapon deposits, see Härke, "Early Saxon Weapon Burials" (p. 54) and Hines, "Military Context" (pp. 38–39). For the making of spears and the materials used, see Arnold, *Archaeology of Early Anglo-Saxon Kingdoms*, p. 102; p. 119 shows their distribution. The major work on spears is M.J. Swanton, *Pagan Anglo-Saxon Spear-Types* (British Archaeological Reports, No. 7. Oxford: BAR Publications, 1974).

[44] See Alcock (*Economy, Society, and Warfare*, p. 298) for a useful summary and for the period's more exotic weapons – the angon and the *fransisca*. In particular, the bow and arrow should be seen primarily as a hunting weapon, and the hand-held axe as more of an all-around tool than a weapon. Their overall utility in everyday affairs might serve to explain their virtual absence from Anglo-Saxon graves (Arnold, *op. cit.*, p. 120). David Gale has shown that the *seax* should be viewed as a hunting knife rather than an effective military weapon (see Gale, "The *Seax*", in Hawkes' *Weapons and Warfare*, pp. 71–84 and Hawkes' remarks in her introduction (p. 5) regarding the "practical demonstration of its total ineffectiveness against both sword and spear").

[45] Jackson, *GOSP*, p. 33.

[46] For a description of shields and bosses and their construction, see Arnold, *Archaeology of Early Anglo-Saxon Kingdoms*, pp. 102–04. For Irish parallels, see Alcock, *Economy, Society, and Warfare*, pp. 298–99.

[47] *Ibid*, p. 299.

[48] The damage that could be wrought by any of these weapons was immense. For an analysis of this damage, based on an analysis of skeletal remains, see Sarah J. Wenham, "Anatomical Interpretations of Anglo-Saxon Weapon Injuries", in *Weapons and Warfare in Anglo-Saxon England*, edited by Sonia Chadwick Hawkes, pp. 123–40 (Oxford: Oxford University Committee for Archaeology, 1989).

CHAPTER FOUR

SOCIAL STRUCTURE

In considering the social structure and internal workings of Dark-Age warbands, several questions need to be addressed: (1) the place of the *comitatus*
within the overall social structure, (2) the levels of social rank and wealth
found within the *comitatus* itself, (3) the relationships between warriors and
lord, (4) the role of the ruling family's members and of kinship ties within the
warband, and (5) the special role played by the lord-retainer relationship, and
its impact upon kinship ties.

Celtic and Anglo-Saxon chiefdoms and kingdoms organized their military
forces along aristocratic lines. The members of these warbands were part of
the dominant social class that presided over the Dark-Age cultures of Britain.
In both a Celtic and a Germanic context, these military-aristocracies formed
the apex of the clearly-graded social structures found among the peoples and
tribes of Britain during these centuries. These social structures were the result
of several factors, and reflect the economic and social changes that were
occurring during these years. Regarding this development, it can be seen that:

> A number of factors deemed to be relevant to the control of the emergence
> of complex ranked societies in early Anglo-Saxon England can be examined
> using archaeological data. These may be summarized as: increased specialization
> in procurement and production; increasing access to resources, producing an
> exploitive elite and authoritarian leadership; trade and limited vengeance
> warfare for resource acquisition. Thus the type of structural hierarchy under
> examination appears as a function of the interrelation of population and activ-
> ity conglomerates, movement minimalization, and differential accessibility,
> often emerging in clusters under conditions of mutual competition.[1]

The social composition of the dominant military class was far from mono-
lithic, with its social structure divided into several distinct grades. It is this
social class as a whole – its martial ideals, activities, and material culture – that
receives the exclusive focus of heroic literature in Britain and elsewhere. As
Chapter 3 showed, the conduct of warfare between Dark-Age kingdoms was
left to this military class in a period that was characterized by varying degrees

---

[1] Arnold, *Archaeology of Early Anglo-Saxon Kingdoms*, p. 164.

of organized violence – ranging from feuds to large-scale (non-ritual) wars of conquest – and by an overall high degree of unorganized violence (such as assaults, murders, and non-aristocratic feuds). While virtually all of the warfare and organized violence can be attributed to the warrior-aristocracy, the other types of violence also were initiated by non-noble kinship groups.

Among the Anglo-Saxons, the social structure in which their tribes functioned had already begun a process of stratification that could be seen among these peoples when they were still in their continental homelands. Based on the thinly spread distribution of weapon-graves throughout Jutland, southern Sweden, and northern Germany, John Hines sees the existence of a:

> thinly spread élite, an élite within which even the non-sword bearers could
> be counted. Warfare would seem to have been the business of this élite and
> few others; the lowest-class fighters represented at Ejsbøl seem to be arch-
> ers, and these would seem to have made up a pitiable supplementary minor-
> ity rather than a massed peasant host supporting their better armed masters.[2]

As Chapter 2 has shown, it was this thinly-spread military élite that had been brought over to Britain as *foederati*[3] during the second quarter of the fifth century by "all the counselors, together with the haughty tyrant" (*omnes conciliarii una cum superbo tyranno*), for use against the Pictish threat. Even after the rebellion of the *foederati* in the mid-fifth century, the entries in the *Anglo-Saxon Chronicle* suggest that the warbands responsible for the early landings and subsequent land-takings were comprised of professional warriors. These small-scale warbands acted as the lead elements in the processes of migration and settlement that involved Angles, Saxons, Jutes, and other Germanic tribes who were crossing over to Britain's shores. Only after the warband had first seized and secured an area would the introduction of the civilian elements of a tribe to that area take place. The *Anglo-Saxon Chronicle* and the *De Excidio* imply that there existed a clear dichotomy in roles and functions between the civilian and military segments of these tribes. Given the small numbers involved in the initial operations, it also seems likely that the military organization of the warbands continued to be along aristocratic lines, as it had been on the continent.

---

[2] Hines, "Military Context", p. 44.

[3] Hines (*ibid.*, p. 45), stated that his model of an élite composition for these continental warbands would have provided "ready-formed bodies of men capable of transplantation into the Roman defensive system as regular *numeri* or *laeti*". However, at least in a British context, I would disagree with his assessment that this type of organization "is of little relevance to the model of the less-controlled *foederati*". Given the evidence in *De Excidio* regarding the initial warbands, it is likely that his model for a small military élite is equally valid for the first warbands which had been introduced onto the island as *foederati*. In any case, even in regard to the *foederati*, Hines noted (*ibid.*) that "in general terms, it does not match with any image of anarchic hordes of barbarians, all men armed to the teeth, divulging upon a civilized Britain from over the North Sea".

It seems likely that the migration itself began to exert an influence upon Germanic society's traditional social structure, as well as upon the social hierarchy within the *comitatus* itself. It was shown earlier that most of these landings, and the subsequent proliferation of kingdoms, probably had been conducted not under the royal auspices of continental dynasties, but rather by adventurers acting on their own behalf. In essence, the overall patterns of Anglo-Saxon settlement had been shaped in their specifics by the boldness, initiative, and military prowess of lesser lords acting independently of their tribal chieftains on the continent. This was a natural result of the political and social chaos that must have accompanied the process of migration, in part because "migration and colonization provide almost a classic situation for social and political divergence between branches of a dividing group".[4] Consequently, it can be assumed that there were greater opportunities for advancement, both within the ranks of the warrior élite itself and within the overall social structure of Germanic society: opportunities that were open to those who possessed the initiative and daring to seize them, regardless of their social standing. Elaborating on this point, Hines has remarked that:

> Despite the evidence for social stratification amongst earlier Germanic folk, there is some justification for regarding the culture of Migration-period England, certainly for the decades after *circa* 475, as being fundamentally egalitarian in the sense that positions of power were open to any with the strength to seize and hold them, not restricted by non-utilitarian qualifications such as birth.[5]

Assuming that weapon-burial distributions found in Britain offer a reasonably accurate portrayal of the military realities of the day, and even assuming that there remained a clear division in both role and status between the tribes' civilian and military segments, the size of the Germanic warrior-aristocracy (*gesiðcund*) in Britain clearly was higher as a proportion of the population than had been seen on the continent.[6] This higher level of weapon-bearing males probably reflects a broadening of membership for the *gesiðcund* as the social structure became less hierarchical in response to the geopolitical situ-

---

[4] *Ibid.*

[5] *Ibid.*

[6] For a comparison between Britain and the continent, see Härke, "Early Saxon Weapon Burials", p. 54 at Table 4.2. Commenting on these differences, Hawkes stated (*ibid.*, p. 4) that this conclusion was reasonable because "obviously the success of the land-takings in England will have depended on the presence and protection of more weapon-bearing males than were needed to maintain the *status quo* at home". In no way, however, should this data be taken to imply the existence of "a large mass of yeoman-warriors", as Alcock would have it (*Economy, Society, and Warfare*, p. 262). In this case, Alcock has misinterpreted the data when he sees an idealized, egalitarian structure where there simply is none, as when he avers (*ibid.*, p. 263) that "archaeological evidence and documentary sources concur in presenting the mass of Wessex peasants as warriors too". I do not concur with his analysis, which equates all free men with free

43

ation on the island during these decades.[7] As a consequence of the number of kingdoms that were founded during the late fifth and early sixth centuries – a result of Germanic settlement of Britain's interior regions and the political fragmentation of some of the recently-established kingdoms – the number of warriors required to defend the Germanic-held territories must have risen to such a degree that the continental military structure, with its restricted membership, was unable to handle the new situation in Britain.[8]

The effects of this slightly egalitarian trend were soon to be reversed. Beginning around the mid-sixth century, Anglo-Saxon society began to regain more of its former social stratification. This restratification is reflected in both archaeological and written evidence. First, the number of weapon-graves, both in terms of absolute numbers and as a percentage of adult male burials, peaks at AD 535/540 and AD 535–555 respectively, after which there is a steady decline.[9] Evidence of this restratification is reinforced by an analysis of Anglo-Saxon weapon-graves, which "suggests that in the earlier cemeteries there was a more equal distribution of the favoured weapon combinations, with a higher proportion of weapon graves; both are reduced with time".[10] The trend toward greater social stratification held true even within the ranks of the *gesiðcund*; it is a trend seen in the introduction, by the end of the sixth century, of princely burials under mounds, such as those seen at Sutton Hoo, Taplow, and Broomfield. In sum, the archaeological record consistently reflects an increasing stratification of Germanic society.[11]

warriors, and think it wiser to follow H. M. Chadwick, who noted in *The Heroic Age* (p. 352) that the conduct of warfare was left to the *gesiðcund* in marked contrast to the Franks and other continental Germans.

7 Hines ("Military Context", p. 45) stated that: "any recasting there was of an inherited hierarchical system, any broadening and simplification of the military élite mirrored by such material remains as cemeteries with more weapon graves and simpler and more practicable weapon sets is best dated . . . to the virtually unrestrained expansion and consolidation of Germanic settlement falling in a conventionaly-datable way between *circa* 475 and 525."

8 Commenting on this point, Hawkes noted (*Weapons and Warfare*, p. 4) that "the evidence from individual Germanic cemeteries established in the fifth century suggests that land could be taken and held in Britain by Anglo-Saxon communities with just one or two major weapon-bearing families in charge".

9 Härke, "Early Saxon Weapon Burials", pp. 51–2 and figures 4.2 and 4.3 (on p. 53).

10 Arnold, *Archaeology of Early Anglo-Saxon Kingdoms*, p. 169.

11 *Ibid.*, pp. 142 and 178–80. Also see Arnold, "Social Evolution in Post-Roman Europe". For the uneven distribution of goods that was the result of, and provides indications for, this stratification, see: M. Carver, "Kingship and Material Culture in Early Anglo-Saxon East Anglia", in *The Origin of Anglo-Saxon Kingdoms* (at pp. 149–50) edited by Steven Bassett, pp. 141–58 (Leicester: Leicester University Press, 1989); Arnold, "Wealth and Social Structure: A Matter of Life and Death", in *Anglo-Saxon Cemeteries*, British Archaeological Reports, No. 82, edited by Rahtz, Dickenson, and Watts, pp. 81–142 (Oxford: BAR Publications, 1980).
   As Hines noted (*The Scandinavian Character of Anglian England in the pre-Viking*

The archaeological evidence dovetails with that found in the period's written sources. The various genealogies of the Anglo-Saxons, whose first credible rulers are dated to the third quarter of the sixth century, reflect the rise of hereditary dynasties among the tribes in Britain as ruling families sought to consolidate their positions of power and validate their pre-eminent social standing within the warrior-élites of this period.[12] By the close of the sixth century, the process of social stratification had resulted in a clearly-graded society, whose existence is seen plainly in the *wergild* or *manbot* (man-price) that early Anglo-Saxon law codes accorded the members of the different social classes. These codes reveal the existence of several classes even within the *gesiðcund*, assigning different monetary values on the lives of common warriors, lesser lords (*thegn*), greater lords (*ealdorman*), princes (*ætheling*), and kings (*cyning*).[13]

The differences that existed within the Anglo-Saxon class structure would be strengthened during the course of the seventh century as warbands made greater use of the horse in the conduct of long-range expeditions, a use whose economic and logistical implications would have called for a reduction of the number of warriors within the *gesiðcund* class as a percentage of the overall population.[14] By Bede's era, these class differences, especially those which

Period, British Archaeological Reports, No. 124. Oxford: BAR Publications, 1984, p. 285), the wide and costly array of grave goods associated with princely burials should be seen as a display of power and wealth that may have helped reinforce the position of the ruling families. In this regard, they would have served the same function as the genealogies.

[12] See Dumville, "Kingship, Genealogies, and Regnal Lists", in *Early Medieval Kingship*, edited by P.H. Sawyer and I.N. Wood, pp. 72–104 (Leeds: University of Leeds, 1977) for dating and use. He states (p. 87) that the reasonably credible and accurate, non-fictionalized elements of these genealogies represent "only that extent (perhaps four or five generations) which is essential to the smooth running of the social structure". In essence, the use of genealogies became an effective method (like panegyric poetry) by which members of the dominant family or social grouping could enhance their status in relation to other members of the warrior aristocracy. See also Yorke, *Kings and Kingdoms*, p. 4.

[13] See Kirby, *The Earliest English Kings*, p. 2. The purpose of these blood-payments was to curtail the number and extent of the incessant blood-feuds between kinship groups that had plagued Germanic society. By accepting a money payment for a death or injury, it was hoped that ongoing acts of vengeance and retaliation between kinship groups, and the social turmoil created by these acts, could be reduced.

In any case, the law codes also show that the *gesiðcund*'s members, whatever their precise social rank, constituted an élite that presided over Anglo-Saxon kingdoms in which peasants, slaves, and native Britons formed most of the population.

The evidence provided by these early law codes is not without some problems of its own. For these, see Patrick Wormald's "*Lex Scripta* and *Verbum Regis*: Legislation and Germanic Kingship from Euric to Cnut", in *Early Medieval Kingship*, edited by P.H. Sawyer and I.N. Wood, pp. 105–38 (Leeds: University of Leeds, 1977).

[14] Anglo-Saxon use of the horse and its logistical implications were seen in the previous chapter. For the social implications that are inherent in such a use, see N.P. Brooks,

separated the members of the *gesiðcund* from the other segments of the population, had become firmly entrenched in social behavior and cultural perception, as Bede's story regarding Imma (a Northumbrian *thegn*) shows. Bede relates (*HE* IV.22) that Imma, wounded and taken prisoner in battle, attempted to deceive his Mercian captors by passing himself off as a peasant (*rusticus*) who worked in the Northumbrian logistics train. He was found out, however, betrayed by the countenance and bearing that showed him to be not a *rusticus*, but a warrior (*miles*).

British culture and society was no less hierarchical and clearly graded than that of the Anglo-Saxons. However, because of its lack of grave-goods, it is more difficult to quantify; due to the problematic nature of the Welsh laws,[15] it is also more difficult to determine the precise legal status and the specific requirements of the different classes within the Celtic social structure during this period. However, even given these limitations, it is possible to say a few things regarding the status of the *comitatus* in the social structure of the British kingdoms.

As for so many other aspects of the *comitatus* during the early sixth century, Gildas is our chief informant for the place of these warbands in British social structure. As was seen earlier, Gildas' *De Excidio* was a wide-ranging condemnation of the ruling British lords of his day, and of the nascent *comitatus* structure over which they presided. It is obvious from Gildas'

"Arms, Status, and Warfare in late-Saxon England", in *Ethelred the Unready*, British Archaeological Reports No. 59, edited by David Hill, pp. 81–103 (Oxford: BAR Publications, 1978).

As noted by Alcock (*Economy, Society, and Warfare*, p. 265), the first specific reference to Anglo-Saxon use of the horse in Britain is found in the *Life of Wilfrid*. The text relates (XIX) that in 672 Ecgfrith "assembled an expedition of cavalry . . . and invaded" (*equitatui exercitu praeparto . . . invasit*) the territory of the Picts in order to crush a rebellion. While this entry denotes the first specific use of cavalry, given the wide geographic range of Germanic miltary expeditions during the seventh century, it is unlikely that this event marked the first instance of the use of horses in an Anglo-Saxon campaign.

[15] In using these law codes, one must assume that there is a reasonable correlation between the legal status and obligations contained in the codes and the actual social realities of the period. In all probability, given the limited organizational resources of the kingdoms, the benefits and obligations associated with one's social class were no doubt less rigid than the codes – both Celtic and Germanic – would imply.

While caution should be used even for the more contemporary Anglo-Saxon law codes, this is true especially in regard to the Welsh laws when they are used as a source for this period, or at least with more caution than is exerted by Alcock in his *Economy, Society, and Warfare*. Without corroborating evidence from either archaeological or other written sources, such anachronistic use is open to criticism, such as that leveled by David Dumville and Wendy Davies. In particular, Davies has cast doubts on the utility of these Welsh laws as sources for this period (*Wales in the Early Middle Ages*, at pp. 202–05). For a partial refutation of her "minimalist stance", see Alcock's arguments (*ibid.*) at pp. 84–88.

attacks on Maelgwn and four other British lords (referred to at *DE* 37.2 as "these five mad and debauched horses") that he viewed their governments as illegitimate and the ruling lords themselves as usurpers (*tyranni*). Gildas' treatment of these contemporary lords is in stark contrast to the approval that he gave to Ambrosius Aurelianus and other earlier rulers, who ruled in a time when, as Gildas (*DE* 26.2–3) relates, "kings, public and private [persons], priests and churchmen, kept to their own ranks" (*reges, publici, privati, sacerdotes, ecclesiastici, suum quique ordinem servarunt*). In part, Gildas' opposition to the recently-established military governments of his day could be seen as a result of his adamant support of the older social structure and political hierarchy (*DE* 26.3), whose "controls of truth and justice have been shaken and subverted" (*veritatis ac iustitiae moderamina concussa ac subversa sunt*). Rather than a nostalgic call for a return to "the good old days", Gildas' writings should be seen as a conservative's reaction to an earlier political and social revolution that evidently had caused both the ruling élite and the old social order of the fifth century to be displaced by the advent and subsequent rise of the warrior-aristocracies in the initial decades of the sixth century.

In fact, it is likely that some of Gildas' lords were members of existing dynasties, while others were not. Vortiper evidently had come to power through legal means. In calling him (*DE* 31.1) the "bad son of a good king" (*boni regis nequam fili*), Gildas is condemning his actions as a ruler and not the method (father-to-son succession) by which he had come to power. On the other hand, Gildas condemns Maelgwn (33.4), who had come by the throne of Gwynedd as a young warrior by "crushing the king your uncle and nearly [all] his bravest warriors with sharp weapons". Similarly, Coroticus, the lord who (as was seen above) Patrick had condemned in his *Epistle* for his men's behavior, should be seen as another self-made lord who had established himself through force of arms amid the social and political wreckage of the late fifth century. Regardless of their precise social origins, these lords established themselves at the apex of a new social order that saw military service and battle prowess as avenues for social and economic advancement. In the political and economic weakness of post-Roman Britain, and especially in the chaos that followed the rebellion of the Saxon *foederati*, the island was rife with opportunities for those with the strength and courage to seize them. As with the Anglo-Saxons, the dominant class in British society became one that was comprised of able-bodied warriors, and one that maintained its power over British society through force of arms, and through a variety of mechanisms (examined in Chapters 6–9) which served to maintain the *comitatus* structure.

However, even with this displacement of the previous social and political order, British society was never as egalitarian as that shown to exist among the Anglo-Saxons. If the evidence of the Welsh laws can be trusted for this period, one finds that British society was more hierarchical, consisting of a sharply tapered pyramid, with the king and his *teulu* at the top, supported by a broad base of bondmen.[16] Though the evidence is far from conclusive, a key difference between Celtic and Germanic social structure might lie in the possible existence of non-noble freemen among the Anglo-Saxons, and their probable absence among the Britons.[17] In part, the more highly-stratified Celtic social structure was the result of an early, consistent reliance on the horse in warfare; the logistical and economic constraints placed on the British by their use of the horse would have acted to restrict the numbers of warriors that could be fielded and maintained by a British *teulu*. As we have seen, the constraints of such use also would have led to several predictable social consequences, while serving to widen the gap between the warrior-aristocracy and the other social classes through its effective preclusion of a peasant infantry. Even given the sometimes anachronistic nature of their texts, the evidence in heroic poetry certainly shows that the warrior-élite had access to a wide array of luxury goods which were not available to other segments of the population. Both the *Gododdin* and Taliesin's poems are replete with detailed references to the material culture of the aristocracy, particularly in their description of the sumptuous gifts given by generous lords to warriors and poets alike. Many of these goods are reflected in the archaeological record for the proposed sites of British courts of this era, and must represent the superior access to these luxury goods that was enjoyed by members of the warrior-aristocracy.[18] Consequently, it is the uneven distribution of luxury items and goods that allows us to equate the military class of the British social structure with the dominant social and economic élite during these centuries. Further, the differences between the warrior-élite and the other elements of British society were reinforced by their adoption of a code of behavior that was specific to their class, and that was promulgated by bards at the courts of Dark-Age chieftains.

Any attempt to discern social gradations within the confines of this warrior-aristocracy is difficult in the extreme. In part, this is a result of heroic poetry's emphasis on military prowess and battlefield deeds rather than on non-utilitarian factors such as birth in a particular social class. This emphasis was warranted: the warrior class among the Britons, like that of the Anglo-

---

[16] Alcock, *Economy, Society, and Warfare*, p. 264.

[17] See *ibid*. See also Wendy Davies, who stated (*An Early Welsh Microcosm: Studies in the Llandaff Charters*. London: Royal Historical Society, 1978, p. 47) in rather non-committal terms that "the existence of untied completely free peasantry is neither demonstrable nor deniable". The absence of such a class, however, does conform to the limited picture of society that is found in the *Gododdin* and in Taliesin's poems.

[18] For the relation between the material culture portrayed in the *Gododdin* and the archaeological finds for this period, see Alcock, *Economy, Society, and Warfare* (pp. 246–49) and Jackson, *GOSP* (pp. 33–35). The heavy concentration of luxury items at these sites makes it clear that Dark-Age courts must have acted as *de facto* centers for the distribution of wealth and goods.

Saxons, constituted an aristocracy of service rather than of birth. Some of the warriors seen in the *Gododdin* were themselves lords, who were noted for their open-handed generosity to their men.[19] Further, though the poem almost always fails to state the precise means – through birth or military prowess – by which these men secured their positions, the poem's constant emphasis on their battlefield skills is perhaps instructive. The poem relates of Buddfan (line 278) that "his leaders were destroyed by [enemy] warriors" (*difa oedd ei gynrain gan wyr*), in a line that would indicate that prominent warriors of a *comitatus* achieved their status through their martial qualities. Even more telling in this regard is the *Gododdin's* stanza (lines 950–57) about a chieftain called Urfai, of whom the poem relates (lines 952–3) that "It was customary for the son of Golystan's words to be listened to, though his father was no prince" (*Gnawd mab Golystan, cyn ni bai gwledig ei dad, yndewid a lafarai*). The clear implication of this passage is that Urfai had advanced to a position of authority that was higher than that of his father. As such, the passage indicates that social advancement within the structure of the *comitatus* was possible, and that such advancement was based on military prowess and service to the warband, rather than on non-utilitarian considerations such as birth. For the most part then, the avenues for social advancement and recognition in a warband, and the economic rewards that such recognition could bring, appear to have wound their way along the campaign trail and onto Dark-Age battlefields, rather than through the bedchambers of an established hereditary elite. The link between service and reward or recognition is best illustrated in *Beowulf* (lines 2183–88) when the poet relates of Beowulf that in his youth, the hero's kinship to the Geatish king did him little good, recalling that:

> He was miserable for a long time,
> as a Geatish child   they thought [him] no good;
> no gifts for him on the mead-bench   nor much honor
> was the lord of the Weders [Geats]   willing to give.
> They were convinced   he was sluggish,
> a lazy noble.[20]

However, it is equally clear that the lord and the members of his immediate family formed a distinct social stratum within the aristocratic class of the

---

[19] For examples of warriors as lords in their own right, see Jarman, *Aneirin: Y Gododdin*, pp. xxxvi–xxxvii.

[20]   *Hean wæs lange,*
swa hyne Geata bearn   godne ne tealdon,
ne hyne on medobence   micles wyrðne
drihten Wedera   gedon wolde;
swyðe [wen]don,   þæt he sleac wære,
æðeling unfrom.

comitatus. As shown above, the evidence provided by Gildas would allow the conclusion that some of the British lords in the old Romanized zone in Britain had inherited their ruling positions through their fathers. This certainly was the situation after the mid sixth century, when father-to-son succession must have been the norm. Of course, outside the confines of the former Roman province, it can be assumed that the Celtic tradtion of succession through tribal kinship would have continued unabated. In any case, to strengthen and maintain their pre-eminent position within the warband's internal social structure, British lords turned to the services of their court poets (*pencerdd*), whose traditional functions included that of keeping the lord's genealogy, and of composing and reciting panegyric poetry in praise of the lord and his family. Beyond this obvious hereditary segment within a British *teulu*, it seems evident that position, honors, and wealth could be granted by the lord to any member of his warband based on service alone, regardless of age or social rank. This distribution also served to reinforce the lord's position in the warband. Above all, the lord maintained his position through his abilities as a warlord.

The major duty of a Germanic or Celtic lord was the conduct of warfare, in which he was expected to take an active part. The lord of a *comitatus* was expected not only to fight, but to fight with a great deal of martial prowess. At least during his younger years, a lord was expected to be one of the most formidable and valiant warriors of his warband. In a Germanic context, these characteristics had been noted long before the migration period by Tacitus, who declared (*Germania* 14) that "When coming into battle it is a dishonor for the chief to be surpassed in warlike deeds; a dishonor for his retinue not to equal the prowess of its chief" (*cum ventum in aciem, turpe principi virtute vinci, turpe comitatui virtutem principis non adaequare*). Similarly, the four lords for whom Taliesin sang were all praised by the poet for their prowess as warriors on the field of battle. In the *Gododdin*, the highest praise of warriors, even of those who were lords in their own right, often revolved around the battlefield skills of a common warrior: the physical abilities and skills required to fight and slay one's enemies in individual combat.

That Dark-Age lords personally took part in battles is best illustrated by the frequency with which they met their deaths on battlefields throughout Britain. On this point, all of the written sources – the various Irish annals, the *Annales Cambriae*, the *Anglo-Saxon Chronicle*, the *Historia Brittonum*, and the writings of Bede and Gildas – are of one accord; battlefield deaths for Anglo-Saxon and Celtic chieftains or kings were frequent during this chaotic period of the island's history. All these sources are replete with entries – so frequent that it is unnecessary to recount them here – that mark the fate of warrior-kings. Death in battle often awaited Dark-Age leaders whose status ranged across the entire gamut of political power, from the weakest *sub-reguli* to the most powerful *bretwalda*. Furthermore, numerous references in heroic poetry, regarding the battlefield deaths of various lords, serve to reinforce the impression that a lord's place in battle was with his men. In fact, some Dark-Age lords appear to have continued in their role as active warriors even when they were quite old. Of several examples, Urien is perhaps the most prominent. Even prior to his assassination during the siege at Lindisfarne it is obvious that Urien was advanced in years. Taliesin describes (*PT* V) Urien's hair as white, and further describes (*PT* VI) Urien's role at the battle at *Argoed Llwyfain* as a supporting one to that of his son Owain. In the same manner, Vortiper, the active warlord of Dyfed, is described by Gildas (*DE* 31.1) as showing the effects of age ("your head is whitening"; *canescante iam capite*). Furthermore, any rudimentary calculation based on the information in the Irish annals will show that Aedan mac Gabran must have been quite old when he led his forces to their destruction at Degsastan in 603. However, this duty to lead and participate in battle was one that could be delegated to members of the ruling family or to his kinship group.

In a Celtic or Germanic warband, the relationship between the lord and his kinship group[21] was an important one. Bound to their lord through the dual ties of kinship and loyalty, the members of a lord's family were entrusted with positions of authority within the warband. Command of the *comitatus* would devolve to them in those instances when the king, either because of old age or illness, was unable to lead it into battle or on a campaign. Also, as was seen in the previous chapter, in battles that involved the use of larger, composite armies, it is probable that members of the ruling family were assigned to lead key elements within the overall force. Finally, within the small-scale *comitatus* that must have constituted the norm for warbands among the smaller kingdoms, the members of the lord's family (that is, the dominant kinship group within a tribe) must have comprised the major portion of a lord's warband. Within larger warbands, the lord's kin would have formed the core of the *comitatus*, whose duty was to defend their lord from attack, and to ensure his personal safety. In effect, they acted as a personal bodyguard for

---

[21] The exact basis for these kinship ties, or what exactly constitutes a "kinship group", is far from certain. For the purpose of this study, the concept of kinship is largely a perceptual one; that is, if the source in question claims that certain people are kin to one another, then they are treated as belonging to the same kinship grouping, regardless of the precise basis for such an affiliation. Put another way, for this study, kinship ties are in the eye of the beholder.

For more on kinship, see: Wendy Davies, *Wales in the Early Middle Ages* (Leicester: Leicester University Press, 1982), pp. 71–81; H.R. Loyn, "Kinship in Anglo-Saxon England", *Anglo-Saxon England* 3 (1974), pp. 197–209; and L. Lancaster, "Kinship in Anglo-Saxon Society", *British Journal of Sociology* 9 (1958), pp. 230–50 and 359–77. A summary of the conclusions of the latter two articles are found in Arnold, *Archaeology of Early Anglo-Saxon Kingdoms* (p. 145). For a much wider and detailed look at Germanic kinship, see Alexander Murray, *Germanic Kinship Structure: Studies in Law and Society in Antiquity and the Early Middle Ages* (Toronto: Pontifical Institute of Medieval Studies, 1983). Lastly, Charles-Edwards has a forthcoming book on Celtic kinship entitled *Early Irish and Welsh Kinship*.

their chieftain during the course of a battle. In fact, in broad terms, there appears to be a correlation between the size of a *comitatus* and the proportion of warriors within that warband that was drawn from among the lord's own kinship group.[22] In any event, while the members of the lord's family owed their social standing and position within the *comitatus* in part to the obvious factor of birth, it remains clear that they retained these positions through service, the same yardstick by which the worth of other warriors was measured.

The most important relationship within a warband, and the one that was most instrumental in protecting and strengthening its social and cultural integrity, was the lord-retainer relationship. It is the internal social relationship that best explains the structure of the *comitatus*, and provides us with the social and cultural context in which Dark-Age warbands functioned. At least for the warrior aristocracy, by the period of the Germanic migrations to Britain, the bonds established between a lord and his men had become more important than traditional kinship ties[23] and, in fact, had usurped some of the duties associated with the older social system.[24] The lord-retainer relationship was one that bound the warriors of a warband to their lord, a relationship whose fundamental and underlying roots lay in a bedrock of personal loyalty, and one whose operational framework is reflected in the series of obligations and duties which the lord and his men owed to one another. In fact, the concept of

---

[22] In theory, the larger the *comitatus*, the smaller the proportion of warriors who were able to count themselves among the lord's kin. Therefore, for many of the British and Anglo-Saxon chiefdoms whose existence can be inferred from the *Tribal Hidage* and other such evidence for this period (presented in the previous two chapters), the small warbands that protected them must have been composed of warriors who were drawn almost entirely from the dominant family/clan of the tribe. As we saw in the case of Guthlac (among other examples), a militarily successful warband could increase its size by attracting warriors from outside its own tribal area, through its increased prestige and wealth, which in turn would have been obtained through a combination of tribute and booty. Less successful warbands would have continued to have been manned primarily by the dominant kinship group until it was defeated or lost control of its territory.

[23] H.M. Chadwick, *The Heroic Age*, p. 344. It is perhaps instructive in this regard to note that the primary emphasis of *Beowulf* certainly is on the lord-retainer relationship, though the importance of kinship ties continued to be stressed by the poet at various points in the poem.

[24] The obligation to protect and/or avenge one's kinsman is an obvious example of one such duty that was incorporated into the lord-retainer relationship. In the non-aristocratic elements of society, traditional kinship obligations must have continued with no little strength, as evidenced by British and Anglo-Saxon attempts to control the extent and duration of blood-feuds by the use of blood-payments (*wergild* and *manbot* in Old English; *galanas* and *sarhad* in Welsh), that are found in their law codes.

Within an aristocratic context, at least for the members of the ruling family or kinship group, the obligations of kinship ties would have had a reinforcing effect on their duties to their lord within the lord-retainer relationship. As is seen in the "Fight at Finnsburg"

loyalty is the "primary concept upon which the ideal society depicted in Germanic heroic poetry is built" and also "implies . . . the entire system of *comitatus* relationships which inheres in the values put forth by Old English heroic poetry".[25]

The loyalty between a lord and his retainers was reflected in the duties and obligations that they owed to one another. We have seen that a principal function of a Dark-Age chieftain or warlord was the conduct of warfare, in which he was expected to take an active part. Within the lord-retainer relationship, this function was important for several reasons, beyond whatever geopolitical gains such warfare might be expected to accomplish. First, by actively pursuing warfare with his neighbors, the lord provided an avenue through which his warriors could put into action the aristocratic, martial ideals of heroic poetry – ideals on which these warriors were weaned. This warrior ethos, seen throughout the period's heroic poetry, found frequent expression on the battlefields of Dark-Age Britain. By allowing the warriors to be engaged often in one of their favorite activities (fighting), the period's endemic warfare offered frequent validation of the warrior class and its way of life. Warfare became the very reason for existence for many warriors in an age in which the power to fight and slay one's enemies was considered a virtue. Warfare also provided the best means by which the lord and his retainers could acquire honor and glory. A warband's victories necessarily brought fame and glory to its lord. In this regard, the fame that Guthlac earned as the young warrior-lord of a *comitatus* (*Guthlac* XVI–XVIII) is instructive. Further, the fame earned by Mynyddog, the lord of Manaw Gododdin, for the efforts of his ill-fated expedition, is well known. Similarly, in *Beowulf*, Hrothgar gained prestige and honor through the earlier victories of his warband. The poem relates (lines 64–7) that:

> Then was Hrothgar   given victory in battle,
> honor in war   that his dear kinsmen
> eagerly served him,   while younger kinsmen grew
> into a great band of warriors.

> *Þa wæs Hroðgare   heresped gyfen,*
> *wiges weorð-my nd,   þæt him his winemagas*
> *georne hyrdon   oðð þæt seo geogoð geweox*
> *magodriht micel.*

episode in *Beowulf* and the *Finnsburg Fragment*, kinship ties were of greater importance in the earlier portion of this period. Beowulf's statements on the proper role of kinsmen reinforce the notion that kinship continued to be an important consideration for members of the aristocracy.

In any event, it is clear that, as the *Chronicle*'s Cynewulf-Cyneheard episode shows in no uncertain terms, duty and loyalty to one's lord took priority over those owed to one's kin.

[25] Cherniss, *Ingeld and Christ*, p. 30.

Second, warfare allowed the lord to share with his warriors the various hardships of the campaign trail and the dangers of the battlefield, shared experiences that would have tended to strengthen the bonds of loyalty among the members of the warband. Third, warfare could provide a lord with the material goods and luxury items, either through the actual seizure of loot and booty or through exacting tribute, with which he could reward his men for their service. It was through this distribution of weapons, gifts, and other forms of wealth that the bonds of loyalty between a lord and his retinue were enhanced and strengthened. As is seen in Chapter 8, the distribution of wealth, in whatever form, was an invaluable cultural support of the *comitatus* structure. In sum, within the lord-retainer relationship, the lord of a *comitatus* was expected to conduct warfare with a certain degree of frequency and daring, to participate personally in campaigns and battles, and to reward his followers with the spoils of war.

For their part of the agreement in the lord-retainer relationship, the warriors were expected to give their lord their full and utter support in whatever matters he deemed important, regardless of where such matters (or the general fortunes of life) might lead. Consequently, the warriors' duties and obligations to their lord would have encompassed virtually every facet of heroic-age life, whether in battle, in the hall, in exile, or in the event of their lord's death. While these topics are covered in the following chapter, a few points can be made here insofar as they touch upon the lord-retainer relationship.

First and foremost, the most important duty expected of these warriors was to fight for their lord in battle so that fame and glory could be won by lord and warrior alike. Tacitus described their role in supporting their lord in this regard when he stated (*Germania* 14) that "The lord fights for victory, the warriors for their chief" (*principes pro victoria pugnant, comites pro principe*). For an individual warrior, the only honorable result of battle could be victory or death. Beyond its cultural and social benefits, victory in battle brought obvious material advantages to Dark-Age warriors. Though technically the lord's property, plunder from warfare normally appears to have been distributed for the most part among the members of a *comitatus*, and thus was an important source of wealth with which the lord could reward his retainers. The importance of plunder to the Germanic tribes had been noted long before by Tacitus, who stated (*Germania* 14) that the goods of a lord's generosity were derived through war and plunder (*materia munificentiae per bellus et raptus*). Plunder continued to play an economic role in the affairs of Dark-Age Britain.

In battle, warriors were expected to fight for their lord, to protect his person to the best of their abilities and, failing that, to avenge his death. As the following chapter demonstrates, these obligations within the lord-retainer relationship were to be fulfilled by the warriors even at the cost of their own lives. There are numerous instances of warriors preferring death in the honorable fulfillment of their obligations, rather than a life of shame and social contempt from their peers. Warriors were obliged to follow their lord into exile. This willingness on the part of a warrior to accompany his lord into exile, and to die for him in battle, shows that the relationship between lord and retainer ran far deeper than one that was purely mercenary in nature. Based on the bonds of loyalty, the relationship could continue to function in good times and bad. During peaceful times, a warrior's other duties were less vigorous and dangerous than the ones just noted. One of these, especially in regard to the younger warriors, was the probable requirement to live in the lord's hall, where they participated with their lord in many of the normal activities associated with hall-life, such as hunting, feasting, and listening to the songs of court poets. Finally, an obligation that is associated with the older, experienced warriors, involved their role in advising their lord in matters concerning their kingdom.

CHAPTER FIVE

DUTIES AND OBLIGATIONS

Our emphasis now shifts to the warriors, examining their motivations in joining a Dark-Age *comitatus* and the manner in which they fulfilled their part of the bargain that is implied in the lord-retainer relationship, in battle, in exile, in the hall, and in the exacting of vengeance.

As Chapter 4 related, a warrior's most important obligation was to fight his lord's battles so that fame and glory (as well as loot and plunder) could be obtained by lord and warrior alike. The lord's task was to fight for victory, while the warrior's was to fight for his lord. Worldly fame and honor could be earned by the lord simply through the military exploits of his *comitatus*. Beyond the cultural and material advantages associated with victory, the lord of a successful warband benefited from its ability to attract warriors from outside its traditional tribal area. In essence, military victories attracted warriors to a successful warband, warriors who in turn would help the (now larger and stronger) warband achieve further victories, which in turn would allow it to attract yet more warriors through its enhanced prestige and economic wherewithal. Beyond enhancing a warband's military capabilities, the addition of warriors to the ranks of a warband was, in itself, a measure of the status of the lord who led it. As Tacitus noted (*Germania* 15),[1] the possession of a large retinue of fierce warriors gave honor and prestige to earlier Germanic lords, whether in times of war or of peace. In effect, the deeds and the reputation of a lord's *comitatus* reflected directly on the lord's own prestige and affected his ability to recruit warriors to the warband.

Among the Germanic peoples, the political and social chaos that had been caused by the processes of migration and settlement must have provided many opportunities for warriors eager to fight for lords who were establishing themselves on the island. Rather than remaining in the Germanic homelands with their traditional tribal groupings and hierarchies, it seems likely that many warriors would have preferred to join the warbands of adventurous

---

[1] *magnaque et comitum aemulatio, quibus primus apud principem suum locis, et principum, cui plurimi et acerrimi comites. haec dignitas, hae vires, magno semper electorum iuvenium globo circumdari, in pace decus, in bello praesidium.*

lords who sought Britain's shores. Given the geopolitical situation in Britain, it can be assumed that these warbands would have offered a warrior a greater chance for social advancement and for the acquisition of wealth – and certainly a greater chance to engage in warfare – than was enjoyed by those who remained on the continent under traditional tribal leaders. However, while it has been argued that some warlords were not members of continental dynasties, it is impossible to determine whether their followers had been drawn primarily from a migrating lord's own tribal group, or whether they had been recruited from other regions or tribes. In the case of the *foederati* units of the pre-rebellion period, it seems reasonable to conclude, assuming that the British authorities recruited established fighting units, that both the lord and his followers were of the same tribal group. It seems unlikely that this would have remained the case during the political and social chaos of the 475–550 period, which saw a rapid, widespread Germanic migration to Britain and the subsequent foundation of numerous kingdoms.

In fact it becomes clear that, once established on the island, the composition of a Germanic *comitatus* was not always along strictly tribal lines. Whether in search of the economic and social benefits associated with warfare, or simply wanting to share in the excitement and exhilaration of battle, there appears to have been a propensity on the part of some warriors to seek out and serve lords outside their own tribal areas. As Chapter 3 showed, this propensity is shown on several occasions. Among these, the story regarding Guthlac's *comitatus* provides one notable example. As his *Life* recounts (XVII), warriors from *diversarium gentium* (various peoples) joined the warband of the youthful Guthlac, which had already won fame and *immensas praedas* (immense wealth) because of its military exploits. Also presented earlier were Bede's story (*HE* III.14) about Oswine and an example regarding Hrothgar (*Beowulf* 64–7).

As seen earlier, the propensity to enter the service of lords from other tribes and chiefdoms also appears to have been a characteristic of warriors of the British kingdoms. While it can be assumed that the composition of a British *teulu* would follow tribal lines for the most part, it seems that the recruitment of warriors from outside a lord's domain was not an unusual event. A prominent example are the numerous warriors from throughout the British kingdoms who had flocked to Mynyddog's court to join the expedition to Catraeth. The *Gododdin* relates that the expedition included warriors who came from Gwynedd, Pictland, Aeron, Elfed, and the south.[2] Also seen in Chapter 3, there is at least one clear instance in Taliesin's poems (*PT* XI) that shows warriors fighting for lords who were not their tribal leaders; entries in *The Annals of Ulster* allow for the proposal that entire British warbands, probably comprised of dispossesed warriors from Rheged, were fighting for Irish chief-

---

[2]   See Jackson's *GOSP* (pp. 18–22, 27–8) or Jarman's *Aneirin: Y Gododdin* (pp. xxxvi–xxxvii).

tains along the east coast of Ireland during the period from 682 to 709. British warriors, whether fighting in the warband of their own tribe or that of another lord's, were motivated by an insatiable desire for fame and by the chance to share in the spoils of war.

For Briton and Anglo-Saxon alike, the faithful discharge of a warrior's duties and obligations in the lord-retainer relationship was known as "earning one's mead". This concept, a fundamental one in the heroic literature, represented a warrior's "repayment" to his lord for the gifts and honors which he had received. Of the various duties that a warrior could perform to repay his lord, none were as important as the obligation to follow his lord into battle. In battle, a warrior was expected to fight and slay the enemies of his lord, to protect his lord to the best of his abilities, and to avenge his death in the event the lord was killed. In heroic poetry, a warrior was expected to fulfill these battlefield duties even at the cost of his own life. For both the Anglo-Saxons and Britons, there are many examples of individual warriors, and sometimes even entire warbands, who met their deaths during the course of "earning their mead".

The *Anglo-Saxon Chronicle* records the annihilation of several warbands in the service of their lords.[3] Elaborating on the entry about the Northumbrian victory over the Dalriadic Scots at Degsastan (603), Bede relates that, "Theodbald, brother to Æthelfrith, was killed with all those whom he led of the host" (*Theodbald, frater Aedilfridi, cum omni illo quem ipse ducebat exercitu,* peremptus est). This entry would imply that all the warriors of Theodbald's *comitatus* had died with their lord while fulfilling their battlefield obligations – that is, while earning their mead. The entries in the *A-Chronicle* for events in 755 and 784 provide a detailed, explicit picture of two bands of warriors who made a conscious and deliberate decision to fulfill their obligations to their lords, even though they knew that such a decision would result in their own deaths. In these entries, the *Chronicle* recounts the final, brutal acts of a particularly nasty feud that began over three decades earlier.

The story begins in 757, when Cynewulf forced King Sigebryht from the throne of Wessex, and then into a life of exile in the Weald. There the exiled king lived for a brief time until he was stabbed to death by a swineherd. Cynewulf then ruled Wessex for thirty-one years, during which he "often fought great fights with the Britons" (*oft miclum gefeohtum feaht wiþ Bretwalum*). In his final year as the ruler of Wessex, Cynewulf decided to drive out Sigebryht's brother, an *ætheling* named Cyneheard. However, Cyneheard

---

3 The much later entries in the *Chronicle*, incorporating *The Battle of Brunanburg* and *The Battle of Maldon* poems, are not discussed here, lying far outside the range of this study. Both poems are replete with the ideals and sentiments of a heroic society, but it is clear that by the tenth century such ideals and sentiments were wholly anachronistic. For more on the Maldon and Brunanburg poems, see Bruce Mitchell, *The Battle of Maldon and Other Old English Poems* (New York: St. Martin's Press, 1965).

caught wind of Cynewulf's plot and decided to strike first. Upon hearing that Cynewulf, accompanied by only a few of his retainers, was with his mistress at a place called *Merantune*, Cyneheard gathered a company of eighty-four warriors and went there. King Cynewulf was slain in the initial foray before his retainers realized that their lord was in danger. Cynewulf's men organized themselves, and went to the chamber where their lord now lay dead. As the *Chronicle* relates, it was at this point that "The prince [Cyneheard] offered each of them wealth and life, and not any of them would accept it; but they all kept fighting until they all lay dead, except for one British hostage."[4] On the following morning, when the rest of Cynewulf's warriors learned of the king's death, they mustered and went to Meratun. Refusing to accept as their lord the murderer of their king, they besieged Cyneheard and his warriors. Trapped and with no hope of escape, Cyneheard's men were given the choice between safe passage – if they would abandon their lord – or certain death. Cyneheard's warriors chose to remain faithful to their lord, and "said [to those outside] that the same terms were offered to their own companions, who before were with the king. They said that they would take no mind of that [offer], any more than those who were slain with the king."[5] During the course of the subsequent battle, Cyneheard and all of his men (except for one) were killed.

The Cyneheard-Cynewulf episode and its tragic consequences were almost inevitable in a period when a warrior's reputation and fidelity to his lord was worth more to him than his own life. The episode also shows that the lord-retainer bond had become more important than kinship ties for the members of the warrior class. In both specific instances an attempt was made to persuade the warriors to surrender, or at least to leave the besieged force, because a number of warriors on the two opposing sides were kinsmen to one another. As things turned out, these arguments fell on deaf ears, with the warriors in both instances preferring to fulfill their obligations to their lord, even if such a decision meant that they might be forced to kill some of their own kinsmen in the process.

Information from the *Chronicle*'s entries is supported by similar data found in *Beowulf*, where this battle obligation is stated in its most forceful terms by Beowulf's kinsman, Wiglaf. In a speech (lines 2865–91) following the death of Beowulf in his fight with the dragon, Wiglaf bitterly condemns the cowardly and unfaithful retainers who had deserted their lord in his hour of need, declaring (lines 2890–1) that "death is better for a warrior than a shameful

---

4 *se æðeling gehwelcum feoh ond feorh gebead, ond hiera nænig hit geþicgean nolde; ac hie simle feohtende wæron oþ hie alle lægon butón anum Brittiscum gisle.*

5 *ond hie cwædon þæt tæt ilce hiera geferum geboden wære þe ær mid þam cyninge wæron. þa cwædon hie þæt hie hie þæs ne onmunden þon ma þe eowre geferan þe mid þam cyninge ofslægene wæron.*

life!" (*deað bið sella eorla gehwylcum þonne edwitlif*). For their failure to uphold their part of the lord-retainer relationship, Wiglaf declares (lines 2884–87) that the unfaithful retainers and their families are to be exiled from the kingdom and from "all hall-joys" (*eall eðel-wyn*) inhered in the *comitatus* system. Later, the poem relates the fate of the Geatish kingdom through the words of a messenger, who tells those assembled in the hall of Beowulf's death and foretells (lines 2911–14), "Now the people may expect a time of war, as soon as the fall of our king is made manifest to Franks and Frisians" (*Nu ys leodum wen orleg-hwile, syððan under[ne] Francum ond Frysum fyll cyninges wide weorðeð*).

Conversely, the poem reserves its highest praise for Wiglaf, the sole member of Beowulf's retinue who risked his life in aiding his lord in his fight with the dragon. It is in fact Wiglaf, the ideal retainer, who manages to wound the dragon enough so that Beowulf – himself gravely wounded – could slay the beast, though he is too late to save his lord. In sum, Wiglaf is praised for fulfilling his battlefield duties to his lord, while contempt and punishment were the fate of those who failed to do so. Such an obvious message could not have been lost on an Anglo-Saxon audience.[6] The performance of the hero's cowardly retainers is in stark contrast to that of Beowulf's hand-picked *comitatus* who had accompanied him to Hrothgar's hall in the first part of the poem. Unlike the cowards who abandoned their lord in his fight with the dragon, Beowulf's earlier companions had made every effort to assist their lord during his fight in Heorot with Grendel. The poem relates (794–7) that:

> Beowulf's warriors
> all drew their swords,   time-tested heirlooms,
> wanted to defend   the life of their comrade,
> their famous chief,   however they could.

> *Ðær genehost brægd*
> *eorl Beowulfes   ealde lafe,*
> *wolde freadrihtnes   feorh ealgian*
> *mæres þeodnes,   ðær hie meahton swa.*

Among the Britons, the best-known example of warriors fulfilling their obligations to their lord, both on an individual and collective basis, is Mynyddog's ill-fated *comitatus*, which met with utter destruction at the hands of the Anglo-

---

6 Another prominent example in *Beowulf* of a warrior's duty to his lord in battle – specifically, the duty to avenge his death – is seen in the "Fight at Finnsburg" episode (lines 1068–1159b). However, because of the belated nature in which the Danish warriors carried out this duty, it is more appropriate to see the destruction of Finn and the Frisians at the hands of Hengest and his men as an act of formal revenge, rather than a desperate attempt to avenge one's lord in the heat of battle. Accordingly, the evidence of the "Finnsburg Episode" and the *Finnsburg Fragment* is presented later in this chapter, in the section addressing the role of warriors in the execution of vengeance.

Saxons at Catraeth.[7] The particulars regarding many of the warriors who comprised the expedition,[8] about the relationship that bound them to their chieftain, and about the conduct of the battle, were all recounted in Aneirin's *Gododdin*. By their unequivocal and unfailing fidelity to their lord and to their oath to him, the warriors of Mynyddog's warband (*gosgordd Mynyddawg*) soon provided a model, a standard of exellence, to which the warbands of other British kingdoms could aspire, and by which they were judged. Despite the disastrous fate that befell them, the warband that set out from Manaw Gododdin became the epitome of an ideal *comitatus*. If the poem called *Moliant Cadwallawn* – allegedly a eulogy to Cadwallon, the powerful king and warlord of Gwynedd who was killed in battle in 634 – is an authentic work of this period, then it would seem that the exploits and fame of Mynyddawg's warband had spread as far as northern Wales no later than the 630s. A reference in *Moliant Cadwallawn* to the warband's destruction is found in its reference to "the grief at Catraeth".

Because of its subject matter (a battle), and its emphasis (on the warriors themselves), the *Gododdin* provides the most comprehensive listing of the battlefield duties and attributes that were expected of a Dark-Age warrior among the Britons.[9] As with the Anglo-Saxons, the fulfillment of a British warrior's obligations to his lord, and particularly the duties that were expected of him in battle, was known as "earning one's mead". As Chapter 8 shows, the *Gododdin* contains many references to warriors, either as individuals or as part of the entire *gosgordd*, who earned their mead by fulfilling their obligations to Mynyddawg. Further, because almost all these warriors met their

---

7 Despite some problems regarding the precise identification of the battle's site, and acknowledging that no other source beyond the poem itself takes note of the battle, the study nonetheless treats the battle at Catraeth as a historical fact. Given the endemic nature of warfare during this period, and given the geographical biases of the *Chronicle* and other English sources, the absence of references to Catraeth in them counts for little, because many other battles are also neglected. Furthermore, given the contemporary nature of the *Gododdin* to the events at hand, the assumption that the events at Catraeth actually took place is a reasonable one.

8 Of the 300 or so warriors who took part in the expedition to Catraeth, perhaps 80 are mentioned by name. For some of these 80, the poem provides more detailed information (i.e., their fathers' names, their kingdoms of origin, the manner in which they were slain, and so forth). For more on this, see Jackson's *GOSP* (pp. 18–22, 27–8) or, for a complete listing of the mentioned warriors, Jarman's *Aneirin: Y Gododdin* (pp. xxx–xxxi).

9 That such duties continued to be valued by British kingdoms in the following century is seen in an interpolation in the *Gododdin* text. This interpolation (B.1 = A.78 in Jackson; 102 in Jarman) is in no way connected to events at Catraeth. Instead, these stanzas commemorate the victory of the Strathclyde Britons over Dalriada's *comitatus* at Strathcarron in 642. In the battle, the king of Dalriada, called "Freckled Donald" (*Dyfnwal Frych*) was killed, and his body evidently left on the field of battle, where his head was gnawed by ravens (*A phen Dyfnwal Frych brain a'i cnoyn*). For more on this interpolation, see Jackson's *GOSP* (pp. 47–8) or Jarman's *Aneirin: Y Gododdin* (pp. lxi–lxii).

deaths while earning their mead, the drink is often viewed as "bitter" or "ensnaring", or given some other non-desirable attribute by the poet.

The chief virtue of a British warrior, and the one most vital in fulfilling his battlefield obligations, resided in his overall martial prowess – the physical and psychological traits required of a warrior to fight and slay his own enemies or those of his chieftain. Not surprisingly, warriors are praised through-out the *Gododdin* for their physical strength and agility, for their skillful use of weapons, and for their courage, steadfastness, and eagerness for battle and fame.[10] Consequently, the poem contains many references to the strength, courage, and ferocity of various warriors, either through straightfoward state-ments or by the poet's frequent employment of metaphors.[11] Thus, one finds that: the sheer strength of Bradwen was such that the warrior (line 452) "held a wolf's mane without spear in his hand" (*A ddalwy mwng blaidd heb bren yn ei law*); the martial abilities of Hyfaidd Hir and Rhufon Hir were so great that, for each warrior, it was said (lines 59, 361) that "five fifties fell before of his blades" (*Cwyddai pum pymwnt rhag ei lafnawr*); the poet says (lines 677–8) of Gwrhafal's battle-prowess, "It was easy that you struck down corpses, with a furious swift sword-stroke" (*Oedd llew y lladdewch chwi ddynin, Cleddyfal dywal ffysgiolen*); of Erthgi's talents for wreaking havoc on the enemy, the poem says (lines 136–7) that "he tore and pierced with spear-points. Above the bloodshed he slew with blades" (*ef rhwygai a chethrai a chethawr, odd uch lledd lladdai a llafnawr*). Similar cases could be cited almost *ad infinitum*.

With its emphasis on the offensive capabilities of these warriors, it is noteworthy that the *Gododdin* also reserves praise for warriors who could defend and hold their positions during the battle. As in its handling of a warrior's offensive qualities, the poem accomplishes this either by overt state-ments or through the use of metaphors.[12] The poem's stanzas record that: (line

---

10 Numerous and specific examples for these traits are presented in far more detail by Jarman and Jackson (in their introductions to their respective editions of the poem) than can be attempted here. The reader is encouraged to review the examples cited in those works; the ones that are presented here represent only a very limited sampling of those found in the *Gododdin*.

11 Jarman notes (*ibid*., p. xli), that "the metaphors used in the poem are almost invariably employed to emphasize the ferocity of the warriors, and frequently do so in terms of the animal world". For his examples, see *ibid*., pp. xli–xlii. Jackson (*GOSP*, p. 41) saw this as one of the poem's stock features, stating that: "the hero is himself often compared to various kinds of savage or wild or stubborn creatures; to a lion (A.57), a bear (A.16, 62), a boar (B.4, A.30, 39, 69), a wolf (A.4, the Gorchan of Tudfwlch, the Gorchan of Cynfelyn), a stag (A.84), an ox (A.39), a bull (A.30, 37, 38, 48, 53, 73, the Gorchan of Tudfwlch), a serpent (A.62), an eagle (A.40, 49, 85), a hawk (A.69), or a dragon (B.3, A.22, 25)."

12 The metaphors employed by the poet to connote a warrior's qualities in the defense center around things which are immovable, or have a sense of strength and longevity. Usually, buildings (especially fortresses) and walls are the metaphors that the poet

62

974) "In the vanguard, Gwawrddur was a palisade" (*Yng nghynnor, gwernor Gwawrddur*); Merin is (line 561) an "anchor, scatterer of Deirans" (*Angor, Dewr daen*); of Graid, the poem says (lines 263–5) that "[Amid] scattered weapons, broken ranks, steadfast, with great destruction, the violent champion overthrew the men of England" (*Arf anghynnull, angyman ddull, angysgoged, Trachywedd fawr, treiglesyd llawr Lloegrwys giwed*).

This praise for warriors in the defense may be due to the way in which the battle had turned against the British warriors. According to Aneirin, for the men of the expedition, retreat was unthinkable, even in the face of overwhelming odds. Engaged in a battle whose outcome had become hopeless, the warriors of Mynyddog's *gosgordd* chose to remain, locked in mortal combat with their enemies, in order to exact whatever retribution they could upon the English hosts for the deaths of their companions. Thus the poem relates (line 70) of Bogdad's son that "the deeds of his hand made slaughter" (*gwnaeth gwyniaith gwraith ei law*); in a stanza (lines 181–4) about Gwrwelling, that for the deaths of his companions, he "avenged them without fail" (*Difefl as talas*). Like their adversaries, they preferred death over the shame of one who fled the battle. At least with such a death in battle, the warriors of the expedition knew that their exploits would win widespread renown and glory through the songs of the warband's poet (*bardd teulu*). In fact, such an expectation was warranted. In one of many passages honoring the ill-fated warband *in toto*, the *Gododdin* records (lines 865–8) that:

> Three hundred gold-torqued [warriors] attacked
> Defending the land, there was slaughter.
> Though they were killed, they slew,
> And until the end of the world they will be honored.

> *Trycant eurdorchog a grysiasant*
> *Yn amwyn breithell, bu edrywant*
> *Cyd ryladded wy, wy lladdasant*
> *A hyd orffen byd edmyg fyddant.*

Beyond his duties on the battlefield, other obligations and duties were required of a Dark-Age warrior. An especially important obligation required a warrior to follow his lord into exile. Given the military and political uncertainties of this turbulent period, this obligation no doubt was fulfilled on many

---

commonly used. Jarman, *ibid.*, p. xlii, says that: "Of the metaphors used to represent the warriors' strength, resilience, and steadfastness, the commonest is that of a wall or rampart (8, 310, 406, 411, 575, 596, 608). Others include the door as 'protector' or 'stronghold' (*dôr*, 395, 466; *tewddor*, 733), the fortress or refuge (*caer*, 597, 609; *din*, 466; *dinas*, 377, 394, 468), the palisade (974), the anchor (395, 561, 577, 587, 827), the shield (319, 738, 887), the pillar (77, 669), the bar or lock (629, cf. 597 and 609), the immovable rock (578, 589), the haven (782, 783), the (back)bone (746), the arm (175)."

occasions. In particular, the *Anglo-Saxon Chronicle* is replete with references to kings and lords who were driven into exile, and subsequently forced to begin new lives outside their native lands. In some cases, these exiled lords met an untimely end in some desolate place, forsaken and far from hearth and home, as was the case for Sigebryht. In other instances, the exiled lords found refuge at the courts of rulers who were willing to shelter them from powerful enemies back home.[13] However, for the most part, the sources take little notice of the warriors who must have accompanied their lords to whatever destination the lonely paths of exile might have led.

There are a few exceptions to this situation, where warriors are specifically mentioned as following their lord into exile. *Guthlac* (XLIX) relates how Æthelbald, who had been driven into exile by Ceolred, sought Guthlac's guidance and spiritual support one day "amid doubts and dangers when his own health and that of his men was failing, and after his strength was utterly failing" (*deficiente virium ipsius valitudine suorumque inter dubia pericula, postquam exinanitae vires defecere*). Similarly, Bede relates (*HE* IV.15) that Caedwalla, banished from his country, came suddenly with an army into Sussex and killed Ethelwalch, its king (*superveniens cum exercitu Caedualla . . . cum exularet a patria sua, interfecit regum Aedilualch*). In this case, the warriors of Caedwalla's force should be seen as men who had followed their lord into exile. A third example is found in the Irish annals in a series of entries that record the arrival of British warbands to Ireland during the last quarter of the seventh century. As Chapter 3 related, these warbands might have been comprised of dispossessed warriors from Rheged, who had come to Ireland following the collapse of that kingdom. It seems reasonable to conclude that these warbands, which fought for various Irish chieftains along Ireland's eastern coastal regions, had followed their own British lords across the Irish Sea. In this regard, these British warbands, following their own lords,

---

13 According to Bede, this was the happier fate that had awaited Edwin, who had been driven from Deira by Æthelfrith in 604. Fleeing beyond the reach of Æthelfrith, Edwin found a safe refuge at the East Anglian court of King Rædwald. Bede relates (*HE* II.12) that Edwin resided there under Rædwald's protection for over a decade, despite repeated attempts by Æthelfrith to pursuade Rædwald (through promises of rewards and threats of war) to kill the exiled prince. Instead, Rædwald helped Edwin regain his throne in 616 by killing Æthelfrith and destroying his army. Consequently, the story continues (*HE* III.1) that it was Æthelfrith's sons who now found themselves in the unexpected role of exiles; fleeing Edwin's Northumbria, they found refuge in Ireland and in Dalriada.

Edwin's nephew, Heretic, was not as fortunate as his uncle. Heretic was in exile, along with his wife and daughter, in the British kingdom of Elmet under the protection of Ceretic. Like his uncle, his death was sought by Æthelfrith, who through a combination of threats and promises attempted to pursuade Ceretic to kill the young noble. No doubt fearing for his own rule, Ceretic decided not to alienate the powerful ruler, and Edwin's nephew was found murdered (by poisoning) within a short space of time.

would have had much in common with those Germanic warbands that had arrived on Britain's shores two centuries earlier.

As their literature demonstrates clearly, the concept of a lord in exile, accompanied by his retainers, is one that was quite familiar to an Anglo-Saxon audience.[14] Several examples[15] in *Beowulf* serve to illustrate this point. Upon their arrival at Heorot, the poem relates (line 339) that Wulfgar, one of Hrothgar's nobles, deduces from the bearing and equipment of Beowulf and his men that they had come to Hrothgar's hall "not on the road of exile!" (*nalles for wræcsiðum*). Conversely, in the poem's Finnsburg segment, Hengest is portrayed (line 1137) as an exile (*wrecca*) from both lord and homeland during the winter in which he and his men were obliged to stay at Finn's hall. A final example was seen earlier in Wiglaf's declaration (lines 2884–87) that the warriors who had abandoned Beowulf in his fight with the dragon would be sent into exile, and their families deprived of all rights. For the members of Dark-Age society – both British and Anglo-Saxon – there was no punishment more feared or dreaded than exile. Placing this punishment in the wider context of heroic society and the lord-retainer relationship of the *comitatus*, it is seen that exile from his warband was catastrophic for a warrior because, in heroic society "to be exiled was to be without protection by lord or kindred, without friends, means, or livelihood, or the respect and trust of others".[16]

Given the economic, social and cultural implications of a life in exile, it is all the more remarkable that warriors chose to accompany their defeated lords into exile, rather than taking the more expedient course of offering their services to the victor. This very willingness of warriors to follow their lord into exile,[17] and to die for him if necessary, demonstrates in no uncertain terms that the bonds uniting lord and man during this period were stronger than those whose basis was founded only on the distribution of gifts and wealth. In a non-battlefield setting, Bede's account about the attempted assassination of Edwin (*HE* II.9) is unequaled in illustrating the utter and unassailable fidelity of a warrior to his lord. In his account, Bede relates that a warrior (Eomer) had been sent by Cwichelm, the West Saxon king, into Northumbria, with the intention of killing Edwin. Once in the presence of the king, Eomer lunged at Edwin in an attempt to stab him to death. Edwin's *thegn* Lille, unarmed and in a desperate attempt to save the life of his lord, threw his own

---

[14] While this study relies primarily on *Beowulf* for its examples, it should be noted that the concept of exile is seen in other Anglo-Saxon poems as well, notably *The Wanderer* and *The Seafarer*. See Chickering, *Beowulf: A Dual Language Edition*, p. 260.

[15] For other examples, see Frank Bessai, "*Comitatus* and Exile in Old English Poetry", *Culture* XXX, pp. 130–44.

[16] Chickering, *Beowulf: A Dual-Language Edition*, p. 260.

[17] For more on the concept of exile in the corpus of Anglo-Saxon poetry, see Chapter 5 in Cherniss' *Ingeld and Christ*.

body between Edwin and the assassin's blade (*mox interposuit corpus suum ante ictum pungentis*). The force of the blow was such that the blade went through Lille entirely, and managed to inflict a wound on Edwin, though not a fatal one. Others of Edwin's men immediately joined the fight against Eomer. In the ensuing tumult, another of Edwin's retainers – a warrior named Forthere – was slain before the other warriors slew Eomer.

The other duties that a warrior owed to his lord were less vigorous and dangerous than those associated with either battle or exile. Most of these duties were associated with the lord's hall or court. One probable duty, though one that evidently was restricted to veteran members of the *comitatus*, was their role as advisors and counselors to their lord. The degree to which these advisors comprised a formal body *per se* – in either a Celtic or a Germanic context – is uncertain. In broad terms, however, it is likely that Anglo-Saxon rulers would have made greater use of such advisors than did the Britons, based primarily on their more egalitarian social structure as well as their prior use of a related institution, the *folkmoot*. Regardless of the precise constitutional underpinnings and authority of these advisors, it is clear that the chieftains and kings of this period did consult them, at least on matters in which they all held a vested interest: the initiation of hostilities, the course of a campaign, and other important matters pertaining to the kingdom. For example, in a passage (*HE* II.13) about Edwin's adoption of Christianity, Bede relates that he consulted his nobles (who in turn debated the merits of the issue) before making a decision on whether or not to adopt the new religion.[18]

Similarly, in *Beowulf*, it is seen that advice is routinely given to Hrothgar. The poem says (lines 171–4) that Hrothgar and his counselors, "mighty, in council, deliberated over all plans" (*rice to rune, ræd eahtedon*) when deciding on the best course of action to be taken against the monster Grendel, who threatened the well-being and very existence of their kingdom. Later in the poem (line 278), Beowulf informs the shore guard that he has come to offer Hrothgar "counsel and advice" (*ræd gelæran*). The poem also (lines 360–70) has Wulfgar address Hrothgar, Wulfgar's "friendly lord" (*winedrihtne*), offering his advice on the newly-arrived troop of Geats led by Beowulf. He first offers sage advice to his lord on how he should handle his audience with these men (lines 366–7), counseling him to "give no refusal to him in your answer, gracious Hrothgar" (*no ðu him wearne geteoh ðinra gegncwida, glædman Hroðgar*). He then (lines 368–70) offers his own estimate of the warband and its leader. Of the warriors, he advises his lord that "in battle-gear, they seem worthy of nobles' esteem" (*hy on wiggetawum,*

---

18 Of course, Bede is using this scene to advance the cause of Christianity, and it should surprise no one that the debate is one-sided. The point to be made here is that a lord's consultation with his leading men in matters of importance would have evoked little surprise on the part of Bede's readers.

wyrðe þinceað eorla geæhtlan), while of Beowulf he says, "surely strong, the chief who led these battle-warriors here" (*huru se aldor deah, se þæm heaðorincum hider wisade*). For the subject at hand, it is instructive that Wulfgar gave his advice without being asked, and clearly expected that Hrothgar would follow it.

Examples of such advice being given by British warriors are more difficult to find. Two entries in *De Excidio* might provide examples of such advisors. During his condemnation of Maelgwn's second marriage, Gildas denounces the union as scandalous, even though the wedding was "public and, as the deceitful tongues of your parasites shout . . . legitimate" (*publico et, ut fallaces parasitorum linguae tuorum conclamant . . . legitimo*).[19] Gildas' second reference is more concise. In condemning the five British lords, whom he calls (37.2) "mad and debauched horses" (*lascivientibus insanisque . . . equis*), Gildas declares (43.1) that they will be judged truthfully, "no place for the poisons that your respectful parasites hiss into [your] ear" (*non ut parasitorum venerata vestorum venena in aures sibilant ora*). In this context, "parasites" must refer to secular counselors who gave advice to their lord in matters pertaining to his rule. If so, they would have been following the precedent established long before by Vortigern and his counselors when they first decided to introduce Germanic *foederati* as a defense against the Picts.

The *Gododdin* provides at least one clear example – seen in the previous chapter as an indication of social mobility – of warriors acting as advisors. In a stanza (lines 950–57) about Urfai, a notable warrior and perhaps a chieftain in his own right, the poem says (lines 952–3) that "it was customary for the advice of the son of Golystan to be heeded, though his father was no prince". The clear inference to be drawn from these lines is that it was typical for the more important warriors of a *comitatus* to offer advice and counsel to their lord. What made Urfai's case unusual was not that he gave counsel often, but that his advice was heeded, "though his father was no prince". The inference is that the advice of other prominent warriors in the warband, whose positions were reinforced by hereditary considerations, was heeded by the lord as a matter of course. In all likelihood, this was true for the lord's own kinship group, which held positions of authority in the warband. In an era when the power and position of a Celtic or Germanic ruler was far from absolute, it stands to reason that a lord who actively sought the advice of his prominent

---

[19] *DE* 35.3. While Gildas had used the term "parasites" to denote court poets, it cannot refer to poets here. After all, it would not have been left to a court poet to decide on the legitimacy of his lord's marriages. The term might refer to clerics, though he never uses this term for them, and in any case describes their manifold shortcomings in a later section of his book. However, it is possible that the leading men of his kingdom, acting as counselors and advisors, may have been required to decide on the legitimacy of this second marriage.

warriors was more likely to enlist their cooperation and support for his political and military agenda than one who did not.

Another obligation commonly associated with the warriors of this period, or at least with the younger, less experienced members of a *comitatus*, was the customary practice of residing in the hall or court of their lord. Also likely to reside at the hall were the lord's family and some of his kinship group, along with hostages and those youths who were being raised there under the system of fosterage. It is evident from historical and literary sources that even the older, seasoned warriors of the warband spent at least some of their time in the company of their lord, both in the hall and during aristocratic entertainments outside the hall. Though examined in the following chapters, a brief listing of these activities is provided here. In the hall, the men shared the lord's hearth, received gifts and wealth from him, and joined the lord in his amusements, which would include hunting and falconry. The evenings would be taken up by feasting and drinking, boasting of deeds to be performed, and listening to the songs of the court poet. These activities – commonly referred to as hall-joys – were instrumental in strengthening the bonds between a lord and his retainers, and reflect the proper functioning of the *comitatus* structure.

The obligation to exact vengeance for the death of one's lord, and even for one's companions, was a fundamental one for the warriors of Dark-Age kingdoms. In both Celtic and Germanic society, the duty to seek revenge as a method of redressing some actual or perceived injury or insult was a basic obligation for the people of this era, regardless of their social standing. For the non-noble segments of society, the duty to exact revenge fell on the members of a kinship group. As the previous chapter related, this duty often led to long-standing feuds between kinship groups, and consequently was a factor that contributed to the high level of endemic violence that characterized this unsettled period.

The introduction of "blood-payments" (*wergild, manbot, galanas,* sarhad) in the early law codes should be seen as an attempt by the rulers of these kingdoms to curtail the number and the extent of blood-feuds between kinship groups. By providing the members of an aggrieved clan with an acceptable social alternative to vengeance in kind, it was hoped that the number of these self-perpetuating feuds, as well as the social turmoil that was the natural result of such acts, could be reduced. Blood-payments may have had some impact on the number of unlawful and socially-destructive acts – banditry, murder, and the like – committed by members of these groups. However, as is evidenced in *Beowulf* (lines 2444–9), the execution of criminals warranted no payment to their kin-groups, as is shown by the old man who watches his son swing from the gallows, knowing that he can neither avenge nor be compensated for his legal death.

Theoretically, such a provision would have been effective, and not only because it offered an acceptable alternative to acts of revenge. Because the law held a kinship group responsible for raising the payment to be awarded on account of an unjustified action by one of its members, it should have been more likely that a kinship group would begin to exert more direct control over the behavior of its individual members than had been seen earlier. In effect, the early law codes rewarded kinship groups that kept the peace, and penalized those that did not. Whether these law codes were ever as effective in practice as they would have been in theory is a matter for debate.

Vengeance, however, was only one of a series of obligations that were inherent within the overall system of kinship ties that formed the basis for interrelationships in Celtic and Germanic culture. In almost all aspects of life, the bonds of kinship formed a strong, underlying support structure for most of the population. Obviously, given the high level of violence during this period, the duty to protect the members of one's kin from outside aggression[20] was a vitally important one. In the event that a man was killed or injured, it was the duty of his kinsmen to avenge him in kind. If one of its members broke the peace, it was his kinship group that had to compensate other kinship groups for his transgressions. Because of their importance in these matters, kinship groups must have played an important role[21] in shaping the social behaviors of their members, and must have possessed effective sanctions that could be employed when needed against errant and delinquent members of their own group.

Among the warrior-class, many of these kinship functions appear to have been incorporated within the lord-retainer relationship. By the beginning of the sixth century, the ties binding a warrior to his lord had become more important than those that bound him to his kin. This is not to imply that kinship ties were not important to members of the warrior élite. It has been seen that Germanic and Celtic lords made use of their own kinship groups in filling key positions in their warbands. Further, there are several cases where the actions of a warlord or his warriors can be seen as a result of their

---

[20] The system of money payments or the exacting of revenge did not apply to deaths and injuries brought about by one's own kindred. As Chickering noted (p. 263) in his edition of *Beowulf*: "One of the most moving scenes of grief in *Beowulf* is the hero's recollection of the case of King Hrethel, Hygelac's father (2435–70), whose eldest son Herebeald was killed accidentally by an arrow shot by his brother Hæthcyn. Hrethel's unappeasable sorrow lay mainly in the fact that this death had to go unpaid and unavenged, since it had occurred within the kindred. The poet has Beowulf liken it to the sorrow and loss of honor, indeed the loss of any meaning to life, felt by an old *ceorl* when he sees his son hanged as a criminal and can expect no compensation since it is a legal death. Hrethel eventually dies of a broken heart. . . . [Both cases] illustrate the central position of kinship obligations in Anglo-Saxon life."

[21] Arnold (*Archaeology of Early Anglo-Saxon Kingdoms*, p. 200) sees the early law codes of the Anglo-Saxon kingdoms and the social practices of kinship groups as acting together to influence the behaviors of, and interactions between, members of society. He relates that, while the seventh century saw the "start towards the codification of laws and punishment . . . kinship as a legal institution may have remained immensely strong in ordinary social life".

obligations within the institution of kinship, rather than as actions based exclusively upon geopolitical considerations. One example (*HB* 63) must be Edwin's expulsion of Ceretic from the throne of Elmet upon the former's return from exile. Edwin's act may have been in retaliation for Ceretic's complicity in the murder of his nephew, who, according to Bede (*HE* IV.23) years before had sought refuge at Ceretic's court while in exile. Another example would be the *Anglo-Saxon Chronicle* (A and B texts) entry for 658, which recounts that Cenwalh had been in exile among the East Anglians for three years. The entry explains that "Penda had driven him there, and seized his kingdom, because he had forsaken Penda's sister" (*Þyder hine hæfde Penda adræfedne 7 rices benumenne forðon þe he his sweostor anforlet*). Penda's action should be seen within the context of kinship obligations. In the same manner, given the probability that many of the warriors seen in the *Gododdin* were kin, the ferocity with which the men of Mynyddog's retinue sought to avenge the deaths of their comrades can be seen as the fulfillment of kinship obligations.[22]

Further evidence for the importance of kinship ties is also found in *Beowulf*. A particularly strong example of this is found in Beowulf's condemnation of Unferth, when the hero declares (lines 587–89) that "you killed your brothers, nearest kinsmen, casting down both, for which you will suffer evil in hell" (*þeah ðu þinum broðrum to baban wurde, heafodmægum; þæs þu in helle scealt werhðo dreogan*). Conversely, Beowulf himself was steadfast in supporting his own kinsmen, particularly Hrethel and his sons. Wiglaf also is praised as a loyal kinsman to Beowulf for his support in the hero's fight with the dragon. Further, the *Beowulf* poet himself saw kinship ties as important, declaring that "Never can kinship be turned aside at all in one who thinks well" (*sibb æfre ne mæg wiht onwendan þam ðe wel þenceð*).

Despite these examples, however, it is clear that protection for these warriors and for their lord was effected not within the context of kinship ties, but primarily within the context of the warband. Furthermore, the behavior of warriors was influenced by the heroic ideals and social code of the *comitatus*, and not by the social dictates of family and clan. Most importantly, the responsibility to avenge the death or injury of the chieftain or his warriors was

---

[22] Is is impossible to determine the extent of kinship ties among those groups from outside the Mynyddog's territory. It is clear that Aneirin had kinsmen among the regular retinue, for he exclaims (550) that "too many are lost of my true kinsmen" (*a rhwy a gollais o'm gwir garant*), and again, (869–70) of the men of the expedition: "And of those kinsmen who went, Alas, except one man, not [any] escaped" (*Ac o'r sawl a aetham o gyd-garant, Tru, namyn un gwr nid enghysant*). Given the importance of the lord's kin-group in comprising the *comitatus* of most Celtic and Anglo-Saxon kingdoms, in most cases it is difficult to determine whether such battlefield vengeance is a function of kinship ties, of the obligations of the *comitatus* system, or of some combination of both. At least in the case of external threats, it is likely that the obligations of kinship and of the *comitatus* would have reinforced one another.

borne by the other members of the *comitatus*. To the chapter's earlier examples (for battlefield vengeance) can be added others portraying revenge in its more traditional sense. Seeking vengeance against Cwichelm because of his assassination attempt, Bede records (*HE* II.9) that Edwin, after recovering from his wounds, went into Wessex with an army and slew or took prisoner all those involved in the plot. Lastly, the *Anglo-Saxon Chronicle* (757) calls the murder of Sigebryht by a swineherd an act of revenge for Sigebryht's earlier slaying of a noble called Cumbra.

However, the best examples of revenge come from *Beowulf*, of which two are presented here. The poem relates that the ravages of the monster Grendel against the Spear-Danes and their hall had not evoked any type of retribution on their part. As such, these unanswered attacks reflected both a failure of Hrothgar to protect his retainers, and a subsequent collective failure of his warriors to exact retribution for the deaths of their fallen comrades. In fact, Beowulf taunts the warrior Unferth for his failure to support Hrothgar against Grendel and for failing to avenge the loss of the fallen warriors, his companions. Addressing Unferth, Beowulf declares (lines 590–7) with obvious contempt that:

> I say to you truly, son of Ecglaf:
> never would Grendel have made so much harm,
> terrible monster, [against] your chieftain,
> humiliation in Heorot, if your thought,
> your spirit were as formidable, as your own words.
> But he has found that he need not fear revenge
> terrible sword-fury, from your people,
> not very many remain, the 'Victory-Scyldings'.[23]

The underlying attitude toward vengeance that is evident in Beowulf's condemnation of Unferth is reinforced by that seen in the "Fight at Finnsburg" episode (lines 1068–1159b) in *Beowulf*.[24] The story as we have it is a classic

---

[23] *Secge ic þe to soðe, sunu Ecglafes,*
þæt næfre Gre[n]del swa fela gryra gefremede,
atol æglæca ealdre þinum,
hynðo Heorote, gif þin hige wære,
sefa swa searogrim, swa þu self talast;
ac he hafað onfunden þæt he þa fæhðe ne þearf,
atole ecgþræce eower leode
swiðe onsittan, Sige-Scyldinga.

[24] This "episode" is written as part of the poem. The text it contains is supplemented by that of the *Finnsburg Fragment*, which has an independent existence from that of the *Beowulf* manuscript. An edition (and commentary) of the *Fragment* is found in Klaeber's edition of *Beowulf*. Though the "episode" and the *Fragment* deal with different aspects of the same tale, even when combined, the story and background as we have it are incomplete.

tale of treachery and vengeance, and illustrates the tension brought about by the conflict of obligations that were part of the *comitatus* system. The tale also shows the often tragic consequences that resulted from acts of retribution and retaliation. These acts of violence were a part of the overall ethos of vengeance that could cause feuds to continue over the course of several generations. Most importantly, the "Fight at Finnsburg" shows clearly that the obligation to exact vengeance could, and did, take precedence over other social and moral considerations in Dark-Age society.

The story opens with a troop of some sixty Danish warriors, led by their lord Hnæf, who were visiting the stronghold of Finn, the Frisian lord. Finn was married to Hnæf's sister Hildeburh. For some unknown reason, Finn's men (or at least some of them) launched an attack on the hall where the Half-Danes were sleeping. The *Fragment* relates that the Danish warriors defended themselves for five days against the Frisian onslaught at the hall's two entrances without losing a man. However, by the time the "Episode" resumes the story, Hnæf had been slain, but the Danes continued to fight under the command of Hengest, Hnæf's chief retainer. Evidently, the battle ended in a stalemate, which was brought to an end when one side offered terms to the other. The pact that allowed this uneasy truce to be established called for Hengest and the remaining Danes to become Finn's retainers. In return, Finn would treat the Danish warriors in exactly the same manner as he treated his own retainers, according them the same honors and rewards as he did his own men. He also forbade his own men ever to mention the battle or the circumstances that surrounded it. After Hengest had sworn his oath to Finn and Finn had paid *wergild* for the death of Hnæf, the slain were burned on a funeral pyre. The Frisians then returned to their homes, while Hengest and his men remained with Finn in his hall for the rest of the winter. However, with the coming of spring, Hengest went back on his pledged word. In exacting retribution for his slain lord, Hengest and his warriors killed Finn and his men, sacked his hall, and carried back everything (including Hnæf's sister, Hildeburh) to their native Denmark.

The destruction of Finn and his men was total and unequivocal, though the poem fails to give the precise nature of the revenge, probably because an Anglo-Saxon audience already would have been familiar with the story's details. The impression one derives from the poem is that the audience would have given its full approval to Hengest's actions, even if those actions would have meant breaking his pledge to Finn. The poem goes to great lengths to explain why the Danes had entered into the truce in the first place, and why the revenge against the Frisians had not been accomplished sooner. Despite the tragic consequences of Hengest's act of retribution upon the honorable and blameless Hildeburh (who lost a brother, a son, and her husband), the poem notes with approval Hengest's decision to seek revenge – called by the poem (line 1142) "the world-wide custom" (*woroldrædenne*) – against Finn. For the poet, such retribution was inevitable and warranted, a natural and expected result of a warrior's duty to avenge his lord. As Beowulf declares (lines 1384–5) to Hrothgar, "Better it is for every man to avenge his friend than mourn overmuch" (*Selre bið æghwæm þæt he his freond wrece, þonne he fela murne*).

CHAPTER SIX

POETS, POETRY, AND HEROIC IDEALS

The court poet[1] had become an integral part of the warband by the onset of this period, and should be listed among the principal cultural and social institutions underlying the ascendancy and the continued existence of the *comitatus* as a viable military and governing structure. For the Germanic tribes seeking to come to the island, and the native Britons who attempted to reverse this migration, the inclusion of a court poet seems to have been integral to the development and structure of the *comitatus*.

Among the Germanic peoples, references to *scops* are found in various sources whose dates stretch over half a millennium. While the evidence found in the works of classical writers is far from unequivocal,[2] references in both *Beowulf* and *Widsith* testify to the presence of *scops* at the courts of Germanic chieftains on the continent during the Migration Period. In *Beowulf*, there are several references to a *scop* who appears to have been a long-standing resident at Heorot. These include: the poet's singing of the creation song in Heorot (lines 90–98), his singing of the Finnsburg tale (lines 1063–1159), and his praise-song to Beowulf (lines 867–74) to honor him for his battle with, and slaying of, Grendel in Heorot. The *Widsith* poem provides evidence for poets who were attached to the courts of Germanic lords and for those who were peripetatic, traveling from court to court.[3] In fact, Cherniss attributes the

---

[1] The study employs interchangably the terms "poet", "court poet", "poet in residence" and their Anglo-Saxon and Welsh equivalents – *scop* and *pencerdd* (court poet), or *bardd teulu* (poet of the warband).

[2] Some of these early references are problematic in regard to the clear existence of what could be seen as a court poet. Still, the references do indicate a strong tradition of aristocratic, eulogistic poetry, a tradition that would have been entirely amenable to the concept of a court poet. For the evidence provided by these classical writers – Tacitus, Ammianus Marcellinus, Priscus of Panium, Sidonius Apollinaris, and Procopius – for poets and poetry among the Germanic tribes before the seventh century, see Opland, *Anglo-Saxon Oral Poetry* (Ch. 2).

[3] Cherniss, *Ingeld and Christ*, p. 14. For more information on *Widsith* and for additional references, see *ibid.*, pp. 12–16. See also Nicholas Jacobs, "The Old English Heroic Tradition in Light of the Welsh Evidence", *CMCS* No. 2 (Winter, 1981), at pp. 13–15. The poem itself is on pp. 149–53 of E.V.K. Dobbie and George P. Krapp (edd.), *The*

widespread knowledge of Germanic heroes and tales to *scops* who had sought service in the courts of the chieftains who ruled the geographically-dispersed Germanic tribes, proposing that:

> The peregrinations of minstrels during the Heroic Age would account for the wide dissemination of tales among tribes remote geographically from the heroes and tribes treated in the poems – minstrels told the stories wherever they went, and learned new stories in turn. Through continual intercourse with foreign tribes a minstrel might accumulate a repertory of considerable size.[4]

It seems clear that a migration of Germanic tales and folklore to Britain was effected by the *scops* who accompanied their lords to the island during the migrations of the fifth and sixth centuries. It seems evident that these stories, regarding the heroes and events of their continental past, were well known to the settlers who had crossed the water to Britain. [5] Evidently, the long tradition of having *scops* in residence at the courts of Germanic lords continued to be of value to the warbands of the pre-Viking Anglo-Saxon kingdoms. Nor was such poetry restricted to the halls of secular lords; heroic poetry appears to have been popular among Anglo-Saxon ecclesiastics as well. This popularity is best illustrated by Alcuin's well-known question: "What has Ingeld to do with Christ?" (*Quid Hinieldus cum Christo?*). This question, in a letter that Alcuin had written to Hygebald, the bishop at Lindisfarne, was meant to admonish the bishop for his monks' predilection for listening to the secular tales of heroic song rather than focusing on spiritual matters.

As with the Germanic tribes, poets had been a familiar feature at the courts of Celtic chieftains before the advance of Roman power into the northern regions of Europe, and ultimately into Britain. The presence of these Celtic poets had been noted long before the Migration Period by several classical

---

Exeter Book, Vol. III of *The Anglo-Saxon Poetic Records: A Collective Edition* (New York: Columbia University Press, 1936); the poem's introduction is on pp. xliii–xlv. Finally, see R.W. Chambers, *Widsith: A Study in Old English Heroic Legend* (Cambridge: Cambridge University Press, 1912).

[4] *Ibid.*

[5] Stanley B. Greenfield, *A Critical History of Old English Literature* (New York: New York University Press, 1965), p. 80. Although the transmission of these tales from the continent to Britain did occur, the precise agent of the transmission remains uncertain. Opland doubts that tribal poets would have accompanied the earlier adventurers who had come to the island, assuming they would have remained in their ancestral homelands along with their kings. He adds that this function may have been fulfilled by someone else in these early warbands (*Anglo-Saxon Oral Poetry*, p. 72), though he views this as unlikely. A court poet was likely among the Anglians, whose ruling dynasty (the Iclingas), in contrast to the other ruling families of their continental homeland, led their people across the Channel and onto Britain's shores.

historians: Posidonius, Diodorus Siculus, Strabo, and Athenaeus.[6] While of little use during the long period of Roman administration, court poets may have been reintroduced in Britain as a result of the collapse of civil authority in the Roman and sub-Roman periods during the course of the fifth century. The resurgence of the Celtic *bardd teulu* appears to have been closely intertwined with the rising fortunes of the *comitatus* as it evolved into the principal governing structure among the native peoples of the former Roman province. Certainly, poets were present at the courts of those British lords condemned by Gildas,[7] earning the special ire and contempt of the cleric in *De Excidio*. In a scathing attack on Maelgwn, one of five lords who had earned his special enmity, Gildas describes the court poets and their functions in highly unfavorable terms. Gildas condemns Maelgwn (*DE* 34.6) for his utter refusal to hear the praises of God from ecclesiastics and other adherents of Christ, or to hear the music of the church. Instead, the British lord preferred to listen to the singing of his own praises by his own court poets – whom Gildas called criminals and raving hucksters (*Arrecto aurium auscultantur captu non dei laudes canora Christi tironum voce suaviter modulante neumaque ecclesiasticae melodiae, sed propriae, quae nihil sunt, furciferorum referto mendaciis simulque spumante flegmate proximos quosque roscidaturo*).

Despite objections such as those voiced by Gildas, bardic activity quickly became associated with the courts of the British princes. Of the five *Cynfeirdd*, or earliest British poets, listed in the *Historia Brittonum*, both Aneirin and Taliesin – the only two bards about whom we have some information – were associated with the courts of prominent lords. Aneirin, whom tradition lists as the author of the *Gododdin*, evidently was attached to the court of Mynyddog Mwynfawr in Manaw Gododdin. On the other hand, Taliesin appears to have seen service with more than one British lord during the course of his career. If the corpus of poetry attributed to him is genuine, then it would appear that Taliesin saw bardic service in the kingdoms of Elmet, Powys, and Rheged with four prominent warlords and chieftains: Cynan Garwyn, Urien and his son Owain, and Gwallawg. It is evident that these poets either initiated or re-established a long tradition in which the poet came to be viewed as an integral part of a British warband.

There are several references pointing to a continuing tradition, dispersed over a wide geographic area, of panegyric poetry being composed among the

[6] For more on these historians and their writings, and for early Celtic society, see Patrick Ford's overview in his introduction to *The Poetry of Llywarch Hen* (Los Angeles: University of California Press, 1974), pp. 4–11. For an in-depth analysis, see J.J. Tierney, "The Celtic Ethnography of Posidonius", *Proceedings of the Royal Irish Academy* LX (1959–60), sec. C, pp. 189–275.
[7] Patrick Sims-Williams, "Gildas and Vernacular Poetry", in *Gildas: New Approaches*, edited by Michael Lapidge and David Dumville, pp. 169–92 (Woodbridge, England: The Boydell Press, 1984).

British kingdoms. If authentic, a poem entitled *Moliant Cadwallawn* (*In Praise of Cadwallon*) – an elegy honoring Cadwallon ap Cadfan, a seventh-century king of Gwynedd[8] – would indicate that this sort of poetry continued to be composed in northern Wales in the second quarter of the seventh century. Second, as was related in Chapter 5, one of the stanzas in the *Gododdin* is an unmistakable interpolation of the poem's original corpus, whose subject matter records a military victory of the Strathclyde Britons over Dalriadan forces at Strathcarron in 642. Again, while the actual method by which the poem found its way into the *Gododdin* corpus of poetry remains unresolved, the poem itself indicates that this type of poetry continued to find favor among the Britons in the northern England/southern Scotland region in the mid-seventh century. Lastly, an elegy to Cynddylan called *Marwnad Cynddylan* (*Death-Song of Cynddylan*), provides yet another indication for the composition of panegyric poetry among the Britons who lived in the southeastern portion of Wales during this same period.[9] In addition to these British references, both Sims-Williams and Moisl[10] have shown that the poetry of these early bards was known on the continent, where it attracted the notice of Venantius Fortunatus (530–609), an Italian living in Gaul who eventually became the bishop of Poitiers. In one of his poems, Fortunatus refers to "British songs" (*crotta Britanna canat*), a reference[11] that would imply that the existence of British poetry was well-known. In sum, after its reintroduction into the British kingdoms by the *Cynfeirdd*, it seems evident that the use of panegyric poetry by British lords became a widespread social and cultural practice at their courts.

As was seen for the Anglo-Saxons, the Celtic audience for heroic poetry was by no means restricted to British halls. Gildas (*DE* 66.4) admonishes his fellow clerics, who he claimed had little tolerance for listening to the precepts of holy men, while they would show alert interest in sports and in the fabulous stories of worldly men (*ad praecepta sanctorum, si aliquando dumtaxat*

---

8 An ally to the Mercian lord Penda, Cadwallon was a powerful warlord and ruler of Gwynedd who, in conjunction with Penda, killed Edwin of Northumbria, and subsequently ravaged the north of Britain. Cadwallon was killed in battle in 634. A difficulty of the *Moliant Cadwallawn* is the lateness of the extant manuscript in which it is found, though this circumstance has not prevented scholars from assigning an early date to the poem.

9 Jackson (*GOSP*, pp. 61–2) describes the elegy of Cynddylan as "Another heroic lay of the first half of the seventh century [whose subject] was a Welsh king of the middle Severn valley and the opposite Welsh border country", and that "the same remarks about metre, style, and language apply to this, *vis-à-vis* the *Gododdin*, as to the Cadwallon poem. The Welsh tradition of a somewhat later period says he fought at the battle of Maserfield in 642 . . . and the elegy itself speaks of him as taking part in an attack on Lichfield in Mercia."

10 Sims-Williams, "Gildas and Vernacular Poetry", p. 179; Moisl, "A Sixth-Century Reference to a British *Bardd*", *BBCS* XXIX (1980–82), pp. 268–73.

11 Found in Sims-Williams, *op. cit.*, p. 179.

audierint, quae ab illis saepissime audienda erant, oscitantes ac stupidos, et ad ludicra et ineptas saecularium hominum fabulas).

In both a Celtic and Germanic context, the primary functions of the poet were centered around those duties which promoted the status of his lord. These duties usually involved the recitation of eulogistic and narrative poetry, and the recitation of the king's or chieftain's genealogies. The two types of poetry would allow a poet who was attached to a *comitatus* different poetic avenues through which he could instruct and entertain its members. The key difference between these two forms of poetry is that:

> Eulogies are not primarily narrative in intent or content; though they can contain sequences of coherent narrative, they are more commonly allusive and elliptical, assuming a knowledge of the narrative content on the part of the audience. Narrative is thus embryonically present in eulogy, but its function is not to tell a story so much as to define a man through a record of his achievements and qualities. Eulogy, as we have seen, plays a part in the ritual life of a people. So too may narrative . . . but the narrative song is more likely to be designed primarily to entertain (perhaps partly to edify or educate) and this is rarely the function of eulogy.[12]

Interwoven with the recitation of eulogistic poetry, with its emphasis on the deeds of current lords or chieftains and their ancestors, was the poet's task of maintaining his lord's genealogy. Like the period's poetry, these Dark-Age genealogies were oral in their presentation and transmission. Also like the period's eulogistic poetry, the early genealogies were instrumental in helping to support the political claims and social position of the newly-established Germanic and Celtic dynasties.[13]

---

[12] Opland, *Anglo-Saxon Oral Poetry*, p. 63. I essentially agree with Opland's definitions and think that the dichotomy presented allows for a reasonable degree of flexibility regarding their use and purpose. As to their use in Britain during this period, there is no reason to assume that the purposes of eulogy and narrative were so strictly defined or mutually exclusive. At least for the warrior-aristocracy, I would doubt that panegyric poetry was devoid of any entertainment value. Conversely, a narrative poem such as *Beowulf* would have contained much "instructional" material that would have helped shape the behavior of the members of the *comitatus*.

[13] For more on the accuracy and historical horizons of these genealogies of Dark-Age kingdoms, see the following by Molly Miller: "Historicity and the Pedigrees of the Northcountrymen", *BBCS* 26 (1974–76), pp. 255–280; "Date-Guessing and Pedigrees", *Studia Celtica* 10/11 (1975–76), pp. 96–109; and "Date-Guessing and Dyfed", *Studia Celtica* 12/13 (1977–78), pp. 33–61. For an general overview, as well as the Celtic genealogies themselves, see P.C. Bartrum (ed.), *Early Welsh Genealogical Tracts* (Cardiff: University of Wales Press, 1966). For the Anglo-Saxons, see Kenneth Sisam, *Anglo-Saxon Royal Genealogies* (London: The Royal Academy, 1953); for the Scots and Picts, see M.O. Anderson, *Kings and Kingship in Early Scotland* (Edinburgh: Scottish Academic Press, 1980).

While their veracity might be a matter of some debate, the oral nature of these Celtic and Germanic genealogies has never been in serious doubt. As an interesting aside,

Beyond these duties at his lord's hall, it seems to have been common practice for a poet to accompany his lord's warband on its expeditions and raids. This practice is better documented for the Britons than for the Anglo-Saxons. Aneirin is likely to have accompanied the ill-fated expedition from Manaw Gododdin and lived to tell, in poignant and stirring terms, of its obliteration at Catraeth. According to later Welsh tradition and references in the poem itself, Aneirin may very well have been wounded, or taken prisoner, or both, during the disaster at Catraeth.[14] Similarly, it seems that Taliesin was present at many of the battles that provided the setting and subject matter for some of his works. Moreover, the sense of immediacy and the attention to detail that pervades the poetry of the two *Cynfeirdd* would tend to support the claim that the place of a *bardd teulu* in battle was among the warriors about whom he sang.

Being an eyewitness to the events recounted in the poems would have made the poet's praise of the men who were a part of them all the more credible and satisfying to the participants than had he relied upon second-hand accounts. In this regard, Taliesin's poems are particularly instructive, making it clear that poets' descriptions were based on eyewitness accounts. In *PT* V, it seems that an anxious Taliesin has been left at court to await the return of Urien and his warriors from a raid against Manaw Gododdin. Taliesin, because he had been left at court, does not recount the events that occurred on the raid. Rather, he describes only those events to which he was an actual witness – the mustering and departure of the raiding party, the events at court as the returning warband is approaching the hall, and the *teulu/ gosgordd's* triumphant return. In his battle poems, Taliesin gives detailed descriptions of the battlefield. In *PT* VI, for example, Taliesin includes even the verbal challenges and taunts that preceded the actual outbreak of battle, verbal exchanges that must have been heard by Taliesin while in the company of Urien and Owain. As a consequence of the poet being an eyewitness to the battles in which his lord fought, in much of this battle poetry it is hardly

Koch has shown that genealogies among the Picts also would appear to have been orally transmitted (see Koch, "Loss of Declension", pp. 219–20).

[14] Given the outcome of the battle, Aneirin's presence at or near the battlefield would have greatly increased his chances of being captured. Regardless of the poet's precise fate, the point to be made is that later Welsh tradition naturally assumed that the place of a *bardd teulu* was with the *comitatus*, whether it was in the hall or marshalled upon a field of battle. References in the poem regarding Aneirin's fate are somewhat contradictory. In CA.XXI (= A.21 in *GOSP*) it is clear that Aneirin was wounded, but managed to escape. However, in CA.XLVIII (= A.45) it is equally clear that Aneirin must have been taken prisoner or perhaps even killed (in CA.LV.A = A.52 and LV.B = B.2). For more on this, see pp. 22–24 in Jackson, *GOSP* or Patrick K. Ford, "The Death of Aneirin", *BBCS* XXXIV (1987), at pp. 41–45.

surprising that one finds that, "The poet plies his epithets as colorfully as the hero his bloody sword."[15]

The fact that the poet shared the same hardships and dangers of the campaign trail as his lord and the warriors of the *comitatus*, rather than remaining at court in relative ease and comfort, undoubtedly would have served to strengthen his ties to those who fought, and accorded him more respect in regard to his position within the warband and in the performance of his duties. Furthermore, in light of what is known regarding the role of the poet in Dark-Age society, it was crucial for the poet to be present at the battles. His observation of events, and especially the events that happened on a battlefield, would lend credibility to a poet's verse. The importance of this point cannot be overstated "since it fell to him alone to interpret and to publicize its acts, alike to a contemporary audience and as a record for posterity, by the means of panegyric, elegy, or satire, as the occasion demanded".[16]

As was seen for Taliesin, the accurate portrayal and publicizing of such acts would have been better served by a poet who actually had been a witness to them, for it provided the poet with the specific details he required to fashion a more credible and interesting account. In an Anglo-Saxon context, *Beowulf* might provide an early example of a *scop*'s search for specific details for the composition of a song. On the morning following Beowulf's slaying of the monster Grendel, it is noteworthy that the *scop* delayed his composition of the poem honoring Beowulf for this feat until after he had viewed (lines 837–52) not only the carnage at Heorot but also the bloody evidence of Grendel's demise, both along the trail leading to the mere and at the mere itself. Only after he had completed his own wide-ranging and thorough survey of the physical evidence did the *scop* (lines 865–74) compose his praise-song about Beowulf's admirable feat.

In summary, it has been seen that the functions performed by Celtic and Germanic poets were essentially the same. The poets of these Dark-Age societies were expected to retain and recite the genealogies of their lords, in addition to composing and reciting narrative or eulogistic poetry. For the most part, the poets were expected to be with their lord and their fellow members of a warband, whether it was in the hall or upon the field of battle. In the performance of these duties, the poet acted as an important support for the proper functioning, as an institution, of the overall *comitatus* structure. This is because:

> Honour and shame were of essence public – they implied reputation, either fame or disgrace. In the absence of developed administrative institutions in the British Isles in the early Middle Ages, fame and disgrace were natural

[15] Barber, *The Figure of Arthur*, p. 22.
[16] Bromwich (ed.), *Astudiaethau Ar Yr Hengerdd: Studies in Old Welsh Poetry* (Cardiff: University of Wales Press, 1978), p. 6.

sanctions. The publicizing of reputations was thus essential to this form of aristocratic organization, and the pre-eminent mode of publication was praise and satire in poetry.[17]

The relationship between a Dark-Age poet and his lord was reciprocal. In return for his services, the poet expected a variety of social and economic rewards. First, as a member of the *comitatus*, the poet participated, along with his fellow warriors, in the various "hall-joys" – feasting, drinking, gift-giving, the swearing of oaths, and so on – associated with the halls that housed Dark-Age warbands. It appears that the poet held an important place within the *comitatus*, based on the special relationship that he enjoyed with his lord and on the influence he exerted in publicizing the reputations of the other warriors of the *comitatus*. The reputations of both lord and retainers effectively lay in the hands of the court poet. While it would have been unlikely, if not impossible, for a poet to criticize his own lord and patron, the obvious controls of patronage did not extend necessarily to the other warriors of the lord's company, who would have had to rely on the poet's good will to have their own deeds included in his poetry. In a society where the active promotion of one's reputation was all-important, the poet's chief weapons – overt satire or subtle omission – must have assured that the poet was treated with respect by all members of a warband. It would have been a foolish warrior indeed who earned the enmity of a court poet. Furthermore, in some cases the importance of the court poet was reinforced through kinship ties to the lord or to other warriors of the *comitatus*, as may have been the case for Aneirin. As we saw in the previous chapter (fn. 22), in the *Gododdin* (line 550), Aneirin refers to a heavy loss of his own kinsmen at Catraeth.

The high esteem in which the Celtic and Germanic chieftains and lords held their poets is reflected best by the lavish gifts they often gave them. For the Germanic tribes, there are clear references to this patronage system and to the types of gifts that a *scop* might expect to receive from his lord as payment for his loyal service. In *Widsith*, the poet:

> tells in some detail about the patronage he received from Guthere (66), Ælfwine (70), Eormanrice (88), Eadgils (93), and Ealhhild (97) in return for his services as a *scop* (*songes to leane* – 67) and even though no one could have lived long enough to have seen all of these rulers, the prevalence of the custom of patronage need not be questioned.[18]

A similar system of patronage, based upon rich rewards, is seen among the British lords and their bards. As an indication of the high esteem in which

---

[17] Charles-Edwards, "Authenticity", p. 46.

[18] Cherniss, *Ingeld and Christ*, p. 14. As Cherniss has noted (*ibid.*), Widsith viewed the lord's generosity toward his poet as having a direct relationship with the poet's praises of his lord. It was, for him at least, a *quid pro quo* arrangement, a payment for services rendered.

they were held by the native chieftains for whom they worked, Aneirin and Taliesin frequently received valuable goods in return for their bardic services. The *Gododdin* (lines 240–7) clearly shows that Aneirin participated in hall feasts and had been given rich ornamentation to wear, as had the other members of Mynyddog's retinue. Aneirin also received gifts from other lords in the warband: Cenau gave him some type of "pay", while Cynfelyn presented him with a "fine gilded spear".[19] The same was true for Taliesin, who had received (*PT* I.3–6) "a hundred horses with silver trappings, a hundred splendid, colourful mantles, a hundred bracelets, and . . . a beautiful sword with a worthy scabbard"[20] from Cynan Garwyn, the lord of Powys, prior to his coming to Urien's Rheged. Urien's reputation for extravagant generosity toward bards in general, and toward Taliesin in particular, at least equaled that of Cynan. Poets were held in high esteem by Urien, who accorded them (*PT* IV.11, 6) a place of honor at his court (*racwed rothit y veird y byt*), and who gave special status of honor and respect (*cyfrifed*) to Taliesin. From Urien, Taliesin received (*PT* IV.3–8) gold (*eur*), possesions or riches (*meued*), and mead (*med*); all that Taliesin desired was given to him (*a rodi chwant. chwant oe rodi*). The phrase *a rodi chwant/chwant oe rodi* is instructive here, because it shows the degree to which the *bardd teulu* was dependent upon his lord for his social and economic well-being.[21]

From the above examples it seems clear that court poets were highly regarded by their Germanic and Celtic patrons. However, this high regard was not rooted in any altruistic appreciation of fine art; instead, the roots for it can be found in the rocky soil of the lord's own self-interest. The poet at a Germanic or Celtic court was rewarded handsomely by his lord because his chief functions – the recitation of his lord's genealogy, the composition and recitation of eulogistic and narrative poetry, and the publicizing of reputations – centered on the promotion of his lord's status in particular, and of the well-being and smooth fuctioning of his *comitatus* in general.

The recitation of heroic poetry[22] by court poets in the halls of their benefactors was a vital social institution acting as a support for the *comitatus*

---

19 Jackson, *GOSP*, p. 41. For examples of other poets receiving gifts from these lords, see Jackson (*ibid.*).
20 As Williams has surmised in his notes (p. 17 at *trefbret*) to that poem, "the gifts which are mentioned would enrich the bard's entire *trefret* [i.e. his house and its adjoining land]". It is impossible to say whether the bard received the farmstead itself from Cynon, or whether he merely provided goods to provision Taliesin's *trefret*. In any case, it is safe to say that the amount of goods that the poem claims was presented to the bard by his grateful lord is a reflection of poetic license or of the requirements of meter rather than any accurate reflection of reality. However, the specific types of gifts (if not their actual quantity) that are listed by the poem are entirely credible.
21 For more regarding this phrase, see Williams, *PT*, pp. 53, 51–2.
22 Heroic poetry, as a genre of literature, has been examined thoroughly in such classic texts as H.M. Chadwick, *The Heroic Age* and H.M. and Nora K. Chadwick, *The Growth*

structure of Dark-Age Germanic and Celtic kingdoms. The influence of heroic literature, orally composed and recited in a hall before a receptive audience, should not be underestimated. Regarding the *Gododdin*, Jarmon observed that the utility of the poem as an institutional support lay well beyond the confines of the *comitatus* itself, noting "its creation, as well as its ceremonial declamation, were functions of the communal life, and contributed to the consciousness of tribal cohesion and identity".[23] In an age when there were few institutional controls, the utility of this poetry lay in the fact that it provided the members of a warband – lord and retainer alike – with a consistent exemplar and model to influence their conduct and behavior. In this regard, heroic poetry was used to reinforce those values and beliefs that tended to strengthen the warband's structure, while condemning those acts that would have had a detrimental effect upon it. In accomplishing this objective, the poetry paid particular attention to the duties and obligations owed by chieftain and warriors to one another in the lord-retainer relationship, the fundamental basis, the permanent foundation, upon which the *comitatus* structure and its heroic value-system were built. In performing this function, these poets made use of the subject matter that most appealed to their audiences: stories concerned with warriors and heroes and the battles in which they fought. Often this function transformed the poet, in figurative terms, into a juggler as he tried to balance his need to promulgate a heroic value-system with that of an audience that did not wish to be lectured or preached to. Regarding the poet's balancing act, Nora Chadwick remarked that:

> Above all he must interest an audience willing to be entertained but not instructed; and a wide unlettered audience has no interest in political conceptions, economic conditions, national boundaries, or city life. The poet knows that the heroes in the hall, both the great heroes and their retainers, want to hear about personal heroes and their feats of valour, their tragic deaths, the loyalties of their followers.[24]

Through his adept use of this subject matter, the poet was able to promulgate the ideals that strengthened the framework of the *comitatus* structure in particular and, in more general terms, gave strength to the entire social fabric from which was woven the complex tapestry of heroic culture in Dark-Age Britain. The ideals that were embodied in the poet's conception of the ideal warband, though focusing primarily upon the lord-retainer relationship, touched

---

of Literature, Volume I (Cambridge: Cambridge University Press, 1932). It is a genre of literature which is not unique to the British and Anglo-Saxon experience, but one that is found among the tribes of pre-Christian Ireland, the pagan Norse, and the Archaic Greeks.

[23] Jarman, *Aneirin: Y Gododdin*, p. xxviii.

[24] Nora Chadwick, *The British Heroic Age*, p. 73.

on all aspects of life (and death) in a warband. Regarding heroic literature, Jackson has declared that:

> It carries with it an implication of a social setting; a military aristocratic society, whether of a primitive or a more highly developed kind, in which the real *raison d'être*, and the chief interest, of the nobility is warfare, and for which the accepted morality is courage and fierceness in war, generosity and liberality in peace, a longing for fame, a horror of disgrace, and a welcome for death provided it leads to immortal glory.[25]

The poetic works cited, Aneirin's *Gododdin*, the historical poems of Taliesin, and the anonymous *Beowulf*, all promulgate heroic ideals and expectations and a code of conduct. Additionally, as has been shown by the introduction of specific historical examples throughout this study, these heroic ideals often manifested themselves in the conduct of both lord and retainer while in the hall, in exile, and on the battlefield.[26] In short, there appears to exist a credible correlation between the ideals established by the court poet of this period and the actual behavior that was exhibited by the members of Dark-Age warbands. The poet's unflagging adherence to, and consistent use of, these ideals also served to validate the existing social structure of the Dark-Age kingdoms. Therefore, the honors and riches with which a lord rewarded a talented poet for the performance of these duties should not be cause for surprise.

For the British tribes, the *Gododdin* in particular sets forth the heroic ideals that were held by the warrior-aristocracy of this period with a force and an unbridled and unabashed passion, that is unequaled by the other poems. The poem does so with such eloquence and single-mindeness of purpose that it has been called "the classic, and only full length, exposition of the ideals of the Heroic Age in Welsh literature".[27] These ideals, a reflection of the aristocratic culture of which they were a part, were the same as those found in other heroic cultures. Writing on the early evolution of heroic ideals whose emphasis centered around the military qualities of the *comitatus*, Ann Matonis asserts that "the *Gododdin*, equally a product of a military aristocratic society, depicts the heroic ideals of the British in the Dark Ages: prowess, courage, generosity,

---

25 Jackson, *GOSP*, p. 38.
26 The purpose of this segment of the chapter is to identify, in broad terms, the major values and ideals of such a system, and to place them in relation to, and in the context of, the institutional health and vitality of the *comitatus* structure.

For a brief synopsis on the relationship between heroic literature and the society that produced it, see (for the Britons) Jarman's *Aneirin: Y Gododdin* (pp. xl–xlvii), or Jackson, *GOSP* (pp. 37–41). For the same in an Anglo-Saxon context, see Chickering, *Beowulf: A Dual-Language Edition*, pp. 259–65.
27 A.O.H. Jarman, *A Guide to Welsh Literature, Volume I* (Swansea: Christopher Davies, 1969), p. 70.

a desire for fame, and fear of disgrace".[28] The ideals of the *Gododdin*, which extol those qualities that acted to strengthen the social and cultural underpinnings of the warband and the lord-retainer relationship, set a standard of conduct and behavior by which the warriors of all the British kingdoms were to be judged. In a society fighting for its very survival, this was of the utmost importance because, against their enemies during this tumultuous period, "the heroic ideals and military exploits of the Welsh dynasties were viable and effective means of defence".[29] Consequently, as was seen earlier, these heroic values continued to be used by the seventh-century British kingdoms throughout the island, as evidenced by the *Moliant Cadwallawn*, the *Marwnad Cynddylan*, and the *Gododdin's* interpolation regarding the battle at Strathcarron.

In any event, by their complete and total fulfillment of their part of the lord-retainer relationship, the warriors of Mynyddog's warband (*gosgordd Mynyddawg*) became the epitome of an ideal *comitatus*, even though their actions led to a disastrous military defeat and to their own unequivocal and utter destruction. Though he was painfully aware of the excesses inherent in a heroic society, Aneirin offers an uncompromising defense of the heroic ideals on which that society was erected. Thus, of the *Gododdin*, it has been said that "While the poem is in form an elegy and is shot through with a sense of the sadness of the losses it records, it is also a eulogy, a poem of celebration, a paean of praise for the warriors who attained undying fame by their utter fidelity to their chieftain and their dauntless and unyielding courage in battle."[30]

When one reads the lines of his poetry, it quickly becomes evident that Taliesin shared with Aneirin this same view of the world. Throughout his poems, Taliesin consistently promoted the same heroic ideals that Aneirin had praised in the *Gododdin*. For the most part, Taliesin's poems differ in mood from the *Gododdin*, in part because he did not, like Aneirin, have to sing of an unmitigated military disaster. Consequently, there are no bittersweet memories of fallen comrades, no compulsive focus on the faithful discharge of one's duties in the lord-retainer relationship, and no doubts whatsoever regarding the wisdom of those heroic ideals that acted to sustain and strengthen the *comitatus* in the larger, heroic value-system of Dark-Age Britain.

Taliesin's poems also differ from Aneirin's *Gododdin* because they present the reader with a greater variety of settings, and provide a much fuller de-

---

[28] Ann Matonis, "Traditions of Panegyric in Welsh Poetry", *Speculum* 53 (1978), p. 686. Jarman's section ("Heroic Society and the Heroic Ideal"), in his introduction to his *Aneirin: Y Gododdin* is replete with specific passages from the poem exemplifying these ideals, as well as the honorable fulfillment of duties that characterized the lord-retainer relationship. Consequently, there is little need to list them here, and the reader is encouraged to see the numerous examples cited by Jarman.

[29] Matonis, *ibid.*, p. 686.

[30] Jarman, *Aneirin: Y Gododdin*, pp. xl–xli.

scription of life in the hall. Further, because his poetry is straightforward praise poetry, Taliesin's poems focus almost exclusively on the chieftain's qualities and roles within the lord-retainer relationship. These differences are only ones of degree and emphasis; the works of both poets promote the ideals of Dark-Age Britain with an equal level of eloquence and fervor. Throughout his poems to the lords for whom he sang – Cynan Garwyn, Urien, Owain, and Gwallawg – Taliesin is utterly consistent in his portrayal of heroic society as he found it at the various British courts where he resided, and unequivocal in his praise of the ideals on which it was erected. Thus, one finds that Taliesin has high praise for a lord who exhibited military prowess and courage in war and open-handed generosity in peace. Allowing for a slight variation in emphasis, setting, and subject matter, the ideals lauded by Taliesin and Aneirin are the same in all their essentials.

The Germanic heroic society found in *Beowulf* shows a remarkable similarity with that found among the Britons. This society, dominated by a warrior-aristocracy, had been brought over from the continent by the Germanic tribes during their migrations to the island during the fifth and sixth centuries. The Anglo-Saxon warriors were organized within a *comitatus* structure that in part was supported by heroic ideals, whose main focus was on the bonds between a chieftain and his warriors within a lord-retainer relationship. A *scop's* support of these ideals, and particularly the ideals that acted to strengthen the bonds between a lord and his warriors, was of the utmost importance to the newly-established Germanic kingdoms of sixth-century Britain.

Not surprisingly, one finds that the ideals and the code of conduct that are set forth by the author of *Beowulf* are the same in their essentials as those that were advanced by Aneirin and Taliesin. The *Beowulf* poet, through his skillful use of heroic ideals, promulgated a set of expectations and a code of conduct by which both the lord (*dryhten*) and the members of his warband (*gedryht*) were to be judged. First and foremost among the ideals lauded by the *Beowulf* poet in his conception of an ideal, heroic society was the overarching concept of loyalty, the fundamental principle that sheltered the lord-retainer relationship from those elemental forces that sought to weaken and destroy it in times of stress and hardship. Elaborating on the importance of this concept, Cherniss certainly was correct in declaring that "Loyalty, the principle of personal allegiance between individual warriors, is the primary concept upon which the ideal society depicted in Germanic heroic poetry is built" and that the word " 'loyalty' . . . implies as well the entire system of *comitatus* relationships which inheres in the values put forth by Old English poetry".[31]

Consequently, one would expect a Germanic *scop* to praise both the concept of loyalty and those actions through which both lord and warrior fulfilled the faithful discharge of their duties and obligations within the lord-retainer

---

[31] Cherniss, *Ingeld and Christ*, p. 30.

relationship. As is seen in the numerous examples from the poem that are presented throughout this study, this is exactly what one finds in *Beowulf*. In broad terms, the poet praises warriors for their strength and courage, and for their devotion to their lord; chieftains are praised, not only for their own martial prowess, but for their generosity toward their warriors as well. The lords and warriors in *Beowulf* have an insatiable desire for fame, and an overwhelming fear of disgrace. For them, death through the faithful discharge of their duties within the lord-retainer relationship is preferable to life through cowardice and disloyalty, a sentiment which has the full and consistent approval of *Beowulf's* composer.

CHAPTER SEVEN

THE HALL

Bede, in relating the story (*HE* II.13) of Edwin's adoption of Christianity, made use of an eloquent and moving metaphor regarding human existence which an Anglo-Saxon audience would have found particularly attractive. Advising his lord on whether to adopt the new religion, one of Edwin's nobles declared:

> It seems to me, my lord, that the present life of men here on earth – for the comparison of our uncertain time to live – as if a sparrow should come to the house and very swiftly fly through; entering through one window and immediately passing out through another, while you sit at table with your thegns and counsellors; the hall being warmed by the fire kindled in the midst of it, but all places outside being troubled by raging tempests of winter rain and snow. While in the house, it is protected from the winter storm, but after a very short time of fair weather that lasts only a moment, it soon passes again from winter into winter and escapes from your sight. So the life of man appears here for a short time, but what follows or what has gone before, we surely do not know.[1]

In addition to Bede's intended use of the hall as an image of man's life, it also illustrates the overarching importance of the hall to the warriors of a heroic society. In this well-known passage, it is evident that Bede, "attributes to the pagan party a use of the hall as a positive existential metaphor; it represents to them the best that life has to offer man, at least until the coming of Christianity".[2]

---

1 *'Talis,' inquiens, 'mihi videtur, rex, vita hominum praesens in terris, ad comparationem eius quod nobis incertum est temporis, quale cum te residente ad coenam cum decibus ac ministris tuis tempore brumali, accenso quidem foco in medio et calido effecto coenaculo, furentibus autem foris per omnia turbinibus hiemalium vel nivium, adveniensque unus passerum domum citissime pervolaverit qui cum per unum ostium ingrediens, mox per aliud exierit. Ipso quidem tempore quo intus est, hiemis tempestate non tangitur, sed tamen parvissimo spatio serenitatis ad momentum excurso, mox de hieme in hiemem regrediens, tuis oculis elabitur. Ita haec vita hominum ad modicum apparet; quid autem sequator, quidve praecesserit, prorsus ignoramus.*
2 Kathryn Hume, "The Concept of the Hall in Old English Poetry", *Anglo-Saxon*

The Hall

For the period's British and Anglo-Saxon kingdoms, the concept of the hall was a fundamental cultural/social support that gave strength and vitality to the warband to which it gave physical shelter, whose importance in this regard is comparable to that of the court poet and his poetry. The hall's supporting role was effected through its physical layout and construction, the activities that took place within its walls, and the importance it is accorded by heroic poetry and the period's other sources. The external situation of the hall[3] did not affect its role in acting as a central, vital support for the *comitatus* structure in general, and for the lord-retainer relationship in particular.

A variety of building forms and materials were employed in the actual construction of these Dark-Age halls.[4] Regardless of the precise nature of the materials and design employed in their construction, the building – both the preparatory excavation and the erection of the structure *per se* – of these large structures constituted a very large undertaking in terms of manpower and materials.[5] Coupled with the large expenditure of resources for other buildings found at many of these sites, along with the enormous amount of work that is embodied in the different types of defensive enclosures that surround many hall-structures, it becomes apparent that the construction of these hall-

England III (1974), p. 69. Hume's article remains a seminal one for understanding the importance of this "hall-idea" to the warrior class in Anglo-Saxon society.

[3] The focus of this chapter is only on the hall itself. Consequently, it is of little relevance whether a particular hall is located on a hill-fort site, on an artificial *crannog*, or on a position of natural strength. Nor does it matter if the enclosure that surrounded a particular hall was of a dry-stone construction or whether it was a wooden palisade. For that matter, the actual utility and effectiveness of these enclosures in actually protecting the hall, or their role in the overall conduct of warfare during this period, also are moot points insofar as this study is concerned. In any case, for those interested in such topics, a useful starting point is Alcock, *Economy, Society, and Warfare*, throughout chapters 10–18.

[4] While the period's poetry and a few references in the historical sources offer some clues regarding the construction and layout of these halls (and of their surrounding outbuildings and fortifications), most of our information about halls in this regard is based on the continuing finds and analysis provided by archaeologists. Accordingly, this section relies heavily upon the synthesis of archaeological research and excavations provided by scholars in that field, and in particular is indebted to the synthesis that is provided by Alcock, *Economy, Society, and Warfare*, and Arnold, *Archaeology of Early Anglo-Saxon Kingdoms*.

[5] A case in point – building C12 at Cowdery's Down – is provided by Arnold, *ibid.*, pp. 98–100. In regard to the construction of that structure (which is the largest of a whole series of buildings that form the complex), Arnold has stated that: "It has been estimated that to construct the rectangular timber building, C12, would have required the movement of c.81 tonnes of topsoil, clay and chalk for the footings, and building materials such as timber, daub and thatch weighing 70 tonnes (Millet 1983, M5/02) . . . A conservative estimate suggests that the principal timber work would have required trees from two hectares of oak forest to construct the building, excluding the floorboards."

complexes testifies to the surprising degree of social control that could be wielded by Dark-Age lords in whatever ventures they deemed necessary. Another indicator of the marked ability of these lords to marshal resources for large-scale construction tasks can be seen in the erection of a series of defensive frontier dykes whose construction can be placed in this period. Given that the resources available to these Dark-Age lords were of a decidedly limited nature, these projects reflect quite favorably on the organizational abilities of these rulers.

While there was some variation in the size and design of these halls, a few of the more common and prevalent features of construction can be addressed here. For the Britons and the Anglo-Saxons, the typical hall was rectangular.[6] In size, halls could range from about 25–30 feet in length, upwards to 80 feet or more and some 30 feet in width, as in the case of the hall at Yeavering. The halls themselves were constructed primarily of timber, their walls usually being constucted of vertical planks set deep into the earth, although wattle-and-daub may have been used in some instances. Evidence for the existence of buttresses to support the walls and roofs of the hall-buildings at many of these sites would indicate structures of no little height. Open in design, with few if any internal divisions, the structures were enclosed by roofs that were made either of wood or thatch.[7] The flooring appears to have been constructed of wooden planking, sometimes set several feet above the excavated ground level. On this last point, the archaeological data is reinforced vividly by a passage in *Beowulf* (lines 1316–17), which relates that "They went through the hall, the distinguished warrior with his handpicked troop – the hall-wood (i.e., floorboards) thundered" (*Gang ða æfter flore, fyrdwyrðe man mid his hand-scale – healwudu dynede*). A few of the following hall-structures illustrate the impressive, open design that characterized many Dark-Age halls.

Though archaeological evidence regarding the precise nature and function of some proposed structures at various British digs is often problematic, especially in regard to proposed halls (*neuadd*) among the northern British kingdoms, an unequivocal example of a large, princely *neuadd* is found at Doon Hill, located within the lands of Manaw Gododdin. The structure, known

6 There may be exceptions. Alcock, *ibid.*, p. 244, has made a plausible case for viewing the round structure located on a *crannog* at Buiston in East Lothian as the hall of a princely stronghold. Conversely, this is not to imply that evidence for the existence of every large rectangular building in Britain automatically denotes the hall of a Dark-Age lord. However, in those structures in which high status finds are unearthed, one can assume with some certainty that they represent a hall building.

7 For more about construction techniques and materials, and for references regarding specific excavations, see Alcock, *ibid.*; Arnold, *Archaeology of Early Anglo-Saxon Kingdoms*, pp. 98–100; Campbell, *The Anglo-Saxons*, at pp. 56–8; and Alcock, *The Neighbors of the Picts: Angles, Britons, and Scots at Home and at War* (Edinburgh: Dornoch Press, 1993), pp. 22–36.

as Doon Hill A,[8] must have been an impressive one, with its internal dimensions measuring some 70 by 32 feet (2,240 sq. feet). The hall itself was divided into a large central room, into which entrance was gained through large doors which were placed along the two long sides of the structure, and two smaller compartments that were located at either end of the structure. Another example of a British *neuadd* is probably evidenced in the large circular[9] structure found at Buiston in Ayrshire. Situated on a *crannog*, the well-preserved seventh- to eighth-century structure is credited by Alcock as a high-status hall of the warrior-aristocracy, based on certain features that the site shared with other royal or princely strongholds: the presence of weapons, evidence of metalworking activities, and indications of imported pottery from the continent.[10] The wooden structure[11] is about 56 feet in diameter (about 2,450 sq. feet), and its open layout surrounds a large hearth that was located near the center of the structure. While larger than other British halls of the period – the *neuadd* at Dinas Powys and Cadbury, for example[12] – both Doon Hill A and the circular hall at Buiston reflect the open design that evidently did characterize, on an almost uniform basis, most Dark-Age halls.

The broad corpus of archaeological evidence relating to the Anglo-Saxon hall (*heall* or *sele*) shows that it shared many of the same features of construction and design as those evidenced for its British counterpart. Evidently, the design of Anglo-Saxon halls followed a regular pattern[13] – uniformly rectangular in shape, open in design, with perhaps a separate chamber located at

---

[8] See Alcock, *Economy, Society, and Warfare*, p. 242, for a fuller description, from which the following is derived.

[9] The exact shape of the structure is of little consequence for the purpose of this study. Whether the hall was rectangular, round, or an illiptical spheroid, the study views the internal divisions (or lack thereof) of halls, and their impact on social interactions and activities of the *comitatus*, as more important than the shape and size of their external walls, or of their surrounding fortifications. However, Alcock is correct in attempting to alter the long-held perception that all halls must of necessity be rectangular (*ibid.*, p. 244). Especially for the British, it is apparent that circular structures were a common architectural feature (*Angles, Britons, and Scots*, pp. 29–32).

[10] *Economy, Society, and Warfare*, p. 244. For the high-status finds at Buiston, see Alcock, *Angles, Britons, and Scots*, pp. 30–2, and Fig. 15 (p. 33).

[11] See *ibid.* for details relating to the hall at Buiston (pp. 30–2) and for a diagram of its excavation (p. 28).

[12] Alcock in large part was responsible for the excavations at both sites, about which he has written extensively. Many of his findings can be found in his *Economy, Society, and Warfare* in chapters 1–9 (for Dinas Powys), and in chapters 12–13 (for Cadbury). The hall-building at Cadbury, for example, was divided into a large hall, with a smaller chamber at one end (see the diagram and reconstruction in *ibid.*, p. 203). Furthermore, other British and Anglo-Saxon sites are mentioned throughout that work. Lastly, a helpful summary and analysis of many of these sites (as well as references to other archaeological studies) also are provided by Alcock throughout his *Angles, Britons, and Scots*.

[13] Arnold, *Archaeology of Early Anglo-Saxon Kingdoms*, pp. 172–3.

either one or both ends. Like the British *neuadd*, the Anglo-Saxon *heall* (especially prior to the eighth century) was constructed primarily of wood, whose walls were often reinforced through the use of buttresses. The architecture of some of the larger halls[14] certainly exemplifies these features. The construction techniques and materials employed for the building of the large timber hall (C12) at Cowdery's Down (enclosing an area of some 1,700 sq. feet), were addressed earlier.[15] Other examples include the large hall-structures found at Northampton and Yeavering. The seventh-century timber hall at Northampton, with a floor area of some 2,300 sq. feet, consisted of "a rectangular centre with square annexes at either end, which appears to have been a highly sophisticated, possibly bayed, structure, which was set out extremely precisely".[16] Similarly, Yeavering was the site of a series of impressive seventh-century timber structures – including perhaps a pagan temple, a church, a grandstand, and a succession of hall-structures – before being abandoned early in the next century or perhaps earlier.[17] The great hall at Yeavering was enormous, its plastered walls measuring some 80 feet in length and almost 40 feet in width (for an enclosed floor area well in excess of 3,000 sq. feet). Furthermore, the structure, one of four successive structures erected at Yeavering, must have been one of considerable height, evidenced by the setting of the posts almost 8 feet into the ground.[18] Despite its great size and

14 Like Alcock, Arnold (*ibid.*, pp. 172 and 174) has cautioned against according every large rectangular structure the status of a princely or royal seat of an Anglo-Saxon kingdom or chiefdom. Like the British sites, such proposed seats of power should also possess those high-status finds normally associated with an aristocratic site to reinforce any argument for such a status.

For other examples of large structures (some of which are not addressed here) and for further references, see Hume, "Concept of Hall", pp. 63–4.

15 See above at fn. 5. For a proposed reconstruction for the hall at Cowdery's Down, see Yorke, *Kings and Kingdoms*, Fig. 9 (located on insert opposite p. 106).

16 Arnold, *Archaeology of Early Anglo-Saxon Kingdoms*, p. 173. The identification as an aristocratic site was made primarily upon the quality of the building itself, which failed to yield any high-status artifacts (though the stone structure that was built upon it, perhaps as a replacement, did contain many high-status finds).

17 Summaries of the site and its principal structures can be found in Arnold (*ibid.*, pp. 173–5), Alcock (*Angles, Britons, and Scots*), or in Campbell ("The First Christian Kings" (pp. 57–8)). The definitive study of the site (and its meticulous excavation) remains that of Brian Hope-Taylor: his findings are related in *Yeavering: An Anglo-British Centre of Early Northumbria* (London: Department of the Environment Archaeological Reports, 1977).

18 Campbell, "The First Christian Kings", p. 57. Given the size of these structures, Campbell is correct to note that "the halls take us straight to the world of *Beowulf*". Similarly, Yorke (*Kings and Kingdoms*, p. 17) is of the opinion that "the excavated halls of Yeavering and Cowdery's Down form a bridge between the world of *Beowulf* and the reality of Anglo-Saxon life".

Beyond *Beowulf*'s detailed descriptions of Hrothgar's hall, it is interesting to note that, on several occasions, the poem specifically mentions (lines 140, 1299–1301) the

evident grandeur, the hall at Yeavering retained the same open design that characterized other Anglo-Saxon halls of this period.

While of little use in a discussion regarding either their design or the methods employed in the construction of Dark-Age halls, our written sources take the forefront in presenting the activities that occurred within their walls, with the notable exception of a warrior's training regimen. In some instances, the archaeological record can verify some of the activities and material culture described by our written sources. A wide range of activities were centered on, and took place within, the physical confines of Dark-Age halls. Many of the activities – feasting, drinking, boasting, the distribution of gifts, and the songs of the poet – are called hall-joys in the period's heroic literature and represent the proper functioning of the *comitatus* structure as it was found among the Britons and Anglo-Saxons. Given the close association of these hall-joys with the structure in which they occurred, it is natural that the hall should have formed a central focus – both in a physical and emotional sense – for the existence of a warrior. The hall, by providing the physical setting for those (bonding) activities that strengthened the social and cultural ties within the warband, acted as a fundamental support mechanism of the *comitatus* structure.

There are many similarities between Germanic and Celtic hall life as it is described by our historical and literary sources, and as it is evidenced by the archaeological record. From what can be inferred from Bede's story (*HE* III.14) concerning Bishop Aidan and King Oswine of Deira, it would seem that a lord's retainers were expected to spend much of their time as his companions, both in the hall and during other lordly pursuits. Bede says of life in Oswine's hall that the lord's men shared their lord's hearth,[19] received often lavish gifts from him, and joined their lord in his various amusements, which included hunting. Evenings at the hall normally would be taken up by feasting and drinking, though the degree of formality and protocol at these feasts remains uncertain. In Bede's account, Bishop Aidan evidently had a designated seat at these feasts; "the bishop for his part took his appointed place" (*episcopus quidem residebat in suo loco*). Similarly, Boniface recounted that Ceolred (709–16) of Mercia died in some sort of convulsive fit "while feasting with his companions".[20] Beyond this, other references to

outbuildings that formed a part of the hall-complex, an attribute that the poem's hall shared with many of its counterparts in the real world. The poem also makes reference (line 785) to the manned palisade wall that surrounded the building-complex at Heorot, another attribute that archaeologists have assigned to halls of this period.

[19] In Anglo-Saxon poetry, the hearth (a physical component of the overall hall structure) could be used to denote the hall itself and, by extension, the entire *comitatus*. The term "hearth-companions" (*heorð-geneatas*) often was used as a synonym for comrades-in-arms or for fellow warriors (*Beowulf*, 261).

[20] Taken from Dorothy Whitelock, *English Historical Documents, Volume I*, pp. 816–22.

hall life in the narrative histories are rare. Bede's story (*HE* II.9) about the assassination attempt on Edwin also illustrates that warriors were in attendance when their lord received emisaries from other rulers. Furthermore, it seems evident that warriors were expected to attend their lord on those occasions when major decisions were to be made regarding a chiefdom's policy, as Bede's narrative (*HE* II.13) regarding Edwin's decision to adopt Christianity shows.

In particular, the scenes in *Beowulf* of Hrothgar's hall, Heorot, present a similar picture to the one drawn by the lives and histories. However, while the latter sources offer only a rudimentary and unfinished sketch of the subject, *Beowulf* paints a much fuller, richly colored, and detailed picture of the hall life that existed among the warriors of the Germanic kingdoms. Many of the scenes depicted in the poem occur in one of several halls of different Germanic tribes. As such, the poem is invaluable in its description of hall life and of the items of material culture (such as mead benches and wall hangings) that were found in the hall. In the poem, Hrothgar frequently is shown as sitting "with his troop of retainers" or "band of kinsmen" (*mid his eorla gedriht* or *sibbehedriht*) in his "gabled hall" (*healreced*), which is claimed to be "the greatest of hall-buildings" (*heal-ærna mæst*). Like the men decribed by Bede, the *Beowulf* poet relates (line 99) that before Grendel's onslaught, Hrothgar's "retinue lived in hall-joys" (*drihtguman dreamum lifdon*): receiving gifts (lines 71–3, 80–1), feasting, drinking, and listening to the songs of the *scop* (lines 88–90).

Compared to Bede and our other sources, *Beowulf* provides far greater detail regarding these activities, and provides further information about hall life and its material culture – in large part substantiated by archaeology – that the other sources do not. Regarding the material culture of the hall, the poem makes it clear at several places in the story (lines 4, 327, 485, 491, 775, 1029) that, while feasting and drinking, the warriors were seated at wooden mead-benches, while the chieftain sat at a designated place called (line 1087) the "high throne" (*heahsetl*) or (line 168) the "gift seat" (*gifstol*). Apparently, these mead-benches could be arranged differently to suit the particular occasion, and were moved out of the way to make space for the warriors who regularly slept in the hall building. For instance, *Beowulf* relates that, upon the hero's return to Geatland, Hygelac orders (lines 1975–6) that "the hall's [internal] furnishings be cleared quickly for the travelers" (*Hraðe wæs gerymed . . . feðegestum, flet innanweard*). Again, prior to the feast at Heorot, the poem tells (lines 491–2) that "Then a bench was cleared in the beer-hall for the Weders [who were] gathered together" (*Þa wæs Geatmæcgum geador ætsomne beorsele benc gerymed*). The poem's references to warriors sleeping in Heorot are even more explicit. In one instance (lines 652–60), Hrothgar entrusts Heorot to the protection of Beowulf and his men, who are asleep by the time that Grendel arrives (lines 728–30). Later in the poem (lines 1237–9, 1242–6), the poet again provides an explicit description of Danish warriors retiring for the night, saying that:

A great host of men
occupied the hall,   as often they did before,
carried away bench-planks,   covered [the floor] entirely
with their bedding and pillows . . .
At their heads were set   their round shields
bright linden-wood.
There was on the bench   above [each] noble
a high-crested war-helmet,   an iron ring-coat . . .[21]

There is ample evidence regarding the interior decorations of these halls. The walls of the poem's various halls appear to have been adorned with tapestries and other woven standards. The poem relates (lines 991–6) that, after Beowulf's slaying of Grendel, Heorot was repaired and refurbished in order to restore the hall to its former grandeur, so that once again "Shining with gold, tapestries shone on the walls" (*Goldfag scinon, web æfter wagum*). Again, the poet tells of Hengest's slaying of Finn and his men by relating (lines 1151–2) that "The hall was decorated with the lives of the enemy" (*Ða wæs heal hroden, feonda feorum*). Though gruesome, the picture drawn by the poet would imply that it was typical for a hall to have wall decorations. Lastly, the poem relates (lines 2767–8) that even the dragon's "hall" had a "gold standard high over the hoard, a weaving of most wondrous skill" (*segn eallgylden heah ofer horde, hondwundra mæst*), and (line 2759) that there were other "wondrous [hangings] on the walls" (*wundor on wealle*) that adorned the "earth-hall" (*eorð-sele*) of the old dragon.

It also seems likely that war-trophies, especially in the form of weapons and shields, were displayed throughout the hall. Unfortunately, the only trophies given prominent display at Heorot are Grendel's arm (nailed to the hall's rafters) and his severed head (raised on a war-spear). However, it is clear that the "hall" of Grendel and his mother displayed weapons on its walls. Beowulf, in relating the story of her destruction, praised God (lines 1662–3) for allowing "that on the wall I might see, brightly hanging, a gigantic ancient sword" (*þæt ic on wage geseah, wlitig hangian, ealdsweord eacen*). Given that war-trophies and heirlooms are earned by, and given to, the principal characters of the poem, it seems reasonable to conclude that these more traditional trophies also would have been displayed on the walls or hung along the rafters of a Dark-Age hall. Doing so would have served two pur-

---

[21]   *Reced weardode*
unrim eorla   swa hie oft ær dydon;
bencþelu beredon;   hit geondbræded wearð
beddum ond bolstrum . . .
Setton him to heafdon   hilderandas
bordwudu beorhtan.   Þær on bence wæs
ofer æthelinge   yþgesene
heaþosteapa helm,   hringed byrne . . .

poses. First, the display of such items would have enhanced the hall's martial atmosphere by acting as constant visual reminders to those inside of earlier victories, and of the rewards that such victories brought. Second, the placement of these items on the walls and along the rafters would have allowed for maximum utilization of the limited floor area, which already doubled as a feasting and sleeping area. Because the poem contains many detailed and accurate descriptions of other items of material culture – weapons, armor, shields, and treasure – we can assume that its references to these items offer an accurate reflection of the situation.[22]

The *Beowulf* poem makes it clear that while the hall provided the physical setting for many of the period's hall-joys, it was the feast that provided the social context in which they took place. The feasting scenes both at Heorot and at the Hygelac's Geatish hall-complex (lines 489–99, 611–46; 1011–68, 1160–1235; 1785–90; 1976–85; 2010–24) are marked by a great deal of formality and protocol.[23] At Heorot and at Hygelac's hall, the chieftain's wife and daughter are portrayed as presenting vessels[24] of mead or wine to the

---

[22] For the similarities between the poet's description of these and other items and those unearthed at Sutton Hoo and other sites, see for example Rosemary Cramp, "*Beowulf* and Archaeology", *Medieval Archaeology* 1 (1957), pp. 57–77; M. Millet and S. James, "Excavations at Cowdery's Down, Basingstoke, Hampshire, 1978–81", *Archaeological Journal* 140 (1983), pp. 151–279. In particular, see Angela Care Evans, *The Sutton Hoo Ship Burial* (London: British Museum Publications, 1986).

[23] The formality and often elaborate protocol that is evidenced in the poem are traits that *Beowulf* shares with the heroic literature of other societies, including those of the Archaic Greeks, the pre-Christian Irish, and the British kingdoms with whom the Anglo-Saxons often fought. The degree to which these scenes offer an accurate representation of reality is problematic. While archaeology can corroborate some of material goods that were used during these feasts (such as glass drinking vessels and silver plates), it can neither verify nor discredit the ceremonial aspects of the feasting activities that are claimed by the poem. Indeed, the formality evidenced at Heorot might be attributable merely to the fact that the Spear-Danes were hosts to Beowulf and his men, or that two of the feasts represented formal celebrations of the destruction of Grendel and his mother.

[24] Made primarily of horn, glass, or (rarely) precious metals. See Evans, *op. cit.* in fn. 22 above. See also Alcock, *Economy, Society and Warfare*, p. 248. The presentation of mead to the warriors by the noblewomen certainly should be seen in a ceremonial context; the poem makes it clear that, with these few ceremonial exceptions, servants were responsible for serving the warriors.

Though women were not part of the *comitatus* (and hence outside the province of this study), it can be noted that the women in *Beowulf* are presented in a favorable light, with the poet creating the distinct impression that counsel and guidance on the part of queens and other noblewomen was part of the normal course of events. Nevertheless, due to the nature of the poem, their role in the affairs of the aristocracy remains understated by the poet, who "uses them mainly to create an impression of splendid civility and heroic pathos" (Chickering, *Beowulf*, p. 264). See *ibid.*, for details regarding the poem's portrayal of women, and how that portrayal differed from the realities of Anglo-Saxon life.

warriors of the *comitatus* in some sort of formal, ordered sequence during the course of these feasts. Further, some of the seating arrangements seem to have been defined by rank and importance. The poem says (lines 1188–91) that, after slaying Grendel, Beowulf is seated on a bench with Hrothgar's two sons, an honor he saw fit to relate (lines 2011–12) to Hygelac upon returning to Geatland. Again, Hrothgar's *scop* sings (line 1067) the lay about Finn's destruction from his place "on the mead bench" (*æfter medobence*). Though the feasts were ostensibly meals, there are no references to what foods were consumed. However, there are numerous and varied references to the types of drink – called alternately mead (*medu*), wine (*win*), and beer (*beor*) – that invariably accompanied feasts, and that were consumed eagerly by lord and warrior alike.

Vows or boasts (*gilp-word*) by warriors, regarding both their previous accomplishments and deeds yet to be performed, also seem to have formed an integral component of the feasting activity. Though Beowulf performs the lion's share of the boasting in the poem, the hero was not unique in this respect. Hrothgar informs Beowulf (lines 480–7) that his own warriors had "often boasted, drinking mead from ale-flagons, that in the beer-hall they would meet Grendel's attack" (*Ful oft gebeotedon, beore druncne ofer ealowæge . . . þæt hie in beorsele bidan woldon Grendles guþe*), but that their boasts had resulted instead in their deaths by the next morning in a "hall bright in blood, all the benches a running slick, the hall red with gore" (*drihtsele dreor-fah . . . eal bencþelu blode bestymed, heall heorudreore*).

As is related in the following chapter, these hall-feasts frequently provided the setting for the ceremonial distribution of wealth and gifts (in the form of weapons, armor, horses, and other treasure) by the lord to his retainers, and for formal recognition and praise of a warrior's service to the *comitatus*. Finally, as we have seen, the songs and poetry of the *scop* constituted another activity and hall-joy that was associated closely with the hall-feast.

Not all hall-joys took place within the physical confines of the hall-structure. Hunting, an activity mentioned by Bede, is seen as an aristocratic activity in *Beowulf*. The poem says (line 854) that, after viewing conclusive evidence of Grendel's destruction at the mere, the warriors returned to the hall "gay as a hunt" (*of gomenwaþe*). Hunting is mentioned again when the poem relates (lines 2435–40) the tragic end of Herebeald, whose accidental death was caused by his brother Hæthcyn during the course of a hunt. The poem's claim (lines 864–5) that the warriors "let [horses] rear, let horses go racing" (*hleapan leton, on geflit faran fealwe mearas*) indicates that horse racing was another leisure activity in which warriors engaged, as do the lines (916–17) that "At times racing, they paced the horses on the road" (*Hwilum flitende fealwe stræte mearum mæton*). Finally, the poem indicates that games were played in the courtyard, saying (lines 2458–9) that, for the slain Herebeald, "there would not be harp music, games in the courtyard" (*nis þær hearpan sweg, gomen in geardum*). Though he offers no specifics regarding their nature or purpose, the poet, by coupling these games with harp music, evidently regarded them as among the hall-joys.

For the warriors of Dark-Age British kingdoms, hall life and its associated activities were similar to those that *Beowulf* and Bede portray as having existed among the Anglo-Saxons. However, unlike the Anglo-Saxons, aside from archaeology, what is known about those subjects is derived exclusively from the surviving poetry of the *Cynfeirdd*. For these hall activities, the written non-poetic sources fail us completely and we are compelled to rely on the works of Aneirin and Taliesin, and trust that the field of archaeology can help reveal any anachronisms that the poems might contain. In any event, despite the existence of several unmistakable anachronisms (such as references to gold torques and filigreed shields), early Welsh poetry nevertheless offers a wealth of information about hall-life and presents a highly-detailed picture of many of its associated activities.

Like *Beowulf*, many of the scenes in Aneirin's *Gododdin* and in Taliesin's poems frequently are set in the halls of their lords, and consequently offer an invaluable description of hall life and its material culture. Of the works of the two poets, Aneirin's *Gododdin* has more to say regarding the specific items that comprised the material trappings[25] of these British halls. The poem (lines 6–7, 818) alludes to hearths when it refers to "the well-fed fire, the logs blazing from dusk to dawn", and mentions (line 148) that the hall's illumination was provided by lighted candles (*leu babir*). There are further references (lines 384, 752, 990, 819) to benches or couches (*baing, lleithig*) upon which the warriors sat during feasts and from which lords would distribute gifts or the drinking horn. Another reference regarding these hall furnishings relates (lines 152–3) that "From his cushion Blaen distributed, the drinking-horn in his opulent hall" (*Blaen ar ei bluddwe dywallofai, Fual yn ei fwynfawr fordai*). However, unlike *Beowulf*, neither Taliesin nor Aneirin make any reference to tapestries or wall-hangings of any type. Given the wealth evidenced on the part of British lords, such an omission should not be granted much weight on this point. After all, the image of an opulent court does not conjure up a vision of an impoverished hall, whose walls are devoid of wall-hangings to brighten up the place.

[25] For those poems whose setting is in the hall, Taliesin's poems are straightfoward, unabashed praise poetry, whose focus is on the attributes of whatever lord is the subject of the poem, and on the gifts that that lord has dispensed (especially to Taliesin). Consequently, Taliesin excels in his descriptions of the sumptuous gifts that were given away by open-handed lords in their halls, but is of little use in describing the physical setting (i.e., the material trappings, such as benches and hearths) of the hall or its associated activities, with the obvious exception of the ceremonial distribution of gifts.

On the other hand, the *Gododdin* contains numerous references to the material trappings and activities of the hall. The poem does so not only for Mynyddog Mwynfawr's hall at Eidyn, but also for the halls of the warriors of the ill-fated expedition who had joined the warband as potentates and lords in their own right.

The central focus of the hall scenes throughout the corpus of *Cynfeirdd* poetry is the hall-feast (*gwledd*), a point that is evident especially for the *Gododdin*, with its frequent references to the year-long feast at Mynyddog's court of Eidyn. Like those of the Anglo-Saxons, the hall-feasts of the Britons provided the social context in which many of the hall-activities – boasting, the distribution of gifts, and the songs of the *pencerdd* or *bardd teulu* – took place. In contrast to the bloody-minded ferocity that often characterized the behavior of the warriors in battle, the hall-feasts are marked by an adherence to formal protocol and civility. In the *Gododdin* (lines 237, 649), an officer of the court called a *maer* (steward) was the official who was responsible for the functioning of the hall and the conduct of its activities, with special regard to feasts. Some of the seating arrangements in the hall would seem to have been predicated on rank and/or service to the *comitatus*. Beyond the references to the lord's couch or bench already cited, the poem relates of Cynon (line 384): "Indeed, he would sit at the end of the bench (couch)" (*Neud ef eisteddai yn nhal lleithig*). Also, the references to blazing fires and lighted candles would indicate that the principal hall-feasts were conducted in the evening, as would the reference (line 116) to Tudfwlch Hir: "Truly he feasted at middle-of-night mead-feasts" (*Neu llewes ev feddgwyn feinoethydd*).

Like the *Beowulf* poet, neither Aneirin nor Taliesin bothers to note what foods were presented at these sumptuous feasts, preferring instead to concentrate their descriptions exclusively on the participants' consumption of mead (*medd*) and wine (*gwin*)[26] during the course of these feasts. The poem relates that wine and mead would usually be served in mead horns (lines 153, 166, 381, 869), though cups of glass (lines 625, 869) and precious metals (line 240) are also mentioned.[27] Especially before a battle, the poem relates (lines 41–2, 114, 227) that the warriors at the hall-feast would boast, give their "pledge" (*amot*) or "intention" (*aruaeth*), of the deeds they hoped to accomplish on the field of battle.[28] Finally, after much drinking and feasting, the warriors would settle down for the night, sleeping in the hall. [29]

---

[26] For the *Gododdin* alone, Jarman (*Y Gododdin*, xliii) counts some thirty-four and fifteen references to mead and wine in his edition. For the lines in the text, see the glossary in *ibid.*, under *medd* and *gwin*. The concept of mead is discussed in the following chapter. For the archaeological validation of these drinks, see Alcock, *Economy, Society and Warfare*, p. 247.

[27] As Alcock has shown (*ibid.*, pp. 247–48), there is little evidence that precious metals or glass were commonly employed in the manufacture of drinking vessels, stating that the available evidence indicates that the numerous glass shards found at these British sites probably were employed exclusively for the production of jewelry. Thus, in this regard, it is likely that the poets are overstating the material wealth of their lords.

[28] Jackson, *GOSP*, pp. 39–40.

[29] I take the phrase "reared in hall" (*magwyd yn neuadd*) at line 859 to imply that most warriors were raised in halls. The line draws a direct comparison between Gwair Hir and all other warriors who were raised in halls, stating that "There was not reared in

In addition to those activities that were associated with the hall structure itself, the poetry presents a few other aspects of life at a British court. A reference in the *Gododdin* (line 949) to a warrior called Urfai demonstrates that hunting was an activity that was pursued by the aristocracy with some degree of avidness. Further, Taliesin specifically relates (*PT* VIII.23) that Urien took great pleasure in both poetry and hunting. Besides hunting, it would appear that horse racing, or a least riding horses swiftly, was another activity in which British warriors often engaged. Because of the unlikely prospect of warriors actually riding their steeds into battle, some of the references to lords riding swift horses, along with other similar terms (lines 13–14, 156, 292, 499) should be taken to imply the existence of racing as a social activity that was associated with life in the hall.

For both the Anglo-Saxon *scop* and the British *bardd*, the concept of the hall was a fundamental and pervasive one, and the overarching importance that it is accorded in their poetry should be seen as a reflection of the hall's instrumental role in supporting the structure of the Dark-Age *comitatus*. The hall's importance is shown in the various images that were employed by the poet to present the concept of the hall and its associated activities to his audience, and the specific methods and literary devices – such as a heavy reliance upon compound-words or the use of the concept of the "anti-hall" – that were used to accomplish this task. For the most part, the literature's emphasis is on the associated activites of the hall and their importance to the proper functioning of Anglo-Saxon and British warbands, rather than on the physical structure of the hall.[30]

Among the poetic works of the Anglo-Saxons, the celebration of the hall as a symbolic, poetic representation of the entire *comitatus* system is best (though not exclusively) illustrated in the *Beowulf* poem.[31] In fact, it has been argued that the image and symbology of the hall provides *Beowulf* with its overarching, unifying theme.[32] Throughout the poem, whose scenes often are

hall one bolder than he" (*Ni magwyd yn neuadd a fai lewach nog ef*). The compliment would have been a meaningless one if only a few warriors were raised in halls.

    Another reference (noted by Jackson *GOSP*, p. 34) can be found in *The Gorchan of Maeldderu*, which had been incorporated into the *Gododdin* text, though it was not part of the original poem. Jackson noted that Maeldderw is referred to as "bed-fellow of the beer-hall" (line 1423 in Williams, *CA*).

[30] Hume, "Concept of the Hall", p. 64.

[31] For the purposes of this study, the examples found in *Beowulf* are sufficient. For those interested in further examples found in other Anglo-Saxon poetic works, see Hume, *ibid*.

[32] Besides Hume's article, this was argued most notably by Edward B. Irving, Jr., throughout Chapter 4 of his *Rereading Beowulf* (Philadelphia: University of Pennsylvania Press, 1989). Equating the image of the hall in *Beowulf* with the "arch-image" that Thomas Greene had posited as a major characteristic of epic poetry, Irving aptly has summarized the importance of the concept in understanding the Old English epic poem,

placed within the physical setting of one of several halls, the *Beowulf* poet clearly equates the physical state of the hall with the fortunes and state of affairs of the warband to which it gave shelter. In essence, the fortunes and ultimate fate of both the hall and its warriors are bound together; their rise and fall, their health and vitality, were one and the same in the eyes of the poet and, consequently, in the eyes of his audience.

While the poem contains at least several examples supporting this important point, three of the more notable ones can be presented here. The first occurs early on in the poem. Prior to the coming of Grendel, during the period in which Hrothgar and his warriors are presented (lines 64–7) as a strong and powerful warband who were given "victory in battle" (*heresped gyfen*), the poem depicts Heorot as a magnificient gabled structure, full of hall-joys and brave warriors (lines 80–2, 88–90, 99–100), calling it at one point (line 78) the "greatest of hall-buildings" (*healærna mæst*). Conversely, when Grendel's onslaughts (lines 114–43) decimate Hrothgar's warband, and drive the noble chieftain and his men from their hall, the poet describes the ravages that Grendel wrought upon Heorot itself (lines 144–6, 164–68). Again, when the fortunes of the *comitatus* are once more on the rise after Beowulf has slain Grendel, the poet chooses to reflect the newly-won ascendancy of the Danes by describing (lines 991–1001) the process through which Heorot was restored to its former glory and grandeur, with the subsequent restoration of hall-joys.

The poem's second example is found in its story about the fight at Finnsburg (lines 1068–1159). In this instance, the closely intertwined fortunes of warrior and hall are obvious: the destruction of one (Finn and his men) is accomplished in tandem with the destruction of the other (the sack and pillaging of the hall); the destruction of both *comitatus* and hall-structure is total, final, and without any hope of reversal. In fact, the poem goes into greater detail in describing the sacking and pillaging of the hall (lines 1151–9) than it does in telling the manner in which Finn and his men met their deaths.

The third example is found in the poem's story about the accidental hunting death of Herebeald at the hands of his brother Hæthcyn. In a moving scene (lines 2455–59), the poem shows the slain warrior's grieving father, King Hrethel, as the old man laments the passing of his son, whose death is represented by Herebeald's abandoned dwelling, now devoid of both its lord and its hall-joys. The poem relates that:

stating that: "In *Beowulf*, there seems little doubt that the major controlling image throughout the poem from beginning to end is the hall. To trace the ways this centered symbol shimmers in the imagination in various changing lights, as halls are built, attacked, restored, abandoned, laid waste, is to gain a sharper understanding of the poem's larger meanings."

Miserable, he looks   upon his son's dwelling
deserted wine-hall,   wind-swept bedding,
emptied of joy. The rider sleeps,
warrior in grave;   no harp music,
no games in the courtyard,   as once before.[33]

Other literary devices employed in the *Beowulf* poem to reinforce the importance of the concept of the hall revolved around the poet's consistent association of the hall with the hall-joys in which the members of the *comitatus* engaged. This was effected primarily by two methods: the poet's use of compound-nouns which directly couple the term for hall with that of a specific hall-joy in order to form such compounds as "gift-hall" (*gifhealle*) or "mead-hall" (*medoheal*), and the poet's use of "deserted-hall" and "anti-hall" images.

The first method is used with great frequency throughout the poem because it: provided the poet variety in the words he could employ to refer to the hall, allowed greater flexibility in meeting the requirements of alliterative verse, and consistently offered a direct and obvious association of the hall structure with the activities that occurred within its walls. In *Beowulf*, the concept of "gift-hall"/*gifheal* (line 838) and its treasures is more commonly represented by compounds involving the treasures themselves: hence "ring-hall"/*hringsele* (lines 2010, 2840, 3053) and "gold-hall"/*goldsele* (lines 1619, 2082). Similarly, the "feast-hall" concept is represented by compounds relating to the drinks associated with these feasts: "wine-hall"/*winreced, -sele, -ærnes* (lines 714, 994; 695, 711; 654), "beer-hall"/*beorsele* (lines 482, 492, 1094), and "mead-hall"/*medoærn, -heal, -sele* (lines 69; 484, 638; 3065). The close association between warriors and the hall-joys (*wynn, dream*) of the war-hall/*guðsele* (lines 443, 2139) is reflected in the poem's use of "hearth-companions"/*heorðgeneatas* (line 3179), "companions-in-hall"/*beodgeneatas* (lines 343, 1985), and "counsellors-in-hall"/*selerædende*.

Beyond the frequent use of compounds, the *Beowulf* poet also employed images of "deserted halls" and "anti-halls" to reinforce the hall/hall-joys association in the minds of his audience. When using the image of the deserted hall, the poet almost invariably portrayed these ruined or abandoned structures as bereft of warriors and all hall-joys. One example of this deserted-hall image, that of the hall of Hrethel's slain son, has been presented. Another is the poem's passage (lines 2231–69) about the only survivor of a warband, whose destruction had come to pass because "An evil death had

[33]   *Gesyhð sorhcearig   on his suna bure
winsele westne,   windge reste
reote berofene, –   ridend swefað,
hæleð in hoðman;   nis þær hearpan sweg
gomen in geardum,   swylce ðær iu wæron.*

sent away many of the race of mortals" (*Bealo-cwealm hafað fela feorh-cynna forð onsended!*). The survivor places the weapons and treasures of his dead comrades in a barrow, or burial mound. Here, beneath the ground in this "hall", amid the decaying weapons and treasures of now-dead and long-forgotten warriors, the poem relates (lines 2262–5) that there would be:

> No harp-joy,
> play of song-wood,   no good hawk
> through the hall swings,   nor the swift horse
> in the courtyard stamps.

> *Næs hearpan wyn*
> *gomen gleow-bearmes   ne god havoc*
> *geond sæl swingeð   ne se swifta mearh*
> *burh-stede beateð.*

Lastly, the poet's skillful use of the image of the anti-hall also serves to equate the halls of warriors with their attendant hall-joys by demonstrating their negation within the context of several anti-halls.[34] This concept is well-illustrated, particularly in regard to Grendel and his mother's lair beneath the mere (lines 1513–18, 1570, 1612–13) and in the barrow-hall of the dragon (lines 2270–80, 2288–2302, 2756–81) who had taken over the burial mound of the plague-stricken warband recounted just above. In both of these examples, treasure-giving is one of the hall-joys that have been eliminated; immense treasure had been amassed at both locations, but their wretched inhabitants, in direct contradiction to appropriate and proper conduct, preferred to hoard their wealth. In fact, early in the poem (lines 86–90), Grendel is seen as "suffering fierce pain" as he listens to Hrothgar's warriors as they participate in various hall-joys, hall-joys in which he himself could never engage. Similarly, the dragon in his *eorð-sele* was jealous of every jewel, of every piece of gold, of his vast treasure-hoard. But because he never shared out his wealth, the poem notes (line 2278) that, despite his treasure, "he gains nothing by it" (*ne byð him wihte ðy sel*). The clear inference to be drawn from this is that good lords share out wealth, while bad lords (along with dragons, of course) hoard it.

The importance of the hall is no less manifest in the poetry of Aneirin and Taliesin than it was in *Beowulf*. Still, there are some marked differences in the methods by which the two *Cynfeirdd* conveyed the hall's importance to their audiences, differences which can be attributed to a variety of factors involving genre, language, and historical context.[35] Consequently, the *Gododdin* in par-

---

[34] See Hume, "Concept of the Hall" (p. 68) for additional characteristics of "anti-halls" as a literary device.

[35] As related in the previous chapter, British praise poetry has a sense of immediacy which Anglo-Saxon poetry does not. The British poets are addressing their poems to the lords

ticular consistently illustrates the importance of the hall by its frequent use of sharply-contrasting images – images often presented within the same stanza – between the peaceful, joyful activities at the hall and the scenes of carnage and bloodshed on the battlefield.[36]

These sharply-contrasting images, "representing the duality between courage and fierceness in war and generosity and liberality in peace",[37] were employed especially in those stanzas whose subjects were lords or lesser potentates in their own right. In these stanzas, the poet recalls earlier instances in which these warrior-lords participated in a wide array of hall-activities during the period before the battle at Catraeth. The images of these happier times in the hall are focused all the more sharply when the poet recounts the violent manner in which these lords fought and met their deaths on that distant battlefield. Thus, among its many examples, the *Gododdin* relates (lines 139–40, 361–2, 593–5) that: "In halls the slayer was humble, Before Erthgi armies groaned" (*Ym mordai ystyngai adleddawr, Rhag Erthgi erthychi fyddinawr*); "Fell five fifties before his blades: Rhufon Hir gave gold to the altar, And gifts and fine largesse to the minstrel" (*Gwyddai bum pynt rhag ei lafnawr: Rhufon Hir, ef rhoddoi aur i allawr, A ched a choelfain cain i gerddawr*); "Senyllt's warband did not bear shame, with its vessels full of mead: He meted out the sword to transgressors, he gave out assaults in battle" (*Nid ef borthi gwarth gorsedd Synyllt, A'i llestri llawn medd: Goddolai gleddyfi garedd, Goddolai lemain i ryfel*).

and warriors who form the subjects of, and perform the actions in, their poems. Since Taliesin's lords appear to have been successful militarily, it is not surprising that there are no abandoned or ruined hall images in his poetry. In like manner, because the disastrous expedition to Catraeth did not entail the destruction of Mynyddog's kingdom or hall, nor those of the lesser lords who had participated (and died), the same statement is true for Aneirin's *Gododdin*. However, one does see this motif gain favor among the Britons several centuries later in the Llywarch Hen cycle of poems as the ruined-hall image came to represent the destruction of a lord and his men. This is not to say that the hall as a representaion of the health and vitality of the *comitatus*, in which the two are equated by the poet, cannot be seen in the poetry of Aneirin and Taliesin. In fact this equation often is made but, unlike in *Beowulf*, it is shown only in its positive sense, in its portrayal of a strong warband accompanied by bright hall-scenes of feasting, boasting, drinking, and the distribution of gifts, treasure, and wealth.

In a further distinction from Anglo-Saxon poetry, the *Cynfeirdd* did not employ the use of compound-words to combine the concept of the hall with those of its hall-joys, in sharp contrast to the *Beowulf* poet, who used the very large number of compounds available to him to wondrous effect. At least in this regard, the language of Old Welsh simply did not provide the same opportunities to Aneirin, Taliesin, and the other *Cynfeirdd* as Old English did to the *Beowulf* poet.

36 For more on the dichotomy of behavior in the hall and on the field of battle within the context of early British society, see either Jackson, *GOSP* (pp. 40–1) or Jarman, *Aneirin: Y Gododdin* (pp. xlii–xliii).

37 Jarman, *ibid.*

In summary then, the hall of this period – its physical construction and design, its activities, and its social/cultural concept – should be viewed as an important support mechanism that acted to sustain the *comitatus* structures of Dark-Age Britain.

CHAPTER EIGHT

OTHER SOCIAL INSTITUTIONS
AND CULTURAL CONCEPTS

Beyond the hall and the poet and his poetry, other social institutions and cultural concepts supported the *comitatus* structure. These are: the concept of mead, the distribution of wealth by the lord to his retainers, and the institutions of fosterage and of hostage-taking. These institutions and concepts, alone or in conjunction with others, acted as fundamental supports for the structure of Dark-Age warbands.

The concept of mead was an important one for the members of a *comitatus*. In heroic poetry, it is the symbol that invariably was chosen by the poet to represent the faithful discharge of duties and the obligations of the lord-retainer relationship. Mead (and to a lesser extent, beer and wine)[1] represented those things – hospitality, patronage, and protection – that the warriors of a *comitatus* expected of their chieftain or lord.[2] In the *Gododdin*, the concept of mead as a metaphor for the lord's obligations is associated with the feasting activities at Mynyddog's hall – referred to as wine-feasts and mead-feasts.[3] Among the Anglo-Saxons, this concept is conveyed usually through the use of compounds, and especially compounds that involve terms for the hall-structure; the most prominent of these are "wine-hall, "beer-hall", and "mead-hall".

---

[1] In both Celtic and Germanic poetry, mead, wine, and beer were employed in this regard. However, mead is the term that was chosen most frequently, and should be viewed as the most important of the stock metaphors used to represent the lord-retainer relationship. Beyond these three drinks, the *Gododdin* mentions bragget, malt, and ale (Jackson, *GOSP*, p. 35) in the same role.

[2] Jarman, *Aneirin: Y Gododdin*, p. xliii. Throughout the poem, mead and wine are employed the most frequently as metaphors reflecting the lord-retainer relationship.

[3] At lines 539 and 545, the poem reads: "After wine-feast and mead-feast they went from us" (*O winfaeth a meddfaeth ydd aethant i gennyn*); "After wine-feast and mead-feast they attacked" (*O winfaeth a meddfaeth yd grysiasant*). At line 84 the expedition is called "a mead-nourished host" (*feddfaest feddwn*), in a reference to the hall-joys at the court at Eidyn. Lastly, at lines 417–18, the poem relates that "Mighty warriors went from among us, They were nurtured on mead and wine" (*Gwyr gormant aethant cennyn, Gwinfaith a meddfaith oeddyn*).

While there was some variation in the methods and metaphors selected for the lord's role in the lord-retainer relationship, there is less variation when it comes to the warriors: mead and wine are employed invariably as the stock metaphors to represent their particular duties and obligations. As related earlier, it was through a faithful discharge of duty – whether in battle, in the hall, in exile, or in the exacting of vengeance – that a warrior repaid his lord for all that the lord had given to him, even if such repayment might cost a warrior his own life. In Germanic and Celtic heroic poetry, this is known, with slight variations, as "earning one's mead".

In *Beowulf*, Queen Wealhtheow tells Beowulf (lines 1230–1) that the Danish nobles and warriors are loyal to one another and to Hrothgar, declaring that "The thanes are united, a people prepared; having been given drink, our retainers will do as I bid" (*þegnas syndon geþwære, þeod ealgearo, druncne dryhtguman, doð swa ic bidde*). Similarly, a close connection between mead and a warrior's deeds is seen when Hrothgar relates to Beowulf (lines 480–3) that his own warriors often had boasted "drinking mead from ale-flagons . . . that they would meet Grendel's attack" (*beore drunce, ofer ealowæge, þæt hie . . . bidan woldon Grendles guðe*). Even more explicit in its association of mead and deeds is Wiglaf's speech to Beowulf's retainers as he tries to shame them into aiding their lord in his fight with the dragon. Beowulf's retainer and kinsman reminds the other warriors (lines 2633–8) of their prior oaths to their chieftain and lord:

> I take notice of the time,   when we were having our mead
> in the beer-hall,   when we vowed to our lord
> who gave us these rings,   this armor,
> that we would repay him   for these helmets and tempered swords,
> if ever it should happen that he needed us.[4]

Lastly, perhaps the finest Anglo-Saxon example of the close association between mead and a warrior's "repayment" to his lord occurs in the *Finnsburg Fragment* (lines 39–40). Attacked without cause or provocation while guests of Finn in his hall, the Danes under Hnæf fiercely battle Finn's warriors. After Hnæf is killed, the battle continues to rage, with Danish command passing to Hengest, as the warriors seek to avenge their dead lord. Of the battle, the *Fragment* relates that "Not ever did warriors better pay for

---

[4]   *Ic ðæt mæl geman   þær we medu þegun
þonne we geheton   ussum hlaforde
in biorsele,   ðe us ðas beagas geaf,
þæt we him ða guðgetewa   gyldan woldon,
gif him þyslicu   þearf gelumpe,
helmas ond heard sweord.*

their sweet mead than did his men repay Hnæf" (*Ne nefre swanas hwitne medo sel forgyldan, ðonne Hnæf guldan his hægstealdas*).[5]

While the concept of warriors earning their mead is seen in Anglo-Saxon literature, it is a concept that reaches its fullest expression in *Cynfeirdd* poetry. This is true especially in the *Gododdin*, where the concept of warriors earning their mead by fulfilling their part of the lord-retainer agreement provided Aneirin with the unifying theme for his poem.[6] While the concept of the hall provided a central theme for the *Beowulf* poet, for Aneirin the manner in which Mynyddog's warriors acquitted themselves of their obligations to their lord at Catraeth became the central focus of the poem.

Given the *Gododdin*'s numerous references to mead and wine, examples of warriors earning their mead – either as individuals or as a group – are not difficult to find. On an individual basis, the poem relates (lines 64–5) about Hyfaidd Hir that "Before his burial his blood flowed down, payment for mead in the hall with the armies" (*Cyn no' i argyfrain ei waed i lawr. Gwerth medd yng nghyntedd gan lliwedawr*). Of Eithinyn, the poem states (lines 407–8) that he would be in the forefront of the battle-ranks "in return for mead in the hall and drinking of wine" (*Gwerth medd yng nghyntedd a gwirod win*). Again, it is told (line 51) that "Gwefrfawr gained [much] in payment for wine from the cup" (*Bu Gwefrfawr goddiwawdd gwerth gwin o fan*). Finally, we learn (lines 965–6) that before he was slain "Edar merited his drink of mead" (*Dyrllyddai Edar ei fedd yfed*). Collectively, the expedition as a whole also earned its mead by fulfilling its obligations to Mynyddawg, a point that finds its most explicit expression when the poem relates (line 340) that "The payment for their feast of mead was their lives" (*Gwerth eu gwledd o fedd fu eu henaid*).

One final point regarding the concept of mead should be addressed, especially as it relates to the *Gododdin*. In several passages, Aneirin describes mead through the use of negative terms such as "bitter", "ensnaring", or even as a "poison". Such terms relate to the fact that the warriors of the expedition were destroyed almost to the last man in fulfilling their part of the lord-retainer agreement; three hundred warriors were slain in the process of earning their mead.[7] Given the unhappy results at Catraeth, it should evoke little surprise that mead is not shown in uniformly positive terms. Thus, of the *Gododdin* warriors, the poem says (lines 79, 102, 148–9) that: "Their feast

---

5 See C.L. Wrenn (ed.), *Beowulf: With the Finnsburg Fragment* (London: Harrap Limited, 1973). The Fragment is on pp. 215–16.

6 See Jarman, *Aneirin: Y Gododdin*, p. xliii.

7 However, as Jackson has noted (*GOSP*, p. 35), at least in the case of "bitterness", such terms could have a twofold meaning, signifying the destruction of Mynyddog's retinue as well as describing the actual physical characteristics of mead. In his description of mead, Jackson informs us (*ibid.*) that it "tastes of honey with a sweet first impression and a slight but distinct aftertaste of bitterness".

was fresh mead and it was bitter" (*Glasfedd eu hancwyn a gwenwyn fu*); "They drank yellow, sweet, ensnaring mead" (*Medd yfynt melyn melys maglawr*); and "Though we drank clear mead by lighted candles, Though its taste was good, long was its bitterness" (*Cyd yfem fedd gloyw wrth leu babir, Cyd fai da ei flas, ei gas bu hir*). These examples are by no means the only ones, but should suffice in making the point that the poet knew full well the sometimes tragic consequences of fulfilling one's obligations to one's lord. In any event, it is evident that the concept of mead was a pervasive one in heroic Anglo-Saxon and British poetry.

While mead is an important concept in the period's heroic literature, and one that played a role in supporting the warband, an even more fundamental support of the *comitatus* structure involved the widespread cultural practice – common to both Anglo-Saxon and Briton – of lords distributing weapons, treasure, and other forms of wealth to their retainers. From the evidence of literary and historical sources alike, it seems that such a distribution of wealth could be based on one of two considerations: either as a reward for services rendered already, or as an expression of confidence in the deeds that were yet to be performed by warriors on their lord's behalf. Regarding the importance of this practice, it has been noted that the vital role played by the lord as "the giver of gifts is reflected in the word used to designate his high seat in the hall; *gifstol*. From the *gifstol* the lord distributed to his followers gold rings, armor and weapons, horses and land from his own personal property."[8]

This widespread cultural practice operated on several levels and in several different functions in its role of sustaining the structure of the *comitatus*. The distribution of wealth can be seen in its capacity as an effective recruiting tool for attracting warriors to a warband, as a social institution that supported the position of the lord within his own *comitatus*, and as a key instrument, within the context of the period's economy, for the distribution of luxury items both between and within Dark-Age kingdoms. Given these important and diverse roles, it is not surprising that the lord's distribution of wealth to his retainers forms an important element in the period's literature.[9]

First and foremost, the distribution of wealth should be seen as an effective recruiting tool that was employed as a matter of course by lords and chieftains in order, on the one hand, to attract warriors to their service and, on the other,

---

[8] Cherniss, *Ingeld and Christ*, p. 42.

[9] While the role of the distribution of wealth within the overall economy is touched upon here, the subject is covered in the following chapter, where specific goods, as well as their role and the impact of their distribution on the economy, are covered in greater detail. Similarly, some of these subjects also have been addressed to some extent earlier in this study, notably the recruitment of warriors from outside a tribal area (Chapter 3) and the distribution of wealth as one of the tools available to a Dark-Age lord in reinforcing his social and political position within his warband (Chapter 4). The purpose of again presenting them here is to place these examples within the context of the distribution of wealth as an institution in its own right.

to reward followers already under their command. While other factors – the endemic nature of warfare, a warrior's desire for fame, the frequency of exile, and the plain fact that fighting was a favorite activity of the warrior-élite – certainly could draw a warrior into service with a particular lord, a lord could exert some measure of control over this by the distribution of his available wealth, whether he was militarily successful or not. Earlier, it was seen that wealth distribution formed a key component in the formation of warbands during this period. Among the Anglo-Saxons, we saw that Guthlac had attracted to his *comitatus* warriors from various peoples (*diversarum gentium*), in part because his warband had amassed immense booty (*immensas praedas*) through its victories in battle. Bede, in describing the qualities that he claimed had attracted warriors to the service of Oswine, stated (*HE* III.14) that the saintly king was "liberal to all" (*manu omnibus . . . largus*). Of course, Oswine's liberality goes a great way toward explaining his success in attracting to his service warriors "From all the nearest provinces on all sides, men even of the highest rank" (*de cunctis prope provinciis viri etiam nobilissimi*).

Similarly, it was seen that British lords were no less adept at attracting warriors from outside their own tribal regions to their service. The most prominent example is the expeditionary force assembled by Mynyddog, whose doomed warriors had been drawn from throughout the British realms of the north and from other kingdoms as well. When considering the factors that induced these warriors to travel to Mynyddog's court, it is instructive to note that Mynyddog's epithet was *mwynfawr* ("the Wealthy"), a point that is reinforced by the *Gododdin*'s frequent references to treasure-giving and its detailed descriptions of the types of goods that were distributed among the members of the expedition. Another case in point might be seen in the British warbands, probably composed of dispossessed warriors from Rheged, that were portrayed by the *Annals of Ulster* as fighting for Irish chieftains along the east coast during a twenty-seven year period. Since the services of these armed and experienced men would have been welcomed (and rewarded) at any British court, it seems more than likely that the warriors from Rheged had sought the shores of Ireland in search of wealthy Irish chieftains who would more richly reward them for their services than would have been the case had they remained among the surviving British kingdoms of their native island.

The distribution of wealth was only one of several methods – including panegyric poetry – that could be employed by a lord to strengthen and maintain his pre-eminent position within the internal social structure of his own *comitatus*. Given the widespread coverage and importance that it is afforded in the period's literature, and given the evidence for its existence in other historical sources, it is probable that the practice of lords distributing wealth to their followers was a widespread and pervasive cultural practice, whose frequency of employment by Dark-Age lords allowed it to achieve the status of a permanent social institution within the period's British and Anglo-Saxon warbands.

The benefits of such a practice to a lord should be evident, especially in regard to supporting his own position within his warband. First, in a point perhaps too obvious to relate, the practice of distributing wealth would have served to strengthen the bonds of loyalty between a lord and his men, and thereby reinforce the entire system that is implied in the lord-retainer relationship. Especially for the younger members of the warband, their lord must have represented an important source of wealth and material posessions, in addition to providing them with food, drink, lodging, and entertainments. Furthermore, given that the distribution of prestige items often was effected with some degree of ceremonial display in the presence of the other hall residents, the practice allowed the lord to enhance a warrior's reputation and prestige through his own public praise and recognition of the man receiving the gift. Such praise might also be accomplished by the lord's poet. Given the warriors' thirst for fame and honor, the importance and social significance of the ceremonial, non-economic aspects of this practice, should not be underestimated. Lastly, as was shown earlier, the distribution of wealth would have tended to enhance the lord's prestige and standing within the *comitatus* by increasing the numbers of a warband, whose size (and by extension, whose capabilities for combat) reflected directly on the status of a Dark-Age lord.

The overarching importance of the lord's distribution of wealth to his retainers is reflected throughout heroic literature, where it forms a frequent and pervasive topic for poets. As with the concept of mead, it is well-evidenced in both Anglo-Saxon and British poetry, where it is employed to represent a key function of the lord within the lord-retainer relationship. For the Anglo-Saxons, this is illustrated by a gnomic statement in *Maxims II*, which asserts, as a matter of course, "So shall a king in hall give rings" (*Cyning sceal on healle beagas dælan*).[10] The same passage relates the importance of such ring-giving for a leader, when it advises that "So ought a young noble assemble good retainers for battle and for ring-giving" (*Geongne æþeling sceolan gode gesiðas byldan to beaduwe and to beahgife*).[11] Similar advice is given by the *Beowulf* poet who, like the compiler of the *Maxims*, knew the importance of generosity to a lord's relationship with his men. Almost at its outset, the poem demonstrates the close, indeed almost causal, relationship between the distribution of wealth on the part of the lord and the loyal service of warriors in its declaration (lines 20–5) that:

> So ought a young man, prepare treasure
> from the largesse in his father's house,
> so that later in life standing by him again,
> his willing companions, when war comes,

---

[10] Found in Dobbie, *The Anglo-Saxon Minor Poems* (ASPR Vol. 6), p. 56 (at lines 28–9).
[11] *Ibid.*, lines 14–15.

his men follow him;   By praiseworthy deeds
and goodness shall   any man prosper.[12]

As the passages from *Beowulf* and *Maxims* make clear, the distribution of gifts and other wealth was not necessarily in payment for services already rendered, but could be effected by a lord in expectation of deeds yet to be performed on his behalf. In essence, the practice of treasure-giving allowed the lord to express, publicly and concretely, his confidence in the abilities and loyalty of his retainers and his full expectation that they would "earn their mead" whenever the necessity arose. However, such an expectation did not always come to fruition, as is seen most notably in *Beowulf* in the case of the hero's cowardly retainers who, save for Wiglaf, abandon their lord during his fight with the dragon.

Nevertheless, most of the instances involving the ceremonial distribution of wealth and gifts in *Beowulf* appear to have been as payment for deeds already performed on a lord's behalf, on an almost *quid pro quo* basis. When at the victory feast (lines 1008–49), Beowulf and his retainers are given sumptuous gifts from Hrothgar's *heordræden* (treasure-hoard) in return for the slaying of Grendel, there is no question in the minds of the warriors present at the ceremony that the gifts were not justly deserved, that they were not an appropriate reward and compensation for the deed accomplished, or that their distribution did not reflect favorably upon the chieftain Hrothgar. The poem relates (lines 1025–6) that "There was nothing in the bounty-giving before the warriors that would be an occasion to cause shame" (*no he þære feohgyfte for sc[e]oten[d]um scamigan ðorfte*)[13] before praising both the treasures and the treasure-giver, saying (lines 1046–9) that:

Manfully,   the famous chieftain,
hoard-guard of heroes,   rewarded the battle-rush
with horses and treasure   that no man will reproach them
who would declare   the truth correctly.[14]

---

12   *Swa sceal [geong g]uma   gode gewyrcean*
        fromum feohgiftum   on fæder [bea]rme,
        þæt hine on ylde   eft gewunigen
        wilgesiþas,   þonne wig cume,
        leode gelæsten;   lofdædum sceal
        in mægþa gehwære   man geþeon.

13 The sentence is of course an understatement, which has been effected by a litote, a type of understatement in which an affirmative is expressed by the negative of the contrary (e.g., the phrase "not shabby" means good). This literary technique is often employed by the *Beowulf* poet, as it is by Aneirin in his *Gododdin*.

14   *Swa manlice   mære þeoden,*
        hordweard hæleþa   heaþoræsas geald
        mearum ond madmum,   swa hy næfre man lyhð,
        se þe secgan wile   soð æfter rihte.

The poem also makes it clear that a lord's public recognition and praise of a warrior's service to the *comitatus* formed an important aspect of the treasure-giving ceremony, and one that might be reinforced to a greater degree if the services of the court poet also were employed in this regard.[15] Given the overwhelming desire for fame and glory among Dark-Age warriors, it comes as little surprise in finding that the poem's heroes and warriors sought public praise and widespread acclaim with almost the same vigor as they used to pursue treasure. Recounting his adventures among the Danes to his lord, Beowulf informs Hygelac (lines 2095–6) that "There, my king, for your people I worked some honor through deeds" (*þær ic, þeoden min, þine leode weorðode weorcum*) while also declaring (line 2134) that he had undertaken the second task (the slaying of Grendel's mother), not only for promised rewards but also that "I might work fame" (*mærðo fremede*). On two occasions – the ceremonial treasure-givings by Hrothgar (lines 1020–54) and by Hrothgar and Wealtheow (lines 1866–7, 1192–1231) – Beowulf seems to have been as pleased with the ceremonial, highly public, aspects of treasure-giving in Heorot as with the actual gifts that he received for slaying Grendel and his mother.

The *Beowulf* poem reinforces the importance of wealth distribution by its unequivocal condemnation of those who failed to do so. Two particularly fine examples of this condemnation are found in the portion of the poem known as "Hrothgar's Sermon" (lines 1700–84), in which the old chieftain offered sage advice to Beowulf on a wide variety of topics relating to the proper conduct that was expected of a good and just lord. In the first, Hrothgar tells Beowulf the story of Heremod (lines 1709–22), an especially evil and despised lord who was sent "from man's joys" (*mondreamum from*), and whose many faults included the sad fact (lines 1719–20) that "never a ring did he give to Danish men for glory" ·(*nalles beagas geaf, Denum æfter dome*).[16] Hrothgar reinforces his lesson to Beowulf by introducing (lines 1725–55) a hypothetical example of a long-reigned king who failed to appreciate the relationship between treasure-giving and the vitality of a kingdom, saying (lines 1749–51) that "Angry and covetous, he gives no rings to honor his men. His future state is forgotton and forsworn, and all that God gave him before" (*Gytsað gromhydig, nalles on gylp seleð fædde beagas, ond he þa*

---

15 As Hume ("Hall", p. 65) has pointed out, such praise was important to a warrior of this period, for it helped to define more clearly his position and status both within the *comitatus* and in the society at large.

16 At lines 1715 and 1719–20. Heremod's behavior is portrayed by the poem to be the direct antithesis of what was expected of a good lord. The poem relates that the erratic and vengeful lord often flew into rages, and "killed Danish men in his own hall, bloodily" and even "cut down companions". Little wonder then, that Heremod was overthrown, with the poem relating his demise with its warning that "Joyless he lived, and unhappy he died" (*dream-leas gebad, þæt he þæs gewinnes*).

forðgesceaft forgyted ond forgymeð, þæs þe him ær God sealde). Lastly, as was seen in the previous chapter, it is the practice of treasure-giving that uniformly is missing in the descriptions of the anti-halls – the lair of Grendel and his mother, and that of the dragon – that are presented by the poem. It is the omission of this vital element of a properly-functioning *comitatus*, this fundamental, underlying basis of the lord-retainer relationship, that helps to distinguish the social arrangements of the poem's monsters as contrary to the proper order of things. In fact, the distribution of wealth is shown to be the exclusive province of a lord when the poem relates (lines 168–9) that Grendel, during those times when he made his lair at Heorot, "could not come near the *gifstol*, the treasure, because of God" (*no he þone gifstol gretan moste, maþðum for Medode*).

As was the case for the concept of the hall, the importance of the lord's role in the distribution of wealth is best shown by the variety and frequency of the compounds that the poet used to join the dual concepts of lord and treasure. The lines of *Beowulf* are rife with such compounds as the poet establishes a powerful association in the minds of his audience between a just lord and treasure-giving. Though only cursory, the following will give some idea as to the variety of terms used by, and the creativity of, the *Beowulf* poet in joining the two concepts. In the poem, the following compounds are some of the ones used to denote a lord or chieftain: "ring-giver"/*beagabrytta* (lines 35, 352, 1487), *beaggyfa* (line 1102); "ring-lord"/*hringafengel* (lines 1507, 2345); "treasure-giver" /*sinces brytta, sinca-baldor* (lines 607, 1170, 1922, 2428); "treasure-giving [lord]" /*sincgyfen* (lines 1342, 2311, 3034); "[treasure] hoard-keeper"/*hordes hyrde* (line 887); "gold-guard"/*gold-weard*, "hoard-guard"/ *hoardweard* (lines 1852, 2594);[17] "guard of the ring-treasure" /beahhorde weard (lines 921); "gold-friend"/*goldwine* (lines 1171, 2419, 2584); "gold-friend of warriors"/*goldwine gumena* (lines 1476, 1602); "gold-giver"/ *goldgyfan* (line 2652); and "friendly lord"/*freawine* (lines 2429, 2357). The degree to which the warriors were dependent upon the lord for their daily upkeep and lodging and their material possessions is reflected in the term *hlaford* (lines 2283, 2634, 3179), meaning literally "bread-lord".

Among the British kingdoms, the lord's distribution of wealth to his retainers also appears to have provided a central focus for the poetry of Aneirin and Taliesin. Like *Beowulf* and the *Maxims*, their poetry presents the widespread practice of treasure-giving as a basic tenet of lordly behavior, viewing a chieftain's generosity as an integral component of his ability to rule and to instill in his followers a deep sense of loyalty and service. Like the Anglo-Saxon poets, Aneirin and Taliesin attempt to weave a firm, associative bond between the practice of treasure-giving and the lords about whom they sang.

---

[17] Also applied to the dragon at lines 2302 and 3061.

Since the bards themselves appear to have been the frequent recipients of their lords' generosity, the reasons why they took great pleasure in describing both the gifts themselves and the reasons for their ceremonial distribution should be evident.

In Early Welsh poetry, munificence and generosity are among the attributes that help to define a good lord. Taliesin says (*PT* X.21–2) of Owain that "Although he hoarded wealth . . . for his soul's sake he gave it" (*Kyt as cronyei . . . ny rannet rac y eneit*). Recounting all that he received from Cynan (*PT* I.1–7), Taliesin clearly shows that generosity was among the admirable attributes of that warlord. Further, the poet often gives high praise to Urien and his sons for their open-handed generosity, which often made the bards quite happy, such as at *PT* III.4–6 (*llawen beird bedyd tra vo dy uuchyd. ys mwy llewenyd gan glotuan clotryd. ys mwy gogonyant vot vryen ae plant*). Taliesin makes an explicit connection between the distribution of wealth and the ability of a lord to procure yet more treasure (evidently through an enhanced military capability that such a distribution would bring). In essence, a generous lord was also a successful one, whose military victories would provide a continuing source of wealth with which he could continue to reward his men.

In the *Gododdin*, Aneirin draws the same picture of the lords of Mynyddog's expedition. The poem (line 257) says of Llif that "He gave a bright array [of goods], shining, to the brave" (*Ef rhoddai gloyw ddull glan i wychiawg*). Of Gwenabwy "the generous chieftain" (*ddraig ehelaeth*), the poem relates (line 285) that "Minstrelsy's benefit did not leave his court" (*Nid edewis ei lys les cerddwriaeth*). Again, the poem tells (lines 305–6) that Isag was renowned "For modesty and liberality and fine mead-drinking" (*O wyledd a llariedd A chain yfed medd*), while saying (line 730) that Mynog would be "praised in song" (*traethiannor*) for his generosity. The poem calls Geraint (lines 823, 825) a "generous, famous lord" (*llary ior molud*) and a "bountiful lord" (*hael fynog*). Lastly, Mynyddog's epithet ("The Wealthy") should itself illustrate the importance of wealth as a key element of one's ability to rule. In sum, it is clear that a firm association was established between generosity (through treasure-giving) and the lord or chieftain of a warband.

As with the Anglo-Saxons, the distribution of wealth could be effected by a lord either as payment for services already performed or as a public and physical manifestation of a lord's good faith that such services would be performed on his behalf in the future. In the *Gododdin* the most obvious example of the latter type of distribution is seen in the year-long feasting activities at Eidyn – activities that are referred to throughout the poem – that had preceded the launching of Mynyddog's warband (*gosgordd Mynyddawg*) to Catraeth. Given the bravery and fierceness that marked the conduct of these warriors at Catraeth, Mynyddog's faith in them was well-placed; his wealth was not squandered in hosting these men nor in giving lavish gifts to them, in stark contrast to Beowulf's ill-advised faith in his retainers after he had become lord of the Geats.

Conversely, there are instances involving the ceremonial distribution of wealth that appear to have been effected for deeds and services that already had been accomplished.[18] Though most of the statements in the *Gododdin* about the rewards given at Catraeth are ironic (that is, death as a reward), at least in regard to tangible gifts and wealth, there are a few examples relating to earlier exploits and battles (and to their subsequent rewards) of some of the Gododdin warriors and chieftains that illustrate this point. Thus, the *Gododdin* says of Gwawrddur (line 970) that "He apportioned (gave out) horses from the herd" (*Goddolai o haid meirch*), and of Gwefrfawr (lines 49–50) it tells that "Wearing a brooch, leading in battle, a wolf in fury, the sharing torqued warrior gained amber beads" (*Caeog, cynhorog, blaidd ym maran, gwefrawr goddiwawdd torchawr am ran*). In an interesting parallel with the the pre-Christian Irish, the poem says (line 894) that Bleiddig was delighted "When he took the renowned portion – that is, the 'champion's portion' – in the hall" (*Pan ddy-ddug cyfran clodfan mordai*) as a reward for his faithful defence of a ford during a battle.[19]

The poems of Taliesin and Aneirin also allow us to believe that a primary motivation on the part of these warriors was to have their deeds to lord and warband publicly acknowledged. Such formal acknowledgment and public praise may have been effected by the lord during events that involved ceremonial treasure-giving, though he may just as easily have had the court poet attend to such praise in his poetry. In fact, the evidence of the *Gododdin*, with its widespread praise of a large number of warriors, would support the view that the latter option was the method that was more widely employed for a warrior's public acclaim. Regardless of the method by which public acclaim and fame were effected, it is clear British warriors held these non-material rewards in high esteem. The poem says (lines 925–6) that Heinif "slew a great host in return for the telling of his [deeds]" (*Ef lladdodd llu mawr, Yng ngwerth ei adrawdd*), and (lines 223–4) Cydywal "Sold his life for the praise of [his] honor" (*A werthws ei enaid, Er wyneb grybwylliaid*). In large part,

---

18 Of course, given the inability of Mynyddog's retinue to receive payment for their admirable service at Catraeth (their deaths, barring divine intervention, making payment difficult), this point is clouded in the *Gododdin*, whose focus is on the battle and the events preceding it. Consequently, many of the instances involving warriors "earning their mead" would refer to their repayment for the gifts and honors that had been accorded them during the year in which they had been Mynyddog's guests.

19 The "champion's portion" refers to the practice of allowing an honored warrior to select the best portion of the meat that was served at a feast. The practice appears to have had a common Celtic origin, and one that is well-attested in such Old Irish works as the *Tain Bo Cuailnge* (The Cattle-Raid of Cooley), the longest and perhaps most important tale of the Ulster Cycle. The common practice might however be attributed to Irish interactions with the Britons at some more recent interval.

fame was the result of actions against an enemy. Of Llif, the poem relates (line 255) that when he made forays against the borderlands "his renown was famous" (*ei glod oedd anfonawg*), and (lines 463–4) of Cynhafal, "When you were a famous warrior, seizing the land of the enemy" (*Pan fuost ti cynifyn clod, Yn amwyn tywysen gorddirod*). Lastly (line 239), because of his deeds, "the renowned Breichiawl was the talk of the world" (*Present gyfad-rawdd oedd Breichiawl glud*).

Though less important than mead or treasure-giving, two other cultural practices – fosterage and hostage-taking – that were common to Briton and Anglo-Saxon,[20] played a role in lending support to the structure of a Dark-Age warband. While both fosterage and hostage-taking had the net effect of introducing other warriors (or boys who had the potential to become warriors) to a Dark-Age *comitatus*, the former practice employed voluntary means to effect this introduction, while the latter involved the use of varying levels of coercion or outright force.

Hostage-taking, the practice of holding warriors or nobles from another kingdom in order to ensure compliance with an accord or treaty, or to maintain a defined geo-military situation, was one of several practices that were available to a Dark-Age lord in his dealings with other potentates.[21] Essentially, hostage-taking was one of the means, short of the initiation of warfare, by which a lord could establish his will on another chieftain. Within the context of supporting the structure of the *comitatus*, the presence of hostages within a warband should be viewed as a reflection of its military prowess and success. Consequently, it is likely that the introduction of hostages to a warband would have tended to bolster the overall reputation of that particular warband as well as enhancing the prestige of its leader. The very presence of hostages was a daily, highly visible reminder to the members of a warband of their military effectiveness and of their lord's ability to capitalize on it. Conversely, giving up some of one's own men as hostages, no matter how few the actual number involved or how reasonable the decision that may have prompted it, must have had an adverse effect on both a lord and his men. Given this situation, it should evoke little wonder that the acquisition of hostages was one of the goals of warfare during this period.

In one of two poems to Gwallawg, the lord of Elmet, Taliesin has the

---

20 The cultural practices of fosterage and hostage-taking are, of course, far from unique to the island of Britain. These practices represent widespread and longstanding social practices that the inhabitants of Britain shared with those of Ireland, Scandinavia, and elsewhere. For more on this, see Davidson, "The Training of Warriors", in *Weapons and Warfare*, pp. 11–23.

21 Other practices include: the exacting of tribute, the ceremonial exchange of luxury goods (as diplomatic gifts), and the use of marriages for diplomatic effect. The last practice, while important, is outside the study's scope. The importance of luxury goods (obtained either through tribute or by ceremonial exchange) to the economy is addressed in the following chapter.

highest praise for that chieftain's ability to demand (and receive) hostages from kingdoms far and wide, declaring (*PT* XII.47–9) that the regions from Caer Clud to Caer Garadawg as well as to Penprys gave hostages to Gwallawg (*rigwystlant greiryd goludawc o gaer glut hyt gaer garadawc. Ystadyl tir penprys a gwallawc*). According to Taliesin, Theodric of Bernicia was less successful in his attempt to obtain hostages from Urien and his son Owain. Taliesin recounts in detail (*PT* VI.7–12) the demands of Theodric for hostages, the refusal of Urien and Owain to comply, and the reasons for their steadfast refusal. In essence, Urien and Owain viewed the giving of hostages as a shameful act, and one that reflected directly on their own prestige. Of course, it was the refusal by the two British lords that led to the battle itself, which Rheged's forces won. The passage clearly shows that a lord's reputation was in part dependent on his ability to obtain hostages or on whether he himself could be forced to give them. Owain viewed giving up hostages as a shameful act, and one to which the red carnage of battle was to be preferred.

As to the hostages themselves, it can be surmised that they were treated well (assuming that their lord complied with the agreed-upon terms) and might well have had the same status as the other members of the warband of which they were now a part. In *Beowulf*, the poem relates (line 1129) that Hengest "stayed without choice" (*[ea]l unhlitme*) in Finn's hall during the winter months as a *de facto* hostage, though the poem makes it clear that he was treated as well as any other of Finn's chief men during his "stay" (lines 1127–37). In fact, it is apparent that a hostage was expected to fight along with the warriors among whom he was a hostage, as was seen in the *Chronicle*'s Cynewulf-Cyneheard episode, which records that all of Cynewulf's men were slain in attempting to avenge his death "except for one British hostage" (*buton anum Brittiscum gisle*), who was badly wounded during the course of the battle.

While the practice of hostage-taking occurred between adversaries or potential adversaries, fosterage was done among allied chiefdoms, or within a chiefdom itself. Fosterage involved sending one's sons to the court of a friendly lord or kinsman, where they would be raised with other boys of similar age and taught the arts of warfare. They would reside at the court from the age of seven or eight until they reached fourteen or fifteen, when they would receive whatever weapons were appropriate to their status and subsequently enter military service. The practice is seen in a variety of sources. *Guthlac* relates (XIV) that, as a young boy in the hall of his father, Guthlac was "affectionate to his fosterbrothers" (*dilectione conlactaneis*).[22] Similarly, in *Cuthbert*, we find that Cuthbert joined a company of boys at the age

---

[22] With *conlactaneis* standing for *collectaneis*. While the term could mean either fosterbrothers or sisters (as Colgrave has translated in his edition), given that the hall in which Guthlac was raised was his own, the term must refer only to the sons of other lords who were being fostered in his father's hall.

of eight, which Bede (*Cuthbert* I) says "was the first year of boyhood suc-
ceeding from infancy" (*qui post infantiam puericiae primus est*). Lastly,
though the *Gododdin's* subjects are of course adult warriors, the poet's famili-
arity with fosterage is shown by a reference to Eiddef (line 831), who "was
fostered with wine from the cup" (*Lledfegin gwin o ban*). For the heroes of
epic literature, the ages at which they were fostered were younger than for
other mortals. In the *Tain*,[23] CuChulainn's fosterage at the court of his uncle
begins at the tender age of five.[24] Similarly, the ripe old age of seven is given
for Beowulf's admission to Hrethel's court. Furthermore, in telling the Danes
of his boyhood, the hero (lines 2428–33) also shows the strong emotional
bonds that could be forged through the practice of fosterage:

> I was seven winters [years] old   when the treasure-lord,
> gold-friend of the people,   took me from my father.
> King Hrethel   kept and looked after me,
> gave treasure and feast,   mindful of kinship.
> Not to him was my life,   more loathsome,
> a warrior of his household   than his own sons.[25]

Whatever the precise age for the beginning of fosterage, it would appear
that the boys received the weapons of true warriors at around fourteen or
fifteen years of age. In *Wilfrid* (II), it is told that at the age of fourteen, Wilfrid
obtained "arms and horses and garments for himself and for his men" (*arma
et equos vestimentaque sibi et pueris suis*). Guthlac must have been the same
age when he received his own weapons, for by the following year (*Guthlac*
XVI) he already was leading his own warband. The archaeological evidence
and anatomical studies of injuries from graves of the period[26] would appear to
substantiate these practices, with little boys being buried with smaller versions of weapons, and young adolescents, who obviously had been slain in
battle, being buried with the full-scale weapons of a warrior.

The practice of fosterage (and the bonds of loyalty inhered in such a
system) provided the lord of a *comitatus* with a useful bridge to allied chieftains and lords, either because he was fostering their sons or because the boys

[23] While the *Tain* is an Irish work, its use as an example here is valid, given that the
practices of fosterage among the Britons and the Irish probably should be seen to be
derived from a common Celtic practice.
[24] Thomas Kinsella (trans.), *The Tain* (Oxford: Oxford University Press, 1969), p. 75.
[25]   *Ic wæs syfanwintre,   þa mec sinca baldor,*
      freawine folca   æt minum fæder genam.
      Heold mec ond hæfde   Hreðel cyning,
      geaf me sinc ond symbel,   sibbe gemunde;
      næs ic him to life   laðra owhite
      beorn in burgum   þonne his bearna hwylc.
[26] For further information, see Wenham's "Anatomical Interpretations of Anglo-Saxon
Weapon Injuries" and the references cited there.

he had fostered had grown up and become lords in their own right. The practice also provided the context and setting in which young boys were brought together and trained in the rigors and arts of warfare, and thus was an important source of future warriors for a warband. It is possible, especially for those boys belonging to the same kingdom or tribe, that the groups in which they were fostered provided a basis for some type of cohesive fighting unit when they became adults.[27] Further, though only a hypothesis, given that boys born to the warrior class were not always fit to serve – because of frailty, physical handicap, or joining a religious order – fosterage may have provided an avenue for the recruitment of strong, promising boys from the humbler classes of society to fill any manpower shortages that may have plagued a warband.

[27] A reasonable, though unproven suggestion advanced by H.E. Davidson in her "The Training of Warriors", p. 16.

CHAPTER NINE

ECONOMIC SUPPORTS

The previous three chapters have examined various cultural and social institutions – the poet and his poetry, the hall and its activities, and other institutions such as hostage-taking, fosterage, and the distribution of wealth – that supported the *comitatus* structure. Together, these chapters have painted a rather pleasant, almost idyllic, picture of heroic life among the members of the British and Anglo-Saxon warrior-élites during this period. In this idealized picture, generous lords are seen distributing weapons and other wealth to their faithful poets and retainers, the members of a *comitatus* are seen engaging in a wide variety of "hall-joys" with their lord, the hall is seen as a physical and emotional focal point of a warrior's life, and the bonds of loyalty uniting lord and man are seen as unassailable and unbreakable.

Attractive as this picture may be, it is a picture that is far from complete, a picture marred by blemishes of omission and inaccuracy. However emotionally sustaining the words of the poet or the gifts of the lord may have been, they played little part in actually sustaining, in an economic sense, the warriors of a *comitatus*. Largely ignored by literary and historical sources, the role played by the underlying, primarily agrarian, economy was of vital importance to the life of the Dark-Age warband, and its marked absence distorts any picture one might see of this society. This omission is most prominent in heroic poetry, whose poets often praise the generosity and liberality of their lords, but who "say little of whence the wealth came; for the corn that the 'well-fed' horses ate, the barley for their riders' food and drink, and much else beside, had to be extorted from impoverished homesteads".[1]

These gaps of omission can be filled and the structure of the *comitatus* placed within the framework of the economy over which it presided by examining: (1) the vital importance of food-renders in their role as the basic economic support of warbands, (2) the economic impact of tribute and the spoils of war, and (3) the role and importance of craftsmen, and the economic and social impact of their goods on the daily functioning of a Dark-Age *comitatus*.

---

[1] John Morris, *The Age of Arthur: A History of the British Isles from 350 to 650* (New York: Charles Scribner's Sons, 1973), p. 246.

Whether Anglo-Saxon or British, the economy[2] that supported the governing structures of the ruling warrior-élites was much the same – an agrarian
one in which the practice of unspecialized mixed farming predominated, and
which was supplemented by cottage industries, some extractive economic
activities,[3] and a limited amount of local and long-distance trade. These
Dark-Age kingdoms or chiefdoms have been classified as "early undevel-
oped states", whose society uniformly was one in which primitive forms of
organization – such as the ties of kinship, family, and community – "still
dominate relations in the political field; where full-time specialists are rare;
where taxation systems are only primitive and *ad hoc* taxes are frequent; and
where such differences are offset by reciprocity and close contacts between
the rulers and the ruled".[4]

Archaeological data – animal bones, farming implements, and pollen analysis – at a number of Dark-Age sites reveal the major products of the period's
mixed farming. On arable lands, the cultivation of cereal grains seems to have
been the major agricultural activity of most farmers, with barley production
dominating in the north of Britain and a mix of barley, oats, and even wheat
found elsewhere.[5] From the great amount of bones that have been recovered
from these sites, it appears that the raising of livestock constituted a fundamental aspect of the mixed farming economy. Though pigs and sheep were raised,
cattle were the most important – in terms of quantities consumed and in social
significance – of the domesticated animals that were raised for food and a
variety of other purposes; this was certainly true for the British and Irish.[6]

2　For overviews on the economy of Dark-Age kingdoms, see Alcock, *Economy, Society,
and Warfare* (pp. 285–89) and *Angles, Britons, and Scots* (pp. 37–46). For a more
detailed analysis, see Arnold, *Archaeology of the Early Anglo-Saxon Kingdoms* (pp.
17–96). For the relationship between social structure and the economy, see Chapters
2–4 in Alcock, *Economy, Society and Warfare*.

3　Though of a limited nature, extractive industries such as mining and timber-cutting
must have played a role in the economy of the period. Mining of course would have
provided some of the raw materials that were needed by specialized craftsmen in the
production of their high-value goods. As we saw in Chapter 7, a great amount of timber
was required in the construction of Dark-Age halls (not to mention their surrounding
palisades), though such timber-cutting need not require specialized labor.

　　Another extractive activity was the harvesting of fish and shellfish. Evidence for this
(Alcock, *Economy, Society and Warfare*) is found primarily at hall-sites located in
coastal regions, though it is impossible to determine if fishing constituted a full-time,
specialized economic endeavor. For the populations of the interior areas, the archaeological evidence suggests that the wild game derived from hunting figured more
prominently in their diets than for those who lived in coastal regions, though in all cases
the amount of game and fish was far less important than that of domesticated animals.
In sum, the resources exploited by these peoples were wide and varied (Arnold, *op. cit.*,
p. 18).

4　Arnold, *Archaeology of the Early Anglo-Saxon Kingdoms*, p. 163.

5　Alcock, *Angles, Britons, and Scots*, p. 36.

6　Alcock, *ibid.* However, it is clear that the Anglo-Saxons did not rely as heavily upon

Besides the warriors and clergy, agricultural surpluses supported two levels of craftsmen. The higher level included those specialists – armorers and jewellers in particular – who made the luxury goods that often are described in heroic literature, and who were closely associated with religious centers and secular halls. The lower level of craftsmanship was represented by cottage and village industries, and involved those who were responsible for the production of basic iron tools, textiles, farming implements, leather goods, and other necessary crafts.[7] Trade, whether it took place within a kingdom or between kingdoms, was limited. In broad terms, it is likely that the lower-value, rather mundane goods of the cottage industries were associated with local, internal trade, while the high-value luxury goods produced by the higher order of craftsmen constituted a major component of the long-distance trade that was effected between kingdoms,[8] regardless of whether such trade can be seen as commerce *per se*. Whether it involved high- or low-value goods, while trade did play an increasingly important role in the economy during the latter part of this period, it is safe to say that its overall significance, either in terms of employment or its impact on the general populace, never approached that of farming and animal husbandry.

Within the overall scheme of this primarily agrarian economy, the Dark-Age *comitatus* played an instrumental role both in the exploitation and allocation of the surplus resources generated by the agricultural sector of the economy, and in the distribution and consumption of finished goods, and particularly of the goods associated with the higher level of craftsmen who were drawn to their courts. Due in large part to the ability of his warband to control the non-noble segments of his territory's population, the lord of a *comitatus* was able to obtain (that is, extort) from his subjects a wide variety of goods and services. Of these, the one that must have been the most critical in maintaining the entire *comitatus* structure was the widely-established system of food-renders, which provided the warband's daily sustenance.

Under this system of food-renders,[9] a Dark-Age potentate obtained the foodstuffs and provisions that were required by him, his family, and whatever

cattle as did the Britons and Irish. See Arnold, *Archaeology of the Early Anglo-Saxon Kingdoms*, p. 19.

[7] Alcock, *Economy, Society, and Warfare*, pp. 287–88.

[8] The assumption is based on a fundamental premise, one of several principles derived from social physics – the application of theoretical physics to the realm of human behavior – that are employed in economic geography. In this case, the premise is that all goods and services have a certain geographic range, or spatial distribution, that is based on their value and on the number of intervening opportunities through which that good could also be obtained. The higher the value of an item, or the rarer a commodity, the longer that item or commodity is able to travel.

[9] An essential article on this subject is found in Thomas Charles-Edwards, "Early Medieval Kingships in the British Isles", in *The Origins of Anglo-Saxon Kingdoms*, edited by Steven Bassett, pp. 28–39 (Leicester: Leicester University Press, 1989).

warriors and miscellaneous personnel resided at his hall. The food that was owed under this system represented a basic diet; in the West Saxon laws of Ine there is a three-fold division of the food-renders that were owed: bread (*panis*), an accompaniment to bread (*companaticum* or *pulmentum*), and drink (*potus*).[10] While it is true that a Dark-Age lord could have obtained food (usually in the form of cattle) through raids or tribute, the system of food-renders should be seen as the primary source of foodstuffs for the members of a warband.

Theoretically, two methods could have been used to effect the acquisition of food-renders; either the ruler and his retinue could have the food-renders brought to them, or they could go on a circuit of the ruler's territory to those designated places where the food-renders would be distributed. Given the primitive road network that characterized the rudimentary infrastructures of the Dark-Age kingdoms, the method that a ruler chose to employ should be seen as a direct function of both the size of a ruler's territory and the number of warriors and other attendants who he could count as being a part of his core, permanent retinue. In other words, the larger a ruler's kingdom and standing retinue (his "hearth-companions"), the more likely that he would have had to embark on a circuit to obtain the necessary food-renders. Conversely, for many of the smallest kingdoms, like those whose existence can be surmised from the *Tribal Hidage*, the short distances over which the food-stuffs were to be transported, and the small numbers of warriors who needed to be provisioned, would probably have made a circuit unnecessary. In short, the amount and extent of logistical requirements that inhered in the transportation and distribution of these food-renders in large part determined the procedure that was employed to effect them. Since the processes of amalgamation and consolidation tended to support the creation of fewer, though larger, kingdoms as the period progressed, it is likely that circuits became increasingly important in food-render collection.

Of course, it is unlikely that such a clear dichotomy existed in historical practice. Some combination of the two methods for obtaining food-renders, at least for the larger and more powerful kingdoms, seems the most likely practice, with the ruler having the food-renders from his own holdings brought to him while he resided at his principal court, and the circuit being employed when he was traveling through his kingdom. Geography also played a role in shaping the food-render system. Because of the lack of an effective road system, Dark-Age centers of power, when they can be located with some degree of certainty, were sited at locations with direct access to a body of water. Given the relative ease of water transport by ship, especially in regard to the efficient transport of bulk cargo, the selection of such sites made economic and political sense. Not only would the sites have allowed larger food-renders to be

[10] See *ibid.*, pp. 29–30.

brought to a ruler's principal (or only) seat from longer distances than could be effected by land transport, but such locations would have provided a ruler with an effective avenue of trade for the introduction of luxury goods from other areas of Britain, from Ireland, and even from the continent. Also, the normal food-render procedure would not apply when a king or chieftain was engaged in warfare. In these cases, regardless of the size of a kingdom or the number of warriors that a lord could field, the food-renders would follow the army in a logistics train that evidently was manned by non-noble segments of the population. Beyond the obvious points that warriors have to eat, and that foraging for food is uneconomical in terms of time and manpower, clear evidence for logistics trains is found in Bede's story (*HE* IV.22) about Imma, the Northumbrian *thegn* who attempted to avoid capture by pretending to be a *rusticus* with the logistics train.

On a ruler's circuit itself, it seems that the distribution of food-renders could have been effected at designated royal sites – the king's own halls or buildings that were scattered throughout his kingdom[11] – or it could have been accomplished by the chief men of the realm who could have hosted the royal party at their own monasteries or halls. Bede refers (*HE* III.26) to these royal sites as *villae regales* and relates that Lindisfarne had a long tradition of hosting secular lords and kings, though his comments also indicate that the adequacy of such hospitality was decidedly mixed. Again, Eddius' *Life of Bishop Wilfrid* provides a contemporary picture of a ruler of a large kingdom while on his circuit, or progress, in the late seventh century (c.681). The passage (*Wilfrid* XXXIX) relates that King Ecgfrith and his queen "had been making their circuit with worldly pomp and daily rejoicings and feasts, through cities, fortresses, and villages" (*per civitates et castellas vicosque cotidie gaudentes et epulantes in pompa saeculari circumeuntes*). The worldly pomp and daily rejoicings may refer to the ceremonial practices associated with a lord that were seen in the previous chapter, or they may simply refer to the interaction of the king with the general population. In any event, the feasts must be a reference to the meals that were given to Ecgfrith and his party through the system of food-renders, either those of his own holdings or those associated with the hospitality that was required of his secular lords and religious notables.

While the system of food-renders allowed a Dark-Age lord to sustain both himself and the members of his *comitatus* by the exploitation of the agricultural surpluses of his own territory, the interrelated practices of tribute and booty represented the principal means by which the surpluses of one's neighbors could be exploited. The exploited surpluses involved in tribute and booty could take the form of agricultural products – primarily cattle – or they might

---

[11] The establishment of these royal sites was a characteristic shared by British and Anglo-Saxon kingdoms, but was one that appears to have been lacking among the Irish kingdoms in Ireland. See Charles-Edwards, *ibid.*, p. 39.

comprise finished luxury products (armor, weapons, jewelry) and other forms of tangible wealth, such as gold or silver. Regardless of their precise nature, tribute and booty involved the transfer of wealth from one kingdom or territory to another, while also providing a warband's lord with an invaluable source of material wealth and luxury goods with which he could reward his followers and pay for the services of craftsmen, poets, and any others who were required for the proper functioning of his warband. The enormous importance to the warband of these luxury items and other forms of wealth that were derived from tribute and booty is best reflected in the period's heroic poetry, where these practices formed a central focus of Dark-Age poets, and where their tangible results (swords, armor, and the rest) are described in affectionate detail.

The acquisition of booty was the direct result of a warband's ability to execute successful raids and achieve battle victories, and of the lord's ability to plan, initiate, and lead such operations. The acquisition of booty therefore reflected directly on the martial prowess of a warband and on its lord's abilities; its subsequent distribution to the members of the warband, beyond the obvious function as payment for services rendered, served as a visible symbol of their strength and as a constant reminder of their earlier military victories and exploits. Especially among British and Irish kingdoms, cattle seem to have been a particularly important form of booty, and one whose acquisition was the object of successful lords.[12] Cattle raids may in fact have been initiated for the purpose of establishing tribute from other kingdoms.[13] In one of Taliesin's poems (*PT* V), we find that the evident objective of a raid led by Urien against Manaw Gododdin[14] was to bring back to Rheged "more wealth" (*chwanec anaw*), which would include "eight-score cattle of the same color" (*wyth vgein vn lliw; o loi a biw*). Furthermore, Taliesin specifically employs (*PT* VIII.16) the term "cattle-reaver" (*gwarthegyd*) in praising his chieftain Urien. Similarly, Cadwallon is praised in *Moliant Cadwallon* for preventing his own cattle from being carried off by Edwin's men (either in a raid as booty or in his refusal to hand them over as tribute); the poem relates

---

[12] Among the Irish this is well illustrated both in their literature (e.g., the *Tain Bo Cualinge* and the *Tain Bo Fraich*) and their annals (e.g., *The Annals of Ulster*, s.a. 720/1).

[13] Charles-Edwards, "Early Medieval Kingships", p. 30. This is certainly true in Ireland, "where it was the recognized custom for a new king to establish his position as overlord by means of a *crech rig* or royal cattle raid". For more on this, see P.O. Riain, "The *Crech Rig* or Royal Prey", *Eigse* XV (1973), pp. 24–30.

[14] As Williams has noted (*PT*, pp. 62–3), the identification of this raid with Manaw Gododdin is likely if, in the phrase *Godeu gweith Mynaw*, the word *Godeu* is seen as a gloss to prevent the site of the battle (listed as *Mynaw*) from being confused with the island of Man. Williams sees it as likely that evidence for the battle is seen in both the *Annals of Tigernach* and the *Annals of Ulster*, which record it (for 582 and 583) as *Cath Manand* and *Bellum Manonn* respectively.

(lines 25–26) that Cadwallon's cattle did not bellow before the spearpoints (used as goads) of Edwin's men (*Ac Edwin arnadynt yn dad rwy tuylluras, ny buglant y warthec*). Finally, two references in the *Gododdin* must allude to cattle-raids when it says of the earlier exploits of both Beli and Eithinyn, evidently initiated against the Germanic tribes in the eastern portion of the island (lines 412, 425), that they made frequent attacks "before the cattle-herds of the eastlands" (*rhag dwyrain alafawr*).

These references clearly show that cattle raids sometimes led to battles, which in themselves constituted another important source of booty for a Dark-Age warband. By stripping the dead of the vanquished side (and of their own side, though undoubtedly with more decorum) of their weapons and gear, a victorious lord could reap a huge windfall of already manufactured, and sometimes luxurious goods with which he could both reward and better equip the warriors of his own *comitatus*, thus enhancing their military capabilities and the prospects of other victories. The *Gododdin* sees booty as a product of battle, relating (lines 133, 435, 722) that: "Harshly they attacked, they gathered booty" (*Crai cyrchynt, cynullynt reiawr*); "Cadfannan, with great renown, took booty" (*Cadfannan ryorug clud, clod fawr*); Erf, is called "The angry slayer of a pillaging army" (*Du leiddiad llu herw*). Taliesin also tells (*PT* VIII.12–14) of the many "plundered gifts" (*preidd lydan*) that he himself had managed to seize from Urien's treasures, by using his poetic talents as a weapon (*pren on hytyw vy awen*) and his smile (*glas wen*) as a shield. Taliesin's metaphors reflect the real method by which plunder and booty were acquired – on the field of battle at the point of a sword or spear.

Beowulf is explicit in its description of plundering in battle. In two passages (lines 2922–90, 2472–89), the poem recounts the events of an earlier battle that had taken place between the Geats and Swedes at a site called Ravenswood. After the Swedes had been defeated and their king (Ongentheow) slain by Eofor, the poem tells of the booty that could be derived from battle, saying (lines 2985–7) that "then [one] warrior plundered the other, took from Ongentheow his iron byrnie, his tempered hilted sword, and his helmet also" (*þenden reafode rinc oðerne, nam on Ongenðio irenbyrnan, heard swyrd hilted ond his helm somod*). Similarly, Beowulf is shown (lines 2501–5) as having taken from the body of Dæghrefn, the champion of the Hugas, his breast-ornament after he had slain him.[15] The poem also states (lines 2361–2) that Beowulf managed to carry off "thirty battle-shirts" (*þritig hildegeatwa*), despite being on the losing side of a disastrous battle against the Hetware in Frisia. Lastly, victory in combat allowed the treasure-hoards of Grendel and his mother, and of the dragon, to become the rightful possessions

---

[15] In one of its many understatements, the poem has Beowulf note (lines 2503–4) that "[Dæghrefn] was never able to bring [back] treasures, his breast-ornament, to the Frisian king" (*Nalles he ða frætwe Fres-cyning[e], breost-weorðunge bringan moste*).

of Beowulf, though in the first case, the hero chose not to avail himself of the immense booty that was his for the taking. In the latter case, he enjoyed the well-earned booty only briefly before he died.

As the example of Dæghrefn shows, besides weapons and gear, dead warriors could also be stripped of any jewelry and precious metals that might have adorned them while they were alive, which in turn would be divided among the lord and his retainers. If the *Laws of Hywel Dda* can provide any indication of the division of spoils during this period, then it seems that a lord was expected to distribute two-thirds of these spoils to his retainers, and to keep one-third for his own use.[16]

After being stripped of everything of value, the bodies of the defeated were left as carrion on the battlefield. The *Gododdin* mourns the loss of its warriors, lamenting (line 350) their lack of burial: "Bitter their rest, no mother's son has cared [for them]" (*Gwenwyn eu hadlam, nid mab mam a'u maeth*). The poem's many references to the beasts normally associated with battle – ravens, crows, wolves, and eagles – reinforce the impression that this was the fate of the British warriors at Catraeth, though not before they had wrought a great deal of carnage of their own. Thus, of the abilities of individual warriors to slay their enemies, the *Gododdin* relates (lines 214–15, 330, 971) that: "In the battle of warriors, [Cynon] made food for eagles" (*Yng nghyfarfod gwyr, Bwyd i eryr erysmygai*); "[Caradog] fed wolves by [the actions of] his hand" (*Ef llithiai wyddgwn o'i angad*); "[Gwawrddur] fed black ravens on the wall of a fort" (*Gochorai brain du ar fur caer*). With their deaths, the warriors themselves become food for animals. Thus, of Graid, son of Hoywgi, the poem says (line 272) that "He was food for ravens, raven's gain" (*Bu bwyd i frain, be budd i fran*).[17] Taliesin describes dead Anglo-Saxon warriors as they lay strewn on the battlefield, relating (*PT* X.13–16) "Sleeps the wide host of England, with light in their eyes" (*Kyscit lloegyr llydan nifer a leuuer yn eu llygeit*).

Given the slaughter and carnage that characterized Dark-Age warfare, it seems natural that the *Gododdin* describes the battles themselves (lines 62, 25, 63, 571–2) as "wolf-feast", "raven's feast", "raven's gain", or "feast for birds". In some instances, it is likely that the bodies of the slain were left after having been mutilated by the victors, in addition to being relieved of their weapons and valuables. One of the *Gododdin's* interpolations would imply that this was the fate of Domnall Brecc, king of Dalriada, whose head was cut off by the Strathclyde Britons after the Battle of Strathcarron in 642;

---

16 Page 112 in M. Richards' edition of the laws.

17 Given the distance from British-held territory and the outcome of the battle, the poem's references to burials for some of these warriors (lines 279, 323, 708, 856, 863, 965) should be seen only as a poetic devise used to signify their deaths, and not as a reflection of events at the site after the battle.

the poet saw (line 996) "the head of Domnall Brecc, ravens gnawed at it" (*phen Dyfnwal Frych brain a'i croyn*). Furthermore, according to Bede and the British poem *Canu Cadwallawn*, King Edwin's head was chopped off and carried away, though the two sources differ as to where the head was taken.[18]

The acquisition and distribution of booty had a direct impact on Dark-Age warbands on several different levels. In purely economic terms, such battle-field collections represent a transfer of wealth from one kingdom to another at its most basic level, aptly summarized by the time-worn adage "to the victor the spoils". At least among the Welsh, the lord's subsequent distribution of some two-thirds of this booty to his retainers allowed these weapons and luxury goods to be further distributed among the military élite within the confines of his own territory. In short, booty provided one of several avenues through which the dominant military class achieved their superior access to luxury goods. In social terms, the underlying spoils system of this social practice helped to validate the period's endemic levels of violence and warfare and the élite status of those who engaged in it by providing the greatest material rewards – rewards derived primarily from booty and plunder – to those who fought well. In cultural terms, the acquisition and distribution of booty served to validate the martial, heroic value-system of the period's literature, a value-system that exerted no little influence on the behavior of the warrior-aristocracy.

Related to booty was the widespread and established practice of exacting tribute from neighboring kingdoms and territories. Tribute was established and maintained by military force or threat of force and, like booty and food-renders, provided an important source of wealth for a king or chieftain. Unlike the obligations that were required under the system of food-renders, the payment of tribute provided little benefit to those who were forced to pay it.[19] Furthermore, there is a clear perception on the part of contemporary witnesses – historians and poets alike – that those who were forced to give tribute were

---

[18] The poem asserts that Edwin's head was taken back to Cadwallon's stronghold at Aberffraw, while Bede states that it was taken by the English to York. In any event, it is certain that Edwin's head did not remain with the rest of his body.

   The Celtic peoples in particular appear to have had quite an affinity for collecting heads. This affinity is evidenced early on in Ireland (in the *Tain* and other works) and continues in much later tales that are found among the Welsh (in the tales that comprise the *Mabinogi* or *Mabinogion*). Among the Britons, the practice should be viewed as an effort to display the heads of one's enemies as a trophy, or to save the heads of comrades from being defiled by the enemy. Among the pre-Christian Irish, the heads *per se* were not displayed, but rather some combination of their brains and some type of gypsum, which would be combined to form balls or spheres, which would be displayed with great pride. See Jackson, *The Oldest Irish Tradition* (pp. 19–20) or Herm, *The Celts* (p. 238).

[19] Charles-Edwards notes ("Early Medieval Kingships", p. 29) that the system of food-renders, concentrated primarily within the core of a king's own kingdom, allowed individuals to approach the king in order to petition him or ask some other favor.

seen to be servile to those who received it.[20] Little wonder then, given the reluctance of rulers to pay tribute, that some campaigns were initiated with the express purpose of enforcing the terms of tribute obligations. Stephanus Eddius states unequivocally (*Wilfrid* XX) that the intent of the warfare initiated by Mercia and its allies against Northumbria (673–675) was "not merely on fighting but on compelling them to pay tribute in the spirit of a slave" (*non tam ad bellandum quam ad redigendum sub tributo servili animo*). Further, it can be argued[21] that Ecgfrith's expedition of mounted warriors that he sent against the Pictish tribes (*Wilfrid* XIX) should be seen as a cattle raid whose purpose was to re-establish tribute obligations. Bede (*HE* IV.26) gives essentially the same purpose – the maintainence of overlordship with its inhered tribute obligations – for Ecgfrith's final campaign against the Picts, which ended with his death in battle at Nechtansmere. The situation among British and Irish kingdoms was much the same; their law codes established a king's right to a hosting for the purpose of raiding (for booty) or to enforce tribute obligations.[22] In short, the evidence indicates that these campaigns had little to do with territorial aggrandizement, and should be viewed instead within the context of enforcing tribute obligations.

It seems likely that cattle constituted the most common form of tribute and non-battlefield booty. In part, the preference for cattle must be attributed to the relative ease with which herds of cattle could be moved from one place to another, either as booty or tribute. Essentially, the cattle transported themselves to the desired location with relatively little manpower required to effect the transfer. Furthermore, especially among the Celtic kingdoms in Britain and Ireland, the ownership of cattle appears to have been linked to social status, while also playing an important role in social and economic transactions.[23]

It was a ruler's ability to exploit the surpluses of his own territory and those of other kingdoms – through various combinations of food-renders, booty, and tribute – that allowed him to pay for the services of his warriors, his court poet, and others as well. Such exploitation also provided him with the economic wherewithal to acquire the finished goods of local craftsmen and the

---

20 See *ibid.*, pp. 30–1 and the references cited there. Also, as Charles-Edwards has related (p. 31), the entire social context differed markedly between tribute and food-renders "Whereas cattle tribute was pure tax, ordinary food renders thus retained an honorable link with hospitality."

21 See Charles-Edwards, "Early Medieval Kingship", p. 30.

22 See Alcock, *Angles, Britons, and Scots* (p. 45), and the references cited there in fn. 125.

23 See Alcock, *ibid.*, pp. 45–6, or Charles-Edwards, "Early Medieval Kingships", pp. 30–1. In Ireland, the role of cattle in social contexts (especially its institution of clientship) was vital. On this, see Marilyn Gerriets, "Economy and Society: Clientship According to the Irish Laws", *CMCS* No. 6 (Winter 1983), pp. 43–61. The article provides an introduction (pp. 44–7) on the applicability of modern economic theory to pre-modern societies.

products introduced to his territory by long-distance trade. This ability to exploit available surpluses is reflected in the archaeological record by the high concentration of luxury goods and finely-made weapons at sites and burial grounds normally associated with the warrior-aristocracy. Given the hierarchical nature of the societies involved, such an uneven distribution of luxury goods is to be expected. This inequality is seen early, and is best reflected in pagan grave-goods. Indeed, it can be said with some confidence that:

> The unequal distribution of such prestigious goods found in the cemeteries may be seen as a reflection of heirarchies in early Anglo-Saxon England and how the maintenence of such hierarchies was closely bound up with the consumption of such valuables. We may predict that there will be a close correlation between the strongest position in the most developed hierarchies and the best contacts for obtaining exotic goods.[24]

The existence of this wide and varied array of luxury goods and prestige items is reflected in heroic poetry. In economic terms, the halls and strong-holds of Dark-Age potentates acted as focal points for the manufacture of locally-produced luxury goods and as receiving centers for the products of long-distance wares. Because of the lord's role in the distribution of luxury goods to his retainers, it is likely that these centers also provided for a further dissemination of goods to other sites of lesser political importance and social status. Especially during this period's later years, with its larger kingdoms and more defined social structures, the social importance of the redistribution of luxury goods, and particularly those imported from the continent, would have been significant, allowing the élite of the warrior-class to reinforce their position.[25] In any case, the archaeological and literary evidence indicates that a high standard of living was maintained by members of British and Anglo-Saxon warbands.

Just as locally-produced prestige items are associated with the halls of this period, the products and goods associated with long-distance trade[26] should

---

[24] Arnold, *Archaeology of Early Anglo-Saxon Kingdoms*, p. 69.

[25] This was noted by Arnold, who saw (*ibid.*, p. 82) that "Goods that had been imported from the Continent may then have become powerful social tools by their redistribution through the social system." Such a redistribution among the warrior-class could also have been effected with goods obtained from neighboring regions, again with the likely result that "such goods could then be channelled through the hierarchy thereby rein-forcing the position of the élite" (Arnold, *ibid.*, p. 50).

[26] Of course, the presence of such products and goods may not be the result of commerce. In many instances, the presence of such items at a Dark-Age site could also have been the result of some other process – diplomatic gifts, dowries, booty, or tribute – by which these items were introduced to a particular site. In short, while archaeologists can reveal the types of items that are present at a site, they can only rarely determine the set of circumstances which allowed for their introduction.

be seen as the province (though one they shared with the Church) of the warrior class; their close association with the period's halls and strongholds should surprise no one. Addressed earlier in regard to the transportation requirements of food-renders, the direct access to a navigable body of water that was enjoyed by most defended Dark-Age sites also indicates that economic considerations regarding the introduction and subsequent maintenence of long-distance trade played an important role in their location. In fact, the geographic distribution of the period's defended sites, mostly along the coast or tidal basins, is in marked contrast to that exhibited for the earlier defended sites of the Celtic tribes of pre-Roman Britain. This distribution represents "a major shift in distribution patterns",[27] a shift that may be attributable to the physical transportation requirements associated with long-distance trade, which would include harbors and perhaps some sort of rudimentary port facilities to act as break-of-bulk sites, where imported goods would be transfered from one mode of transport (such as ships) to another (such as carts or wagons).

Long-distance trade involved both raw materials and finished products. Among Anglo-Saxon territories during the sixth and seventh centuries, the commodities involved in this trade – gold coins, amethyst beads, glass vessels, garnet, crystal spheres, and wheel-thrown pottery, along with amber, crystal beads, and ivory rings – appear to have had two distinct patterns of spatial distribution within Britain, based on the geographic origins of these commodities on the Continent and elsewhere.[28] Regardless of their precise source and distribution patterns, the sites at which these imported commodities were used (at varying levels of consumption) were centers of political and economic power;[29] that is, the halls and strongholds of secular lords. Whether such items figured prominently in a primitive exchange system or were employed as "primitive valuables moving horizontally and cementing relationships between major and minor allies",[30] the acquisition and distribution of commodities was controlled by local potentates, who used this control to reinforce their positions within their own warbands.

Even after the introduction of gold and silver coinage during the seventh century, Bede informs us that valuables in the form of ceremonial gifts continued to play an important role in Anglo-Saxon affairs, and makes reference to: fine clothing, a silver mirror, an ivory comb worked in gold (*HE* II.11),

27 Alcock, *Angles, Britons, and Scots*, p. 40.
28 Arnold, *Archaeology of Early Anglo-Saxon Kingdoms*, pp. 51–2. The first five commodities are from the Mediterranean region and are found concentrated in only a few areas, having been introduced to the island primarily through Kentish auspices. The other three items, coming mostly from northwest Europe or the Baltic Sea, are more widely dispersed throughout the Anglo-Saxon kingdoms. For the specific geographic distributions of some of these commodities, see the series of figures in Arnold, *ibid.* (pp. 54, 55, 57, 65, 68).
29 *Ibid.*, p. 67.
30 *Ibid.*, pp. 66–7.

gold coin (*HE* II.12), a horse and trappings (*HE* III.14), "royal treasure and presents exceeding belief" (*HE* III.24), and silver and gold plate (*HE* IV.1). Among the British kingdoms, there is clear evidence for imported commodities from as far away as the Byzantine Empire. In particular, shards of pottery amphorae (post-Roman B-ware) found at British sites indicate an early trade in wine coming from Byzantium, though this came to be replaced with wine imported from the Bordeaux region of Gaul.[31] Other imported pottery, known as E-ware, probably manufactured in western Gaul, has been found at a variety of British strongholds, as have glass shards of various hues, though whether they were introduced as glass vessels or as scrap cullet (to be used in making glass beads and bangles, or as inlays for fine jewelry) continues to be problematic.[32]

The archaeological evidence also shows a clear and close association between Dark-Age centers of power and the production of fine metalwork, whether in the form of jewelry or weapons.[33] The production of this metalwork was accomplished by the higher level of craftsmen, represented by the jeweller and the armorer. Due to the high level of skill and expense that were involved in the manufacture of their goods, it is likely that, like some of their contemporary poets, some proportion of these craftsmen were peripatetic, traveling from court to court as they sought the patronage of chieftains and lords. Whether peripatetic or attached to a specific court, their presence certainly should not be sought at the village level. According to later Welsh tradition, these craftsmen were held in the highest regard by British lords for their services.[34] The *Gododdin* also refers (line 193) to a goldsmith (*eu-*

---

[31] For more on this wine trade, see Alcock, *Angles, Britons, and Scots*, pp. 37–9 and the references cited there.

[32] *Ibid.*, p. 39. See also Alcock, *Economy, Society, and Warfare*, at pp. 287–8.

[33] As Alcock relates (*ibid.*, p. 287): "The sites which produce copious evidence for the manufacture of fine metalwork – crucibles, moulds, scrap bronze and glass, 'sketch pads', and so on – are either monasteries like Nendrum, royal sites like Lagore or Garranes, or forts like Garryduff I, Mote of Mark and Dinas Powys where the total evidence argues for a high social status."

[34] A reference found in *Culhwch and Olwen*, one of four Welsh tales that, along with three stories of Arthurian romance and the *Four Branches of the Mabinogi*, comprise the corpus of tales known collectively as the *Mabinogion*. The *Mabinogion* is found in two manuscripts known as The Red Book of Hergest (*Llyfr Coch Hergest*) and The White Book of Rhydderch (*Llyfr Gwyn Rhydderch*). Though both manuscripts are late, the tale's orthography and other features make its compilation in the tenth century likely. The tale itself may reflect earlier social practices and attitudes. For more, see Gwyn and Thomas Jones, *The Mabinogion* (London: J.M. Dent & Sons, 1949; 1975 reprint).

The tale itself implies that courts welcomed craftsmen, and that they were held in high esteem. Attempting to enter Arthur's hall, Culhwch is told by the porter (pp. 97–8) that "Save the son of a king of a rightful dominion, or a craftsman who brings his craft, none may enter" (*Namyn mab brenhin gvlat teithiavc. neu y gerdavr a dycco y gerd atter y myvn*). The Welsh is found on p. 228 of Evans' and Jones' diplomatic edition of *Llyfr Gwyn Rhydderch* (*The White Book of Rhydderch*).

ruchog). The same can be said of Anglo-Saxon craftsmen who worked in metal, and who were praised for their work in two Old English poems: *The Gifts of Men* and *The Fortunes of Men*.[35] In *Gifts*, the poem (lines 58–60) refers to the one who is "cunning in gold and gems whenever a prince of men bids him to prepare a jewel for his adornment" (*sum searocræftig goldes ond gimma, þonne him gumena weard hateð him to mærþum, maþþum renian*). In *Fortunes*, reference is made (lines 72–3) to the one who is "given wonderful ability in the goldsmith's art" (*Sumum wundorgiefe þurh goldsmiþe gearwad weorþað*).

The wide variety of luxury goods and prestige items that jewellers and armorers produced are attested to in literary and historical sources and are evidenced in the archaeological record. In particular, numerous detailed descriptions in *Beowulf*, in the *Gododdin*, and in Taliesin's poems of finely-wrought and highly-decorated weapons and accoutrements, of sumptuous silken clothing, and of beautifully-made jewelry and other treasures, have been confirmed (with few exceptions)[36] by archaeology. These craftsmen made a wide array of circular and penannular brooches and pins, gold and silver-chased goblets, silver chains, ceremonial hanging bowls, and a variety of ornaments and baubles using gold, tin, silver, bronze, and inlaid glass. Furthermore, at least among the Anglo-Saxons, it appears that helmets, sword hilts, and harness-buckles were often decorated, as may have been shields among the Britons.[37] In any event, this varied corpus of luxury items are better and more fully described elsewhere.[38] What is important to note here is that the work of these highly-skilled craftsmen provided (along with tribute and booty) a lord or chieftain with the material goods – the weapons and treasures – with which he could reward the warriors and poet of his *comitatus*. As such, the products of these craftsmen became an important economic support, along with the proceeds derived from loot and booty and the subsistence provided by food-renders, of the overall *comitatus* structure.

---

[35] Found in Volume III of the Krapp and Dobbie, *Anglo-Saxon Poetic Records*: *The Gifts of Men*, pp. 137–40; *The Fortunes of Men*, pp. 154–6.

[36] The *Gododdin*'s many references to gold torques are anachronistic. What archaeologists have recovered, however, are massive chains of silver, which may have been worn around the neck as torques, or (more likely) worn as chest pendants. While not of gold, these are ornaments that warriors would certainly seek to gain through service to the *comitatus*.

Because of the obvious limitations of archaeology in regard to clothing, the *Gododdin*'s references to rich and sumptuous clothing (lines 648, 693, 901) cannot be validated. However, given the other far-ranging imports that were presented above, it is not unreasonable to assume that such silken cloths could have been introduced for use at these British courts.

[37] Alcock, *Economy, Society, and Warfare*, pp. 246–8.

[38] For a detailed description of the artifacts, see Evans, *The Sutton Hoo Ship Burial*, and the wide-ranging references cited on pp. 40–3 in Alcock, *Angles, Britons, and Scots*.

CHAPTER TEN

SUMMARY AND CONCLUSIONS

Many things have been said regarding the structure of the Dark-Age *comitatus* as an identifiable, distinct, and unique institution, and about the cultural, social, and economic practices and institutions that were employed in its support.

Chapter 2 provided an overview of the historical context in which the rise and subsequent development of the *comitatus* took place and emphasized, insofar as was possible, the *comitatus'* impact on social and political developments in Britain, and on the course of events that transpired on the island from the late-fifth to the mid-eighth century. The processes of political and military amalgamation and consolidation and their impact on state-formation and on the rise and fall of the Dark-Age kingdoms was reviewed. Lastly, the migration of Germanic tribes to Britain – itself a chief contributor to the chaos and turbulence of this period – and the British response to it, were placed within the wider social processes of amalgamation and consolidation.

Chapters 3, 4, and 5 addressed the formal structure of the *comitatus*. Chapter 3 examined the role and the military organization of the *comitatus*, determining that, in an age when varying levels of warfare and other forms of unorganized violence were endemic, the primary role and function of these warbands was the conduct of warfare. Beyond this military role, the structure of the *comitatus* provided the organizational framework for the governments of the numerous British and Anglo-Saxon kingdoms and chiefdoms that were established, and subsequently proliferated, during the late-fifth and early-sixth century. The structure and effectiveness of these governments should of course be seen as rudimentary. The chapter presented a wide range of evidence – theoretical, literary, historical, and archaeological – that showed in no uncertain terms that the number of warriors who comprised these warbands could not have exceeded a few hundred at most, and in most cases numbered far less. The large corpus of archaeological evidence, particularly that for the pagan Anglo-Saxon tribes, is convincing in this regard: the numbers involved in weapon-bearing graves, and the size of the halls and forts of the period, uniformly indicate the small-scale numbers of Dark-Age warbands. Under certain circumstances, these warbands could be combined to form larger, composite forces, an organizational technique that became more frequent as the period progressed, as more powerful kingdoms absorbed their weaker neighbors.

While a warband's purpose and organization seem clear, the overall strategy and tactics that were employed by its lord remain cloudy, shrouded in the fog of heroic battle-scenes or lost among the dimly-lit corridors of Dark-Age politics, where an affront to a lord's dignity could weigh more heavily on questions of state than any set of geopolitical considerations. About the only unequivocal trend that could be noted in this regard was that military campaigns appear to have ranged over increasingly longer distances as the period progressed. Dark-Age weaponry presented an easier task, with the chapter concluding that the spear (used either as a pike or javelin) and shield represented the basic weapon-set of a British or Anglo-Saxon warrior, who was afforded the additional protection of a leather jerkin. Swords were rare and chain-mail rarer still, and both should be viewed as prestige items, whose ownership must have been restricted to the lord and other prominent warriors of a warband. Other weapons (the bow and arrow, the military knife, the axe, etc.), while used in some instances, could not have been a regular piece of equipment for either a British or Anglo-Saxon warrior.

Chapter 4, in its examination of the social structure of the Dark-Age warband, concluded that its members constituted a small warrior-aristocracy that exerted social and political dominance over the other segments of a clearly-graded society. Despite a slight egalitarian trend that was evidenced during the Germanic migrations to the island, the dominance of this military élite became as firmly established as it had been on the continent. It is likely that British social structure was even more restrictive than that of the Germanic tribes, with a newly established warrior-élite merely replacing an earlier, civil one. Though at the apex of a clearly-graded pyramid that marked the class structure of both Anglo-Saxon and British society, whose existence is reflected in law codes, in heroic poetry, and in the archaeological record (and especially in the distribution patterns of luxury goods), the social structure that was found within the *comitatus* itself appears to have comprised several distinct social sub-strata. At the apex of these sub-strata were the lord and the members of his family and/or kinship group. For both Anglo-Saxons and Britons, it was the members of a lord's own kinship group who often filled key positions within the *comitatus*. In the case of smaller warbands, the lord's own kinship group would have comprised the bulk of the warband, while in larger ones they were likely to have formed the lord's personal bodyguard, in addition to their role of filling key positions. The lord made use of the court poet and the common cultural practice involving the distribution of weapons and luxury items to reinforce his pre-eminent social and political position, and perhaps that of his family or kinship group as well, within the warband. Still, despite these hereditary considerations, it appears that the fundamental basis of the Dark-Age warrior-class was service to the warband, rather than non-utilitarian considerations such as birth. Though birth was a factor, the evidence indicates that, by and large, the lord and his family/kinship group retained their positions through service, as did any other warrior of the *comitatus*.

After concluding that the bonds between lord and retainer had become more important than those between kin (whatever the precise nature of those kinship ties), the chapter reviewed the role and duties of the lord in the lord-retainer relationship, which in fact must have usurped many functions that previously had been performed within the context of kinship ties. The evidence showed that, at least within the *comitatus* structure, the lord-retainer relationship was most important, and the one that exerted the greatest influence on the other interrelationships that were found in a warband. Finally, the chapter showed that the principal duties of a Dark-Age lord were related to the conduct of warfare (in which he was expected to take an active part) and the distribution of wealth to his retainers.

Chapter 5 presented the duties and obligations owed by the warriors in the lord-retainer relationship, and their motivations in joining a Dark-Age warband. The chapter examined the extent to which warriors joined warbands from outside their own tribal or territorial areas, and saw that such actions were not unusual. It then reviewed the obligations and duties of a Dark-Age warrior: those that were required in battle, in exile, in the hall, and in the execution of vengeance.

A warrior's duties and obligations in battle were the most important. In battle a warrior was expected to fight and slay the enemies of his lord, to protect his lord to the best of his abilities, and to avenge his death in the event he was slain. A warrior was expected to perform these duties even at the cost of his own life, an expectation that often is seen in the documented and historical actions of these warriors. Regarding the duty to follow one's lord into exile, it was found that the histories and chronicles contain few overt references to such a duty, though this may be attributable to the focus of these sources, which rested on the lords and kings who had been driven into exile rather than on the warriors who shared their plight. The dearth of references also might be the result of the fact that, for the period's chroniclers and historians, the following of one's lord into exile was treated as a given, a statement of fact so obvious that its written declaration would have constituted a waste of parchment. In any case, heroic poetry contains clear references to warriors in exile.

A warrior's other duties and obligations were less arduous and dangerous than risking his life in battle or accompanying his lord into exile. For a warband's older, experienced members, a likely duty entailed their role as counsellors and advisors to their lord in matters relating to the conduct of war or to other policies affecting the entire kingdom. Given that the power of a Dark-Age lord was far from absolute, the inclusion of his more prominent warriors in the decision-making process would have been a prudent course of action on the lord's part, and one that is evidenced in historical and literary sources. For the younger warriors, a likely requirement (or at least an established social practice) stipulated that they reside at their lord's hall. Conversely, regardless of age or social standing in the *comitatus*, it is evident that a warrior often participated with his lord in various activities – feasting, drinking, hunting, boasting, and listening to the songs of the court poet – which were known collectively in heroic poetry as "hall-joys".

Finally, Chapter 5 examined a warrior's duty to exact vengeance on behalf of his lord or his companions. It was seen that vengeance, in both an aristocratic and non-noble context, was a persistent problem that plagued Dark-Age society, and one that could act to perpetuate longstanding and bloody feuds. In fact, the "man-price" accorded to the members of various social classes by Anglo-Saxon and Welsh law codes might be seen as a concerted effort by Dark-Age rulers to limit the scope and duration of feuds, though it is impossible to tell if such codes were effective. While this fundamental obligation appears to have fallen on the kinship group in a non-noble setting, it was seen that within the the warrior class this duty was relegated to other members of the *comitatus*. However, vengeance could be effected through kinship ties as well as the bonds of the warband. It is evident that vengeance was pervasive – called the "world-wide custom" in *Beowulf* – and should be viewed as a factor that regularly influenced the behavior and decisions of warriors and kings alike.

Chapters 6, 7, 8, and 9 presented the supporting cultural, social, and economic institutions that acted to stengthen and maintain the *comitatus* structure. Chapter 6 examined the role of the court poet and his poetry in this regard. The chapter saw that the advent of the court poet was an early development, and one common to both Celt and German. The evidence indicated that poets were attached to a specific court, or that their bardic activities were peripatetic, allowing them to offer their poetic services to more than one lord during the course of a career.

Whether peripatetic or not, once established at the court of a Dark-Age lord or chieftain, the poet's functions were comprised of those specific duties that served to maintain the pre-eminent social and political position of his patron (and perhaps that of his family and kinship group) within his warband. In particular, the poet's role of supporting his lord revolved around two tasks: his recitation of the lord's genealogy, and the composition and recitation of panegyric poetry, whose praises seem to have been directed primarily toward the lord. For these services, lords rewarded their poets with social honors and material riches.

The influence exerted by a Dark-Age *bardd* or *scop* was not restricted to a lord or his family because the poet praised other warriors of the *comitatus* as well. More importantly, the martial, heroic ideals of his poetry allowed the poet to both propagate and validate the entire value-system of the ruling élite. Whether panegyric or narrative, the poetry of the *bardd* and *scop* provided a model of behavior, a set of expectations, for the warrior class of Dark-Age

Britain. Heroic poetry consistently praised those attributes of lord and retainer alike that would have acted to strengthen the warband, while condemning those behaviors that would have had a detrimental effect on the *comitatus*. In particular, these poets exhibited a steadfast support of the duties and obligations of the lord-retainer relationship.

Chapter 7 examined the Dark-Age hall. For warriors, the hall provided a focal point – in a physical, intellectual and emotional sense – around which their lives were centered. Many of the scenes in heroic poetry take place within the confines of the hall as the poets offer their view of life and customs within the shelter of its walls. Poets used the hall as a powerful symbol that represented both the health of the warband to which it gave protection and shelter and the proper functioning of a *comitatus*. Conversely, Anglo-Saxon and, to a lesser extent, British poets employed the concepts of the "ruined hall" and "anti-hall" to represent either the destruction of a warband or as a literary juxtaposition to reinforce the proper values and functioning of a warband. While the centrality of the hall in the existence of warriors is best seen in heroic poetry, its importance also is seen in Bede and other sources.

Chapter 7 also saw that the physical layout and construction of Dark-Age halls would have assisted in promoting a sense of fellowship and communal well-being that was essential to a warband. Open in design, containing few interior partitions, their walls adorned with shields and weapons of war, Dark-Age halls provided an open stage on which most of the activities of the lord, his warriors, and the poet were performed for all to see. The close association of these activities with the structure in which they were conducted is reflected in the name – "hall-joys" – given to them in heroic poetry. The feasts and drinking at mead-benches, the distribution of wealth and gifts from the lord's seat, the boasting by warriors of deeds to be done in service to lord and warband, and the praises of the court poet – were activities that were performed within the physical confines of the hall in the full view of the entire warband. These hall-joys, by their bonding effects on a warband's members, gave strength to the *comitatus*. Thus, both the concept of the hall and the hall itself was a vital social and cultural support for the Dark-Age *comitatus*.

Chapter 8 presented the other social and cultural practices, common to both native and invader, that supported the structure of the warband in an institutional sense. The chapter showed that the concept of mead was a fundamental one among the Britons and Anglo-Saxons, representing the fulfillment of the entire set of duties and obligations that comprised the lord-retainer relationship. While evidenced in all the period's heroic literature, the concept of mead in this role is best shown in the *Gododdin*. The chapter also demonstrated that the distribution of wealth – primarily in the form of weapons, horses, and other treasure – by the lord to his warriors was an important support for both the lord and his warband. The chapter saw that this distribution of wealth, beyond its obvious effect of strengthening the bonds between a lord and his men, also would have had the effect of reinforcing the lord's political and social position within his own warband. That the lord's distribution of wealth to his followers was a vital one perhaps is reflected best by the Anglo-Saxon term (found only in poetry) for the lord's seat, the *gifstol*. The longstanding practices of fosterage (initiated among allies) and hostage-taking (effected between enemies or potential enemies) were other practices that supported the *comitatus*.

After placing these warbands within the context of the agrarian economies over which they presided, Chapter 9 presented those economic practices – food-renders, tribute and booty, and the role of craftsmen – that played a vital role in supporting Dark-Age warbands. It was seen that food-renders played the most vital (though unheralded) role in sustaining warriors in their day-to-day existence. However, while food-renders provided warriors with the basics of life, tribute and booty provided the wherewithal – in the form of weapons, jewelry, and other prestige and luxury items – with which the lord could reward his retainers for their service. These goods often are described in great detail by the court poets, and the lords who were able to seize booty and exact tribute from their neighbors had little trouble attracting warriors to their service. Finally, the chapter examined the role of specialized craftsmen, whether peripatetic or not, in the manufacture of prestige items and goods, and concluded that the courts of Dark-Age kingdoms acted as centers of distribution of these items, based upon the archaeological evidence.

The written sources that derive from this period – both historical and literary – portray the concept of the *comitatus* in remarkably similar terms. It is clear that the image of the warband was a fundamental one, and one that found frequent expression in our Dark-Age sources. Further, through its presentation of a wide, diverse array of evidence regarding the formal structure of the *comitatus* and the social, cultural, and economic practices that supported the warband as an institution, it might be advanced that the *comitatus* was a viable institution of Britain's Dark-Age kingdoms, though the exact manner and extent to which the image of the *comitatus* manifested itself in the historical record at any specific time or place must remain unknown.

THE DATING OF HEROIC POETRY

This appendix justifies the study's use of heroic poetry as a contemporary source for Dark-Age Britain. It does so by providing a brief, and admittedly cursory, overview of some of the major arguments that have been used to advance early dates for *Beowulf*, the *Gododdin*, and the historical poems of Taliesin. It is not meant to be a definitive and comprehensive work on the dating and oral-formulaic nature of these poems, but rather a brief introduction. In fact, the arguments presented here are among other arguments and topics which are addressed in far greater detail in my forthcoming book, *The Heroic Poetry of Dark-Age Britain: An Introduction to Its Dating, Composition, and Use as a Historical Source* (Lanham, Maryland: University Press of America, 1997).[1]

In any case, the focus of the appendix rests primarily on codicological and palaeographical arguments, as well as those of historical linguistics, these being the most valid and reliable indicators for the dating of these poems. Arguments based on historical context, style, or other factors are not presented if they are at variance with the dating schemes that are indicated by the orthography of the texts themselves.

In discussing *Beowulf*, it should be noted at the outset that the composition of the poem occurred much earlier than c.1000, the date given to the poem's only extant manuscript. *Beowulf* is found in the Nowell Codex, the second of two codices that comprise BL MS. Cotton Vitellius A.XV. The Nowell Codex has been dated c.975x1025.[2] Several arguments support the contention that the poem's composition was far earlier than the date of the extant manuscript.

The first of these was advanced by Leonard Boyle in reaction to Kevin

---

[1] For those readers who are interested in a much fuller and detailed analysis of these and other arguments regarding the dating of *Beowulf* in particular, see either Sam Newton, *The Origins of Beowulf and the Pre-Viking Kingdom of East Anglia* (Cambridge: D.S. Brewer, 1993), or R.D. Fulk's seminal *A History of Old English Meter* (addressed below).

[2] Neil R. Ker, *Catalogue of Manuscripts Containing Anglo-Saxon* (Oxford: Oxford University Press, 1957), MS. no. 216. Ker dates the manuscript as 's.X/XI', equivalent to 975–1025.

Keirnan's claim[3] that *Beowulf* represented a composite poem whose composition (as we now have the poem) can be placed during the reign of Cnut. Boyle's article[4] makes it clear the the two scribes responsible for the extant manuscript were copying separate sections of an earlier manuscript that lay before them. Also opposing Kiernan's methodology and conclusions was Katherine O'Brien O'Keefe, whose argument concerned the amount of "pointing" (i.e., visual cues – such as capital letters, periods, and colons – that help a reader to decipher a text) found in the Nowell Codex. The style and amount of pointing used by Scribes A and B are at variance with the practices of their day, but are consistent with works of the third quarter of the tenth century.[5]

Other arguments all point to an early date for *Beowulf*. One of these, proposed by Ashley Crandell Amos, is based on the consistent alliteration of velar *g* and palatal *g* that is clearly demonstrated in *Beowulf*, and which must place an exemplar for the poem before the end of the ninth century.[6] Furthermore, Wrenn's argument, regarding the evident scribal confusion of *d* for *ð* (*eth*), is evidence that the poem existed in written format by the late eighth century, when *ð* was introduced as a letter.[7] Finally, Klaeber advanced the fourth argument, that posited the existence of a written exemplar for the poem c.750, based upon the evidence provided by stray language forms.[8]

More recently, early eighth-century dates have been advanced, in particular by Sam Newton and R.D. Fulk. Among his many arguments for an early East

---

[3] Kevin Kiernan, *Beowulf and the Beowulf Manuscript* (New Brunswick, N. J.: Rutgers University Press, 1981), especially pp. 65–169 and 219–43, as well as his summary article, "The Eleventh-Century Origin of *Beowulf*", in *The Dating of Beowulf*, edited by Colin Chase (Toronto: University of Toronto Press, 1981), pp. 9–21.

[4] Leonard E. Boyle, "The Nowell Codex and the Poem of *Beowulf*", in *The Dating of Beowulf*, edited by Colin Chase (Toronto: University of Toronto Press, 1981), pp. 23–32.

[5] O'Keefe dismisses Kiernan's proposal that *Beowulf* is a composite poem compiled during the reign of Cnut, stating that "it is quite unlikely that the pointing in *Beowulf* represents eleventh-century practice or was added by the scribes who copied this work". *Visible Song: Transitional Literacy in Old English Verse*, Volume 4 in Cambridge Studies in Anglo-Saxon England (Cambridge: Cambridge University Press, 1990), p. 174.

For a lengthy refutation of Kiernan's proposal, see Ashley Crandell Amos's review ("An Eleventh-Century *Beowulf*?", *Review* 4 (1982), pp. 335–345) of Kiernan's book.

[6] Ashley Crandell Amos, *Linguistic Means of Determining the Dates of Old English Literary Texts* (Cambridge, Mass.: The Medieval Academy of America, 1980), at pp.101–2 and p. 167. Essentially, poems in which velar and palatal *g* are found to alliterate are older than those in which there is only a partial alliteration and older still than those in which they do not alliterate at all.

[7] C.L. Wrenn, *Beowulf: With the Finnsburg Fragment* (London: Harrap Ltd., 1973 [third revised edition]), p. 17.

[8] Fr. Klaeber, *Beowulf and the Fight at Finnsburg*, 3rd edn with supplements (Lexington, Mass.: D.C. Heath & Co., 1950), pp. lxxxviii–xc.

142

Anglian provenance for *Beowulf*, Newton has rehabilitated the long-held view that evidence of contraction due to the loss of intervocalic *h*, *j*, and *w* (and especially *h*) is a clear indication for an early eighth-century date for *Beowulf*,[9] a claim that has been supported in part by Fulk in his analysis of the contraction caused by the loss of these letters.[10] Fulk also has proposed that the composition of *Beowulf* must precede c.725 at the very latest,[11] based on the *Beowulf* poet's strict adherence to Kaluza's law; that is, the poem almost invariably preserves the "original quantities in final vowels with Indo-European and Germanic broken intonation: after these vowels were shortened, it was no longer possible to observe Kaluza's law in many words".[12] Finally, recent work – on the *Epinal Glossary* in particular – has shown that Wrenn was overly cautious in his dating for the introduction of the letter *ð*. Recent scholarship has dated this development much earlier than Wrenn had supposed, perhaps even to the final decades of the seventh century.[13]

In any event, to advance a date for a written exemplar that greatly precedes the first decades of the eighth century cannot be accomplished with any degree of certainty, though Anglo-Saxon orthography had developed sufficiently to allow the poem to have been written down as early as the 670s.[14] Though theoretically possible, a written exemplar for *Beowulf* that is earlier than c.685 is unlikely, based on the differences between *Beowulf* and the early glossaries regarding the frequencies of noncontracted words.[15]

A date for the poem's oral composition cannot be advanced, except to state the obvious: that an oral form of the poem is likely to be found somewhere in the seventh century, prior to the first written version of the poem.

Beyond this, a few things can be said. First, because the "author" of *Beowulf* is undoubtedly a Christian, the poem as we have it must be later than 597, the date of Augustine's mission to the island. The degree to which Christianity is evidenced in the poem itself, however, has been a matter of some debate. In this matter, the study concurs with Cherniss' assessment that "*Beowulf* appears to be a Christianized heroic poem, in which the Christianity

---

9 Newton, *The Origins of Beowulf*, p. 13.
10 R.D. Fulk, Chapter 2 ("Contraction"), in his *A History of Old English Meter* (Philadelphia: University of Pennsylvania Press, 1992). In fact, in regard to contraction, Fulk saw the loss only of intervocalic *h* as a reliable basis for any proposed chronology of Anglo-Saxon texts.
11 *Ibid.*, pp. 389–90, based on the shortening of *æ*. The date 725 would apply only if the poem were written by a Mercian or someone from the southern kingdoms. A date c.825 would apply if the poem had Northumbrian origins, which Fulk thought unlikely. His reasons for a Mercian origin are found *ibid.*, pp. 390–91.
12 *Ibid.*, p. 389.
13 Malcolm Parkes, "Palaeographical Commentary", in *The Epinal, Erfurt, Wurden, and Corups Glossaries*, edited by B. Bischoff (Copenhagen: Rosenkilde and Bagger, 1988).
14 Dumville, "The Uses of Evidence", p. 120.
15 Fulk, *Old English Meter*, pp. 380–81.

is pervasive but superficial".[16] Further, the study agrees with Stevick's assertion that the poem acquired its Christian trappings during the process of being sung by one or more converted poets.[17] Over the course of several generations, this Christian material became incorporated into the overall poem with varying degrees of intensity and success, depending on the part of the narrative in question. A likely explanation for the uneven incorporation of this Christian material and for the poem's other discrepancies is Foley's proposal that *Beowulf* is probably a "song amalgam", a joining together of two or more songs,[18] that may have aided in its oral presentation.[19] Because of the poem's general unity and the essentially uniform densities of formulas and formulaic expressions that are found in the poem's various parts, it seems evident that this process of amalgamation was completed before the poem had been written down.

This said, a date for *Beowulf*'s oral composition – in roughly the same form as that found in the manuscript – to somewhere within the period 650x700 can be proposed. This period is late enough to have allowed sufficient time for Christianity to have taken hold among the Germanic peoples. It also is late enough to have allowed several generations of poets the time to mold *Beowulf* (or its component parts) into some semblance of a Christian poem, but early enough to account for its uneven handling of Christian motifs. Furthermore, the proposed dating is late enough to have allowed the various stories within the poem to coalesce into a fine epic by the time it assumed written form during the first quarter of the eighth century, but early enough to still show the various cloths from which its epic tapestry was woven. Of course, this does not preclude later interpolations from entering the text of the poem, such as the well-known "Offa Digression". It is likely that this digression worked its way into the written text as it was being copied during the latter half of the

---

[16] Michael Cherniss, *Ingeld and Christ*, p. 133. For more on the Christianity in the poem, see *ibid.*, pp. 120–150.

[17] Robert D. Stevick, "Christian Elements and the Genesis of *Beowulf*", *Modern Philology* LXI (1963), pp. 79–89.

[18] John Miles Foley, "*Beowulf* and Traditional Narrative Song: The Potential and Limits of Comparison", in *Old English Literature in Context: Ten Essays*, edited by John D. Niles, pp. 117–36 (Cambridge: D.S. Brewer, 1980), at p. 136. He states: "Distinctive tales, such as Beowulf's account of his adventures before Hygelac, for example, may at some point have existed apart from the main frame of the monster-fights. And if we find narrative inconsistences in Homer and *Beowulf*, we should consider the possibility that they arose from an amalgamation of stories which once existed (and perhaps still did exist at the time of the composition of our *Beowulf*) as individual tales."

[19] Even once joined, the separate tales would have retained their usefulness to a poet as units of presentation to be recited before an audience. In no case should we see the poem as being presented in its entirety at one sitting. For more regarding this, see Jeff Opland, "From Horseback to Monastic Cell: The Impact on English Literature of the Introduction of Writing", in *Old English Literature in Context: Ten Essays*, edited by John D. Niles, pp. 30–43 (Cambridge: D.S. Brewer, 1980), at pp. 42–3.

eighth century, perhaps in Mercia during Offa's reign.[20] Finally, due to its oral-formulaic nature,[21] even if the poem's oral composition were assigned the same date as that proposed for its exemplar, the poem nevertheless could contain accurate information about people, events, or material culture that is far older than the initial decades of the eighth century.

This brings us to a brief review of the arguments concerning the dating for the poetry of the *Cynfeirdd*, or "earliest poets". Of the five *Cynfeirdd* whose names are recorded in the *Historia Brittonum*, the poetry of only two of them – Taliesin and Aneirin – has survived. The dating of the corpus of poetry that traditionally has been attributed to these two bards, can be effected with less controversy than that surrounding the *Beowulf* poem, even though the earliest extant manuscripts are much later than the *Beowulf* manuscript.[22] In part this is because, unlike the *Beowulf* poem, the poetry of the *Cynfeirdd* can be assigned more readily to a specific historical period, based upon the persons and events which they purport to describe. Second, the poetry of the *Cynfeirdd* is not considered as "epic" literature, and consequently takes little note of long-dead and distant heroes.[23] Rather, this Welsh poetry is panegyric,

---

[20] The digression has long been seen to be an indication for the poem's dating. For example, see Whitelock's *Audience*, pp. 57–9. For an overview of this subject, see Colin Chase, "Opinions on the Date of *Beowulf*, 1815–1980", in his *The Dating of Beowulf* (Toronto: University of Toronto Press, 1981), pp. 3–8, at p. 5.

[21] There is little doubt that *Beowulf* is an oral-formulaic poem. Though overstated and somewhat dogmatic, an article by Francis P. Magoun was the first to apply Lord and Parry's oral-formulaic theories to Anglo-Saxon literature in his "Oral-Formulaic Character of Anglo-Saxon Narrative Poetry", *Speculum* 28 (July 1953), pp. 446–67. Despite its shortcomings, Magoun's article remains a seminal one for the application of Oral Theory to Anglo-Saxon literature. For further information, see Lord, *Singer of Tales*, pp. 198–99. Much has been written regarding the poem's orality since Magoun's article. For an brief overview of the debate over the oral-formulaic question and its application to *Beowulf*, see Cherniss, *Ingeld and Christ*, pp. 16–17. For a more detailed overview of the debate, see Foley, "The Oral Theory in Context", in *Oral Traditional Literature*, pp. 51–91.

[22] The *Gododdin* poem is found in the *Book of Aneirin* (*Llyfr Aneirin*). The manuscript itself is called South Glamorgan County Library MS. 2.81 (formerly Cardiff MS. I), and is dated c.1250. Taliesin's "historical" poems are found in the *Book of Taliesin* (*Llyfr Taliesin*), along with *The Great Prophecy of Britain* (*Armes Prydein Vawr*) and other poems of the tenth, eleventh, and twelfth centuries. The manuscript is named Peniarth MS. 2 (formerly Hengwrt MS. 17), and has been dated alternatively either to c.1275 or to the second quarter of the fourteenth century.

[23] It is important to note that the poems of the earliest British poets, while heroic in nature, were not works of epic literature. Unlike works of epic literature, the heroes and events that are portrayed in these poems appear to have been contemporary with the composition of the poems themselves. Thomas Jones ("The Early Evolution of the Legend of Arthur", *Nottingham Medieval Studies* VIII (1964), p. 13) has remarked that "there are no references in early Welsh heroic poetry to legendary or unhistorical figures". Similarly, Richard Barber (on p. 24 in his *The Figure of Arthur* (Cambridge: D.S. Brewer, 1972)), remarking on the immediacy and the contemporary nature of the

a type of poetry whose main purpose was to offer praise, and particularly praise for the lord by whom the poet was employed. Furthermore, in yet another contrast to *Beowulf*, references to both the poets and their poetry are provided by other early sources. The review continues with Aneirin's *Gododdin*,[24] before concluding with Taliesin's "historical" poems.

South Glamorgan County Library MS. 2.81 contains two distinct versions of the *Gododdin*, called the A and B texts, which were written down by two scribes who are referred to as Scribes A and B.[25] Each of these two scribes used a different exemplar to copy his portion of the poem. The exemplar for the A-text was far more modern in its orthography than B's exemplar, and has been dated to the twelfth century with little controversy. The B Scribe, using a much older text as his guide, gave up his initial attempt to modernize the archaic words and phrases that he encountered in his exemplar before he was half-way through his task of copying it. These archaic words and phrases, along with the very limited use of *y*, allow a written exemplar of the B-text (perhaps at one or two removes), to be dated on orthographic grounds to the first half of the ninth century.[26]

Gododdin and the poems of Taliesin, has stated that, "there are rich epithets, but no appeals to tradition or to heroes or days gone by".

It is this sense of a contemporary context that separates the poetry of the *Cynfeirdd* from that of later traditions. The keen laments of these bards over the deaths of their lords and friends simply are not found in other literary traditions.

[24] This section of the appendix is indebted to Charles-Edwards' "Authenticity" article, which provides an excellent overview of the controversy, and subsequently uses various and wide-ranging arguments to date the poem and assign its composition to Aneirin. The article should be viewed as a seminal one in this discussion. Like the dating controversy over *Beowulf*, the debate regarding the authenticity of the *Gododdin* has seen a long evolution. For more of an historical perspective on the debate, see A.O.H. Jarman, *The Cynfeirdd: Early Welsh Poets and Poetry* (Cardiff: University of Wales Press, 1981), at pp. 5–13.

[25] While this is the traditional method of viewing the manuscript, it has come under attack by Brendan O'Hehir, Kathryn Klar, and Eve Sweester in "The Components of Cardiff MS. Welsh I, *Llyfr Aneirin*", *BBCS* XXXII (1985), pp. 38–49. Essentially, this group prefers a different labeling system for the poem's major components, while also postulating the existence of a third scribe, who was responsible for part of the material that has been traditionally assigned to Scribe A. For a summary of these contentions, see Kathryn A. Klar, "What are the *Gwarchanau*?", in *Early Welsh Poetry: Studies in the Book of Aneirin* (Aberystwyth: National Library of Wales, 1988), p. 120 at endnote 4.

[26] For a fuller discussion of these arguments, see Charles-Edwards, "Authenticity" (pp. 50–51) and Ifor Williams, "The *Gododdin* Poems", in *The Beginnings of Welsh Poetry: Studies by Sir Ifor Williams*, 2nd edn (Cardiff: University of Wales Press, 1980), p. 46. At least initially, Dumville had reservations about the poem's dating schemes (see his "Palaeographic Considerations in the Dating of Early Welsh Verse", *BBCS* XXVII (1976–1978), p. 249). However, evidently swayed by the arguments of Charles-Edwards and others, Dumville later admitted that, "From the evidence of orthography we can see the possibility that the exemplar of the B-text predated the tenth-century *computus*-fragment . . .". ("Early Welsh Poetry: Problems of Historic-

Recent developments, in large part due to Wendy Davies' work on the charters in the Book of Llandaff (*Liber Landavensis*),[27] have allowed later scholars to assign the *Gododdin* poem to a much earlier period, based upon the evidence of its orthography. In particular, the frequent confusion of *e* and *wy* indicates that a written exemplar existed in the early eighth century or earlier.[28] Furthermore, Koch has claimed that a manuscript exemplar must have existed prior to c.625, based upon the number of cases in the *Gododdin* that have *Uu-* for *gu-*, as well as instances where *ew-* can be seen as "defective modernizations" of pre-Old Welsh *gu-*.[29] Despite some disagreement over the precise date of some of these orthographic features, these examples, and the phonology which their spellings represent, make it clear that the system of orthography that is displayed in the *Gododdin* manuscript was already established by the mid-sixth century.[30] The orthography evidenced in the poem itself, therefore, points to the latter half of the sixth century as the period in which the *Gododdin* was composed.

This contention is supported by linguistic and historical arguments that support and reinforce the orthographic arguments calling for a late sixth-century date for the poem. One of these relates that the full effects of radical syncope and apocope are shown in the poem, evidence that indicates that radical syncope and apocope are completed processes in the *Gododdin*, and that would provide, consequently, an approximate *terminus a quo* (located within the first half of the sixth century) from which to date the poem's oral composition.[31] Furthermore, while the events and heroic milieu portrayed in

---

ity", in *Early Welsh Poetry: Studies in the Book of Aneirin*, edited by Brynley F. Roberts, pp. 1–15 (Aberystwyth: National Library of Wales, 1988), at p. 4.

27 See Davies, "The Orthography of Personal Names in the Charters of *Liber Landavensis*", *BBCS* XXVIII (1978–80), pp. 553–57, and her *The Llandaff Charters* (Aberystwyth: The National Library of Wales, 1979). For the enormous impact of her research on Welsh orthography and its use in dating schemes, see Patrick Sims-Williams, "The Emergence of Old Welsh, Cornish, and Breton Orthography, 600–800: The Evidence of Archaic Old Welsh", *BBCS* XXXVIII (1991), pp. 20–86; especially pp. 29, 45, 71–73, 78–79.

28 John Koch, "When Was Welsh Literature First Written Down?" *Studia Celtica* XX–XXI (1985–86), at pp. 48 and 58, and his "Gleanings From the *Gododdin* and Other Early Welsh Texts", *BBCS* XXXVIII (1991), p. 113.

29 See Koch, "Gleanings", pp. 112–13, and his "Welsh Literature", pp. 54–55. See also Davies, "Orthography", p. 555. It is Koch's contention that *uu-* went out of use by 625 ("Welsh Literature", p. 55), a view that by no means is held universally. See the comments of Sims-Williams ("Archaic Old Welsh", p. 29) for further information on opposition to Koch's views.

30 Sims-Williams, *ibid.*, p. 78.

31 Sweester's protests notwithstanding in her "Line-Structure and *Rhan*-Structure", in *Early Welsh Poetry: Studies in the Book of Aneirin*, edited by Brynley F. Roberts, pp.139–54 (Aberystwyth: National Library of Wales, 1988), p. 140, that the processes of radical syncope and apocope must be viewed as a *fait accompli* by the mid-sixth century. This also would be in accordance both with the orthographic evidence already

the poem could be used to place the poem comfortably almost anywhere within the period 550–640, it is most likely that the poem's oral composition should be assigned to the third quarter of the sixth century. This premise is based upon two observations. First, our earliest external source for the validation of Aneirin and the other *Cynfeirdd*, the *Historia Brittonum*, clearly saw these earliest British poets as belonging to the mid-sixth century, viewing their *floruit* (*HB* 62) as contemporary with the reign of Ida (547–59), the first king of Bernicia. Second, evidence is found in both the *Gododdin* and Taliesin's poems that is at variance with the commonly-held assumption that the battle at Catraeth (which forms the subject matter of the *Gododdin*) must be later than the assasination of Urien, the ruler and warlord of Rheged. Instead, the internal evidence of the poetry itself points to the third quarter of the sixth century as the likely period for the *Gododdin's* composition. In particular, the absence of any reference to the Bernicians in the B-text of the *Gododdin* might indicate an earlier date than those usually proposed for the Catraeth disaster.[32] Conversely, references in Taliesin's poetry to Urien as "lord of Catraeth" make more sense if we assume a date for the events portrayed in the *Gododdin* that is earlier than the expansion of Rheged's military power under Urien.[33]

In summary, we can place the oral composition of the *Gododdin* to within the decades between 550 and 570, and do so with a good deal of confidence. This degree of confidence is based upon various types of evidence – orthographic, linguistic, and historical – all point to these specific decades as the period in which the oral genesis of Aneirin's *Gododdin* should be sought.

Many of these same arguments also can be used to assign a date for the "historical" poems of Taliesin. These poems, along with other material of varying antiquity, are found in the *Book of Taliesin* (*Llyfr Taliesin*), in Peniarth MS. 2 (formerly Hengwrt MS. 17), which has been dated to the period between 1275 and 1350.

presented and with Sims-Williams' contention that the orthographic system of Archaic Old Welsh that is displayed in the *Gododdin* text already was in existence by the mid-sixth century. For Jackson's dating of these processes, see his *Language and History in Early Britain*, §182.

Furthermore, while I agree with Sweester on many points, I do not agree with her contention that the poetry of the *Cynfeirdd* antedated these processes of apocope and syncope (*ibid*. p. 145).

32 See Charles-Edwards, "Authenticity", p. 64 (at fn. 70) for the original observation. See also Dumville, "Problems of Historicity", pp. 2 and 11 (fnn. 15, 16, 19, 20), who used this initial observation to argue for an early date for Catraeth.

33 *PT* II and VII refer to Urien and his warriors as "lord of Catraeth" and "men of Catraeth". The naming of this specific place makes sense as a compliment if the site was the location of a previous British loss, which Urien now held. After all, Urien was the "lord of" a great many places; that he was lord of Catraeth showed that he had evened the score for an earlier British loss.

Ifor Williams has concluded, on the basis of the content and layout of *Llyfr Taliesin* and on the archaic language forms that he claimed were in evidence in the text, that much of *Llyfr Taliesin* was derived from manuscript sources of both the early and very late tenth-century period.[34] Furthermore, Williams regarded the twelve "historical" poems of Taliesin as the authentic works of that sixth-century bard, basing his conclusion on a series of scribal misunderstandings and misspellings of early Welsh language forms, as well as examples of archaic forms which had remained in the manuscript.[35]

Subsequent research by other scholars has tended to validate Williams' claims. Marged Haycock has demonstrated clearly that much of the material in question must have been composed when the accent still remained on the final syllable, a metrical pattern that indicates in no uncertain terms that the composition of these poems must be placed at some time before the accentual stress shifted from the ultima to the penultimate in the early eleventh century.[36] Furthermore, using evidence found in the Llandaff charters, subsequent research has allowed scholars to advance a much earlier date for these poems, based solely upon orthographic considerations, than had been possible when Williams addressed the subject. In particular, John Koch has advanced the position that the poems are of a very early date. He based his position of several arguments. First, he viewed the absence (or at least the rarity) of unique Welsh innovations of Common Brittonic – such as the use of *-awd* as the 3 sing. pret., as well as the distribution of *-is* and *-es* endings when these are based on vowel harmony – as indicative of an early date for this poetry.[37] Secondly, as was shown for the *Gododdin*, Koch viewed the clear existence of anachronistic *cyflythyraeth* (alliteration) in these poems as another indicator

---

[34] Ifor Williams, *The Poems of Taliesin*, English version edited by J.E. Caerwyn Williams (Dublin: Dublin Institute of Advanced Studies, 1975), at pp. xviii–xx and p. xxviii. Specifically, Williams stated that the *Book of Taliesin* "was derived partly from a manuscript written at the beginning of the tenth century, i.e. 900–950, and partly from manuscript material written perhaps c.1000".

[35] For additional information regarding this, see Williams, *PT*, at pp. xvii–xix and scattered throughout the introductory material and the notes sections to the poems in question.

[36] See her "Metrical Models for the Poems of Taliesin" in *Early Welsh Poetry: Studies in the Book of Aneirin*, edited by Brynley F. Roberts, pp. 155–78 (Aberystwyth: National Library of Wales, 1988), at p. 166. For more regarding the dating of the Welsh accent shift, see T. Arwyn Watkins, "The Accent in Old Welsh – Its Quality and Development", *BBCS* XXV (1972), pp. 1–11, who argued for a ninth-century shift. However, it is more likely that the accent shift occurred in the eleventh century (Sims-Williams, "Archaic Old Welsh", p. 79).

[37] For additional information, see John Koch, "The *Cynfeirdd* Poetry and the Language of the Sixth Century", in *Early Welsh Poetry: Studies in the Book of Aneirin*, edited by Brynley F. Roberts, pp. 17–41 (Aberystwyth: National Library of Wales, 1988), at p. 20.

that pointed to their early composition.[38] Finally, Koch has demonstrated that there are a number of cases in *Llyfr Taliesin* which have *Uu-* for Old Welsh *gu-* (or where *eu-* and *ew-* can be seen as "defective modernizations" of pre-Old Welsh *uu-*), which indicated a manuscript exemplar that could be assigned to the first quarter of the seventh century, and perhaps even earlier.[39] As noted earlier, it is this particular aspect of seventh-century orthography, and the sixth-century phonology that its spellings represent, which carries these poems back to the historical milieu of Taliesin and the court of Urien Rheged.

The argument for this late sixth-century date is reinforced by some of the same historical arguments and sources that had been used earlier in the dating of the *Gododdin* corpus of poetry. In fact, these sources allow Taliesin's poetry to be assigned a date within a much narrower historical period than had been the case (at least initially) for Aneirin's *Gododdin*. In large part this is because, in marked contrast to the *Gododdin*, the historical *floruit* for *both* the poet and the subjects of his poetry have been established by the *Historia Brittonum*. Along with Aneirin, Taliesin was one of the five British poets whose *floruit*, according to the text (*HB* 62), was roughly contemporary with the mid-sixth century reign of Ida. Furthermore, while the *Historia Brittonum* was unable to produce any information for the heroes of the *Gododdin*, it plays an important role in establishing a firm *floruit* for the subjects – both friend and foe – of Taliesin's poems. In short, at least for the compiler of the *Historia Brittonum*, the *floruit* of Taliesin, as well as his British lords and their Germanic enemies, could be found in the years that centered on the third quarter of the sixth century. This precise period is substantiated to an even greater degree by the internal evidence provided by the poems themselves.[40]

In summary, we can place the composition of Taliesin's twelve historical poems – addressed to Cynan, Urien, Owain, and Gwallawg – to the third quarter of the sixth century, on the basis of a variety of evidence – orthographic, linguistic, and historical – that uniformly points to these decades as the period in which the events and people portrayed in Taliesin's poems, as well as the oral genesis of the poems themselves, can be found.

---

[38] *Ibid.*, pp. 21–3.

[39] It will be remembered that the same orthographic characteristic held true for the *Gododdin*. For examples from Taliesin's poetry, see Koch, "Gleanings", pp. 112–13.

[40] Beyond the references to Urien and his men as "lord of Catraeth" and "men of Catraeth", the Bernicians under Theodric are specifically named. Further, Taliesin's poem to Cynan Garwyn fits this period. See Jarman (*The Cynfeirdd*, p. 25) for details.

SELECTED BIBLIOGRAPHY

Alcock, Leslie. *Arthur's Britain: History and Archaeology AD 367–634*. London: Alan Lane, The Penguin Press, 1971.

Alcock, Leslie. *Economy, Society, and Warfare Among the Britons and Saxons*. Cardiff: University of Wales Press, 1987.

Alcock, Leslie. *"Gwyr y Gogledd*: An Archaeological Appraisal", *Archaeologia Cambrensis* 132 (1983), pp. 1–18.

Alcock, Leslie. *The Neighbors of the Picts: Angles, Britons and Scots at War and Home*. Glasgow: Dornoch Press, 1993.

Amos, Ashley Crandell. *Linguistic Means of Determining the Dates of Old English Literary Texts*. Cambridge, Mass.: The Medieval Academy of America, 1980.

Amos, Ashley Crandell. Review article ("An Eleventh-Century *Beowulf?*") of *Beowulf and the Beowulf Manuscript*, by Kevin Kiernan. *Review* 4 (1982), pp. 335–45.

Anderson, Alan Orr and Margorie Ogilvie. *Chronicle of the Kings of Scotland* (Version A), in their *Early Sources of Scottish History AD 500 to 1286* (two volumes). Edinburgh: Oliver and Boyd, 1922.

Anderson, A.O. and M.O., edd. and tr. *Adomnan's Life of Columba*. Edinburgh: Edinburgh University Press, 1961.

Anderson, Margorie O. *Kings and Kingship in Early Scotland* (revised edition). Edinburgh: Scottish Academic Press, 1980.

Anstee, J.W., and Biek, L. "A Study of Pattern-Welding", *Medieval Archaeology* 5 (1961), pp. 71–93.

Arnold, C.J. *An Archaeology of the Early Anglo-Saxon Kingdoms*. London: Routledge, 1988.

Arnold, C.J. *Roman Britain to Saxon England: An Archaeological Study*. London: Croom Helm, 1984.

Arnold, C.J. "Stress as a Factor in Social and Economic Change: Anglo-Saxon England in the Seventh Century", in *Ranking, Resource, and Exchange*, edited by A.C. Renfrew and S. Shennan, pp. 124–31. Cambridge: Cambridge University Press, 1982.

Arnold, C.J. "Territories and Leadership: Frameworks for the Study of Emergent Polities in Early Anglo-Saxon Southern England", in *Early Historical Archaeology*, edited by Stephen Driscoll and Margaret Nieke, pp. 111–27. Edinburgh: Edinburgh University Press, 1981.

Arnold, C.J. "Wealth and Social Structure: A Matter of Life and Death", in *Anglo-Saxon Cemeteries*. British Archaeological Reports, No. 82, edited by P. Rahtz, T. Dickenson, and L. Watts, pp. 81–142. Oxford: BAR Publications, 1980.

Attenborough, F.L. *The Laws of the Earliest English Kings*. Cambridge: Cambridge University Press, 1922.

Bannerman, J. *Studies in the History of Dalriada*. Edinburgh: Edinburgh University Press, 1974.

Barber, Richard, ed. *Arthurian Literature VI*. Cambridge, England: D.S. Brewer, 1986.

Barber, Richard. *The Figure of Arthur*. Totowa, New Jersey: Rowman and Littlefield, and Cambridge: D.S. Brewer, 1972.

Bartrum, P.C., ed. *Early Welsh Genealogical Tracts*. Cardiff: University of Wales Press, 1966.

Bassett, Steven, ed. *The Origins of the Anglo-Saxon Kingdoms*. Studies in the Early History of Britain. Leicester: Leicester University Press, 1989.

Bately, Janet, ed. *The Anglo-Saxon Chronicle, MS A*. Vol. 3, The Anglo-Saxon Chronicle: A Collaborative Edition. Cambridge: D.S. Brewer, 1986.

Bessai, Frank. "Comitatus and Exile in Old English Poetry", *Culture* XXV, 1964, pp. 130–44.

Binchy, D.A. *Celtic and Anglo-Saxon Kingship*. Oxford: The Clarendon Press, 1970.

Bischoff, B., *et al.* edd. *The Epinal, Erfurt, Werden and Corups Glossaries*. Copenhagen: Rosenkilde and Bagger, 1988.

Blair, Peter Hunter. *Anglo-Saxon Northumbria*, edited by Michael Lapidge and Pauline Hunter Blair. London: Variorum Reprints, 1984.

Bone, Peter. "The Development of Anglo-Saxon Swords from the Fifth to the Eleventh Century", in *Weapons and Warfare in Anglo-Saxon England*, edited by Sonia Chadwick Hawkes, pp. 63–70. Oxford: Oxford University Committee for Archaeology, 1989.

Bonnell, Victoria E. "The Uses of Theory, Concepts, and Comparison in Historical Sociology", *Comparative Studies in Society and History* (April 1980), pp. 156–73.

Bowra, Cecil Maurice. *Heroic Poetry*. London: MacMillan, 1952.

Boyle, Leonard E. "The Nowell Codex and the Poem of *Beowulf*", in *The Dating of Beowulf*, edited by Colin Chase, pp. 23–31. Toronto: University of Toronto Press, 1981.

Brady, C. "Weapons in *Beowulf*: An Analysis of the Nominal Compounds and an Evaluation of the Poet's Use of Them", *Anglo-Saxon England* 8 (1979), pp. 79–141.

Brandon, Peter, ed. *The South Saxons*. London: Phillimore, 1978.

Bromwich, Rachel and R. Brinley Jones, edd. *Astudiaethau Ar Yr Hengerdd: Studies in Old Welsh Poetry*. Cardiff: University of Wales Press, 1978.

Bromwich, Rachel, ed. *Trioedd Ynys Prydein: The Welsh Triads*. Cardiff: University of Wales Press, 1978.

Brooks, Nicholas. "The Formation of the Mercian Kingdom", in *The Origin of the Anglo-Saxon Kingdoms*, edited by Steven Bassett, pp. 159–70. Leicester: Leicester University Press, 1989.

Bruce-Mitford, Rupert, ed. *Aspects of Anglo-Saxon Archaeology: Sutton Hoo and Other Discoveries*. New York: Harper and Row, 1974.

Bruce-Mitford, Rupert. *The Sutton Hoo Ship-Burial* (3 Volumes). London: Gollancz, Ltd., 1975, 1978, 1983 (Vols 1, 2, and 3).

Campbell, James, Eric John, and Patrick Wormald, edd. *The Anglo-Saxons*. Ithaca, New York: Cornell University Press, 1982.

Campbell, James. "The First Christian Kings", in *The Anglo-Saxons*, edited by Campbell, *et al.*, pp. 45–69. Ithaca, New York: Cornell University Press, 1982.

Carver, Martin. "Kingship and Material Culture in Early Anglo-Saxon East Anglia", in *The Origin of the Anglo-Saxon Kingdoms*, edited by Steven Bassett, pp. 141–58. Leicester: Leicester University Press, 1989.

Chadwick, H.M. and N.K. *The Growth of Literature, Volume I*. Cambridge: Cambridge University Press, 1932.

Chadwick, H.M. *Early Scotland: The Picts, the Scots, and the Welsh of Southern Scotland*. Cambridge: Cambridge University Press, 1949.

Chadwick, H.M. "The Foundation of the Early British Kingdoms", in *Studies in Early British History*, edited by Nora Chadwick, pp. 47–60. Cambridge: Cambridge University Press, 1954.

Chadwick, H.M. *The Heroic Age*. 1967 reprint. Cambridge: Cambridge University Press, 1912.

Chadwick, Nora K., *et al.*, edd. *Studies in Early British History*. Cambridge: Cambridge University Press, 1954.

Chadwick, Nora K., ed. *Celt and Saxon: Studies in the Early British Border*. Cambridge: Cambridge University Press, 1963.

Chadwick, Nora K. *Celtic Britain*. New York: F.A. Praeger, 1963.

Chadwick, Nora K. *The British Heroic Age: The Welsh and the Men of the North*. Cardiff: University of Wales Press, 1976.

Chambers, R.W. *Widsith: A Study in Old English Heroic Legend*. Cambridge: Cambridge University Press, 1912.

Charles-Edwards, Thomas. "Early Medieval Kingships in the British Isles", in *The Origins of Anglo-Saxon Kingdoms*, edited by Steven Bassett, pp. 28–39. Leicester: Leicester University Press, 1989.

Charles-Edwards, T.M. "Bede, the Irish and the Britons", *Celtica* 15 (1983), pp. 42–52.

Charles-Edwards, T.M. "The Authenticity of the *Gododdin*: An Historian's View", in *Astudiaethau Ar Yr Hengerdd: Studies in Old Welsh Poetry*, edited by Rachel Bromwich and R. Brinley Jones, pp. 44–71. Cardiff: University of Wales Press, 1978.

Chase, Colin, ed. *The Dating of Beowulf*. Toronto: University of Toronto Press, 1981.

Chase, Colin. "Opinions on the Date of *Beowulf*", in *The Dating of Beowulf*, edited by Colin Chase, pp. 3–8. Toronto: University of Toronto Press, 1981.

Cherniss, Michael. *Ingeld and Christ: Heroic Concepts and Values in Old English Heroic Poetry*. The Hague: Mouton, 1972.

Chickering, Howell D., ed. and tr. *Beowulf: A Dual-Language Edition*. New York: Anchor Press/Doubleday, 1977.

Clancey, J.P. *The Earliest Welsh Poetry*. London: MacMillan, 1970.

Colgrave, Bertram and R.A.B. Mynors, edd. *Bede's Ecclesiastical History of the English People*, 1992 rpt. Oxford: Oxford University Press, 1969.

Colgrave, Bertram, ed. and tr. *Felix's Life of Saint Guthlac*. Cambridge: Cambridge University Press, 1956.

Colgrave, Bertram. *The Life of Bishop Wilfrid by Eddius Stephanus*. Cambridge: Cambridge University Press, 1927.

Colgrave, Bertram. *Two Lives of Saint Cuthbert*. Cambridge: Cambridge University Press, 1940.

Cramp, Rosemary J. "Anglo-Saxon Settlement", in *Settlement in North Britain: 1000 BC – 1000 AD*. British Archaeological Reports, No. 118. Edited by J.C. Chapman and H.C. Mytum, pp. 263–98. Oxford: BAR Publications, 1983.

Cramp, Rosemary J. "Beowulf and Archaeology", *Medieval Archaeology* I (1957), pp. 57–77.

Cross, J.E. "The Ethic of War in Old English", in *England Before the Conquest: Studies in Primary Sources Presented to Dorothy Whitelock*, edited by Peter Clemoes and Kathleen Hughes, pp. 269–82. Cambridge: Cambridge University Press, 1971.

Davidson, Hilda Ellis. "The Training of Warriors", in *Weapons and Warfare in Anglo-Saxon England*, edited by Sonia Chadwick Hawkes, pp. 11–23. Oxford: Oxford University Committee for Archaeology, 1989.

Davidson, H.R.E. *The Sword in Anglo-Saxon England: Its Archaeology and Literature*. Oxford: The Clarendon Press, 1962; reprinted Woodbridge, England: The Boydell Press, 1994.

Davies, K. Rutherford. *Britons and Saxons: The Chiltern Region 400–700*. London and Chichester: Phillimore, 1982.

Davies, Wendy. *An Early Welsh Microcosm: Studies in the Llandaff Charters*. No. 9, Royal Historical Studies In History Series. London: Royal Historical Society, 1978.

Davies, Wendy. *The Llandaff Charters*. Aberystwyth: The National Library of Wales, 1979.

Davies, Wendy. "The Orthography of Personal Names in the Charters of *Liber Landavensis*", *Bulletin of the Board of Celtic Studies* XXVIII (1978–80), pp. 553–57.

Davies, Wendy. *Wales in the Early Middle Ages*. Studies in the Early History of Britain. Leicester: Leicester University Press, 1982.

Davis, R.H.C. "Did the Anglo-Saxons Have Warhorses?", in *Weapons and Warfare in Anglo-Saxon England*, edited by Sonia Chadwick Hawkes, pp. 141–44. Oxford: Oxford University Committee for Archaeology, 1989.

Denholm-Young, N. *Handwriting in England and Wales*. Cardiff: University of Wales Press, 1954.

Dobbie, E., ed. *The Anglo-Saxon Minor Poems*. Vol. VI, *The Anglo-Saxon Poetic Records: A Collective Edition*. New York: Columbia University Press, 1942.

Doble, G.H., ed. *Lives of the Welsh Saints*. Cardiff: University of Wales Press, 1971.

Drew, Katherine Fisher. *The Burgundian Code*. Philadelphia: University of Pennsylvania Press, 1949.

Drew, Katherine Fisher. *The Laws of the Salian Franks*. Philadelphia: University of Pennsylvania Press, 1991.

Drew, Katherine Fisher. *The Lombard Laws*. Philadelphia: University of Pennsylvania Press, 1973.

Driscoll, Stephen T. and Margaret R. Nieke, edd. *Early Historical Archaeology*. Edinburgh: Edinburgh University Press, 1981.

Driscoll, Stephen T., and Margaret R. Nieke, edd. *Power and Politics in Early Medieval Britain and Ireland*. Edinburgh: Edinburgh University Press, 1988.

Dumville, David, and Kathryn Grabowski, edd. *Chronicles and Annals of Medieval Ireland and Wales: The Clonmacnoise-Group Texts*. Vol. IV, Studies in Celtic History. Woodbridge, England: The Boydell Press, 1984.

Dumville, David. "Beowulf and the Celtic World: The Uses of Evidence", *Traditio* 37 (1982), pp. 109–60.

Dumville, David. "Early Welsh Poetry: Problems of Historicity", in *Early Welsh Poetry: Studies in the Book of Aneirin*, edited by Brynley F. Roberts, pp. 1–15. Aberystwyth: National Library of Wales, 1988.

Dumville, David, ed. *The Historia Brittonum, Volume 3: The Vatican Recension*. Cambridge: D.S. Brewer, 1985.

Dumville, David. "Essex, Middle Anglia, and the Expansion of Mercia", in *The Origin of the Anglo-Saxon Kingdoms*, edited by Steven Bassett, pp. 123–40. Leicester: Leicester University Press, 1989.

Dumville, David. "Kingship, Genealogies, and Regnal Lists", in *Early Medieval Kingship*, edited by P.H. Sawyer and I.N. Wood, pp. 72–104. Leeds: University of Leeds, 1977.

Dumville, David. " 'Nennius' and the *Historia Brittonum*", *Studia Celtica* X/XI (1975–76), pp. 78–95.

Dumville, David. "On the North British Section of the *Historia Brittonum*", *Welsh History Review* 8 (1977), pp. 345–54.

Dumville, David. "Palaeographical Considerations in the Dating of Early Welsh Verse", *Bulletin of the Board of Celtic Studies* XXVII (1976–78), pp. 246–51.

Dumville, David. "Sub-Roman Britain: History and Legend", *History* LXII (1977), pp. 173–92.

Dumville, David. "The Anglian Collection of Royal Genealogies and Regnal Lists", *Anglo-Saxon England* 5 (1976), pp. 23–50.

Dumville, David. "The Historical Value of the *Historia Brittonum*", in *Arthurian Literature VI*, edited by Richard Barber, pp. 1–26. Cambridge, England: D.S. Brewer, 1986.

Dumville, David. "The Origins of Northumbria: Some Aspects of the British Background", in *The Origins of Anglo-Saxon Kingdoms*, edited by Steven Bassett, pp. 213–24. Leicester: Leicester University Press, 1989.

Dumville, David. "The Tribal Hidage: An Introduction to its Texts and their History", in *The Origins of the Anglo-Saxon Kingdoms*, edited by Steven Bassett, pp. 225–230. Leicester: Leicester University Press, 1989.

Dumville, David. "The West Saxon Genealogical Regnal List and the Chronology of Wessex", *Peritia* 4 (1985), pp. 21–66.

Etzioni, Amitai, and Frederick L. Dubow, edd. *Comparative Perspectives: Theories and Trends*. Boston: Little, Brown, and Co., 1970.

Evans, Angela Care. *The Sutton Hoo Ship Burial*. London: British Museum Publications, 1986.

Evans, H. Meurig and W.O. Thomas. *Y Geiriadur Mawr: The Complete Welsh-English English-Welsh Dictionary*, Eleventh Edition. Llandybïe, Wales: Salesbury Press, 1983.

Evans, J. Gwenogvryn, ed. *Facsimile and Text of the Book of Taliesin*. New York: 1978 AMS Reprint, Llanbedrog: 1910.

Evans, J. Gwenogvyrn, and R.M. Jones, edd. *Llyfr Gwyn Rhydderch: Y Chwedlau a'r Rhamantau*. Cardiff: 1973 University of Wales reprint, Llandbedrog, Wales: 1907.

Evans, Stephen S., *The Heroic Poetry of Dark-Age Britain: An Introduction to Its Dating, Composition, and Use as a Historical Source*. Lanham, Maryland: University Press of America, 1997.

Farrell, R.T., ed. *Bede and Anglo-Saxon England*. Oxford: Oxford University Press, 1978.

Finley, M.I. "Myth, Memory, and History", *History and Theory* 4 (1965), pp. 281–302.

Finnegan, Ruth. *Oral Poetry: Its Nature, Significance, and Social Context*. Cambridge: Cambridge University Press, 1977.

Foley, John Miles. "*Beowulf* and Traditional Narrative Song: The Potential and Limits of Comparison", in *Old English Literature in Context: Ten Essays*, edited by John D. Niles, pp. 117–36. Cambridge: D.S. Brewer, 1980.

Foley, John Miles, ed. *Oral Traditional Literature: A Festschrift for Albert Bates Lord*. Columbus, Ohio: Slavica Publishers, 1981.

Foley, John Miles. *Oral-Formulaic Theory and Research: An Introduction and Annotated Bibliography*. Vol. 6, Garland Folklore Bibliographies. New York: Garland Publishing, 1985.

Foley, John Miles. "The Oral Theory in Context", in *Oral Traditional Literature: A Festschrift to Albert Bates Lord*, edited by J.M. Foley, pp. 27–122. Columbus, Ohio: Slavica Publishers, 1981.

Foley, John Miles. *The Theory of Oral Composition: History and Methodology*. Bloomington and Indianapolis: Indiana University Press, 1988.

Ford, Patrick K. *The Poetry of Llywarch Hen*. Los Angeles: University of California Press, 1974.

Frank, Roberta. "Skaldic Verse and the Date of *Beowulf*", in *The Dating of Beowulf*, edited by Colin Chase, pp. 123–39. Toronto: University of Toronto Press, 1981.

Fulk, R.D. *A History of Old English Meter*. Philadelphia: University of Pennsylvania Press, 1992.

Gale, David. "The Seax", in *Weapons and Warfare in Anglo-Saxon England*, edited by Sonia Chadwick Hawkes, pp. 71–84. Oxford: Oxford University Committee for Archaeology, 1989.

Gerriets, Marilyn. "Economy and Society: Clientship According to the Irish Laws", *Cambridge Medieval Celtic Studies* 6 (Winter 1983), pp. 43–61.

Goffart, Walter. "Hetware and Hugas: Datable Anachronisms in *Beowulf*", in *The Dating of Beowulf*, edited by Colin Chase, pp. 83–100. Toronto: University of Toronto Press, 1981.

Goodier, A. "The Formation of Boundaries in Anglo-Saxon England: A Statistical Study", *Medieval Archaeology* 28 (1984), 1–21.

Greenfield, Stanley B. *A Critical History of Old English Literature*. New York: New York University Press, 1965.

Grew, Raymond. "The Case for Comparing Histories", *American Historical Review* 84 (1980), pp. 763–78.

Gruffydd, R. Geraint. "Canu Cadwallon ap Cadfan", in *Astudiaethau ar yr*

Hengerdd: Studies in Old Welsh Poetry, edited by Rachel Bromwich and R. Brinley Jones, pp. 25–45. Cardiff: University of Wales Press, 1978.

Hall, J.R. Clark. *A Concise Anglo-Saxon Dictionary, Fourth Edition*. Medieval Academy Reprints for Teaching 14. Toronto: University of Toronto Press, 1984.

Halsall, Guy. "Anthropology and the Study of Pre-Conquest Warfare and Society", in *Weapons and Warfare in Anglo-Saxon England*, edited by Sonia Chadwick Hawkes, pp. 155–78. Oxford: Oxford University Committee for Archaeology, 1989.

Härke, Heinrich. "Early Saxon Weapon Burials: Frequencies, Distributions, and Weapon Combinations", in *Weapons and Warfare in Anglo-Saxon England*, edited by Sonia Chadwick Hawkes, pp. 49–62. Oxford: Oxford University Committee for Archaeology, 1989.

Hawkes, Sonia Chadwick, ed. *Weapons and Warfare in Anglo-Saxon England*. Oxford: Oxford University Committee for Archaeology, 1989.

Hawkes, Sonia Chadwick. "Weapons and Warfare in Anglo-Saxon England: An Introduction", in *Weapons and Warfare in Anglo-Saxon England*, edited by Sonia Chadwick Hawkes, pp. 1–10. Oxford: Oxford University Committee for Archaeology, 1989.

Haycock, Marged. "Metrical Models for the Book of Taliesin", in *Early Welsh Poetry: Studies in the Book of Aneirin*, edited by Brynley F. Roberts, pp. 155–78. Aberystwyth: National Library of Wales, 1988.

Henige, David P. "Oral Tradition and Chronology", *Journal of African History* XII (1971), pp. 371–89.

Henige, David P. *The Chronology of Oral Tradition: Quest for a Chimera*. Oxford: Oxford University Press, 1974.

Herm, Gerhard. *The Celts: The People Who Came out of the Darkness*. New York: St. Martin's Press, 1975.

Hills, Carla. "The Archaeology of Anglo-Saxon England in the Pagan Period: A Review", *Anglo-Saxon England* 8 (1979), pp. 297–329.

Hines, John. "The Military Contexts of the *adventus Saxonum*: Some Continental Evidence", in *Weapons and Warfare in Anglo-Saxon England*, edited by Sonia Chadwick Hawkes, pp. 25–48. Oxford: Oxford University Committee for Archaeology, 1989.

Hines, John. *The Scandinavian Character of Anglian England in the Pre-Viking Period*, British Archaeological Reports, No. 124. Oxford: BAR Publications, 1984.

Hodges, R. "The Evolution of Gateway Communities: Their Socio-Economic Implications", in *Ranking, Resource, and Exchange*, edited by C. Renfrew and S. Shennan, pp. 117–23. Cambridge: Cambridge University Press, 1982.

Hodges, R. "State Formation and the Role of Trade in Middle Saxon England", in *Social Organization and Settlement*, British Archaeological Reports, No. 47, edited by D. Green, C. Haselgrove, and M. Spriggs, pp. 439–54. Oxford: BAR Publications, 1978.

Holt, Robert T. and John E. Turner, edd. *The Methodology of Comparative Research*. New York: The Free Press, 1970.

Hood, A.B.E., ed. and tr. *St. Patrick: His Writings and Muirchu's Life*. London: Phillimore, 1978.

Hooke, D., ed. *Anglo-Saxon Settlements*. Oxford: Blackwell, 1988.

Hooper, Nicholas. "The Anglo-Saxons at War", in *Weapons and Warfare in Anglo-Saxon England*, edited by Sonia Chadwick Hawkes, pp. 191–202. Oxford: Oxford University Committee for Archaeology, 1989.

Hope-Taylor, B. *Yeavering: An Anglo-British Centre of Early Northumbria*. London: Her Majesty's Stationery Office, 1977.

Hughes, Kathleen. *Celtic Britain in the Early Middle Ages: Studies in Scottish and Welsh Sources*. Vol. II, Studies in Celtic History. Woodbridge, England: The Boydell Press, 1980.

Hume, Katherine. "The Concept of the Hall in Old English Poetry", *Anglo-Saxon England* III (1978), pp. 63–74.

Hutton, Maurice, ed. and tr. *Germania*, Vol. I of *Tacitus: Agricola, Germania, and Dialogus*. 1980 reprint. Loeb Classical Library. Cambridge, Mass.: Harvard University Press, 1914.

Huws, Daniel, ed. *Llyfr Aneirin: A Facsimile*. Aberystwyth: South Glamorgan County Council and The National Library of Wales, 1989.

Irving, Edward B., Jr. *Rereading Beowulf*. Philadelphia: University of Pennsylvania Press, 1989.

Jackson, Kenneth. "Gildas and the Names of the British Princes", *Cambridge Medieval Celtic Studies* 3 (Summer 1982), pp. 30–40.

Jackson, Kenneth. "The 'Gododdin' of Aneirin", *Antiquity* (1939), pp. 25–34.

Jackson, Kenneth. *Language and History in Early Britain*. Edinburgh: Edinburgh University Press, 1953.

Jackson, Kenneth. "On the Northern Section in Nennius", in *Celt and Saxon: Studies in the Early British Border*, edited by N.K. Chadwick, *et al.*, pp. 20–62. Cambridge: Cambridge University Press, 1963.

Jackson, Kenneth. *The Gododdin: The Oldest Scottish Poem*. Edinburgh: Edinburgh University Press, 1969.

Jackson, Kenneth. *The Oldest Irish Tradition: A Window on the Iron Age*. Cambridge: Cambridge University Press, 1964.

Jacobs, Nicholas. "The Old English Heroic Tradition in Light of the Welsh Evidence", *Cambridge Medieval Celtic Studies* 2 (Winter 1981), pp. 9–20.

James, Edward. "The Origins of Barbarian Kingdoms: The Continental Evidence", in *The Origins of Anglo-Saxon Kingdoms*, edited by Steven Bassett, pp. 40–54. Leicester: Leicester University Press, 1989.

Jarman, A.O.H., and G.R. Hughes, edd. *A Guide to Welsh Literature, Volume I*. Swansea: Christopher Davies, 1969.

Jarman, A.O.H. *Aneirin: Y Gododdin, Britain's Oldest Heroic Poem*, Vol. 3 The Welsh Classics. Llandysul, Wales: The Gomer Press, 1988.

Jarman, A.O.H. *Llyfr Du Caerfyrddin (The Black Book of Carmarthen)*. Cardiff: University of Wales Press, 1982.

Jarman, A.O.H. *The Cynfeirdd: Early Welsh Poets and Poetry*. Cardiff: University of Wales Press, 1981.

John, Eric. "*Beowulf* and the Margins of Literacy", *John Rylands University Library of Manchester* 56 (1973–74), pp. 388–422.

Jones, Gwyn, ed., *The Oxford Book of Welsh Verse in English*. Oxford: Oxford University Press, 1977.

Jones, Gwyn and Thomas Jones, edd. and trans. *The Mabinogion*. London: J.M. Dent, 1974 revised edition.

Jones, Thomas. "The Early Evolution of the Legend of Arthur", *Nottingham Medieval Studies* VIII (1964), pp. 3–21.

Ker, Neil R. *Catalogue of Manuscripts Containing Anglo-Saxon*. Oxford: Oxford University Press, 1957.

Kiernan, Kevin S. *Beowulf and the Beowulf Manuscript*. New Brunswick, N.J.: Rutgers University Press, 1981.

Kiernan, Kevin S. "The Eleventh-Century Origin of *Beowulf* and the *Beowulf* Manuscript", in *The Dating of Beowulf*, edited by Colin Chase, pp. 9–21. Toronto: University of Toronto Press, 1981.

King, J.E., ed. and tr. *Historia Ecclesiastica Gentis Anglorum*, in Volumes I and II of *Baedae Opera Historica*. 1979 rpt, Loeb Classical Library. Cambridge, Mass.: Harvard University Press, 1930.

Kinsella, Thomas, ed. and trans. *The Tain*. Dublin: The Dolmen Press, 1969.

Kirby, D.P. "Bede and Northumbrian Chronology", *English Historical Review* LXXVIII (1963), pp. 514–27.

Kirby, D.P. *The Earliest English Kings*. Boston: Unwin Hyman, 1991.

Klaeber, Fr., ed. and tr. *Beowulf and the Fight at Finnsburg*. 3rd edn w/supplements. Lexington, Mass.: D.C. Heath & Co., 1950.

Klar, Kathryn A. "What Are the *Gwarchanau*?", in *Early Welsh Poetry: Studies in the Book of Aneirin*, edited by Brynley F. Roberts, pp. 97–137. Aberystwyth: National Library of Wales, 1988.

Koch, John. "Gleanings From the *Gododdin* and Other Early Welsh Texts", *Bulletin of the Board of Celtic Studies* XXXVIII (1991), pp. 111–18.

Koch, John. "The *Cynfeirdd* Poetry and the Language of the Sixth Century", in *Early Welsh Poetry: Studies in the Book of Aneirin*, edited by Brynley F. Roberts, pp. 17–41. Aberystwyth: National Library of Wales, 1988.

Koch, John. "The Loss of Final Syllables and the Loss of Declension in Brittonic", *Bulletin of the Board of Celtic Studies* XXX (1983), pp. 201–32.

Koch, John. "When Was Welsh Literature First Written Down?", *Studia Celtica* XX–XXI (1985–86), pp. 47–59.

Krapp, G.P. , and E. Dobbie, edd. *The Exeter Book*. Vol. III, *The Anglo-Saxon Poetic Records: A Collective Edition*. New York: Columbia University Press, 1936.

Krapp, G.P., and E. Dobbie, edd. *The Anglo-Saxon Poetic Records: A Collective Edition* (6 Volumes). New York: Columbia University Press, 1931–1953.

Lancaster, L. "Kinship in Anglo-Saxon Society", *British Journal of Sociology* 9 (1958), pp. 230–50 and 359–77.

Lang, Janet, and Barry Ager. "Swords of the Anglo-Saxon and Viking Periods in the British Museum: A Radiographic Study", in *Weapons and Warfare in Anglo-Saxon England*, edited by Sonia Chadwick Hawkes, pp. 85–122. Oxford: Oxford University Committee for Archaeology, 1989.

Lapidge, Michael, and David Dumville, edd. *Gildas: New Approaches*. Vol. 5, Studies in Celtic History. Woodbridge, England: The Boydell Press, 1985.

Lewis, Ceri W. "The Historical Background of Early Welsh Verse", in *A Guide to Welsh Literature, Volume I*. Swansea: Christopher Davies, 1969.

Lord, Albert Bates. "Homer, the Trojan War, and History", *Journal of the Folklore Institute* 8 (1971), pp. 85–92.

Lord, Albert B. *The Singer of Tales*. Cambridge, Mass.: Harvard University Press, 1960.

Loyn, H.R. "Kinship in Anglo-Saxon England", *Anglo-Saxon England* 3 (1974), pp. 197–209.

MacAirt, Sean, and Gearoid MacNiocaill, edd. *The Annals of Ulster*. Dublin: Dublin Institute for Advanced Studies, 1983.

MacAirt, Sean, ed. *The Annals of Insfallen*. Dublin: Dublin Institute for Advanced Studies (DIAS), 1977.

Mac Cana, Proinsias. "Conservation and Innovation in Early Celtic Literature", *Etudes Celtiques* 13 (1972–73).

Mac Cana, Proinsias. Review of *The Gododdin: The Oldest Scottish Poem*, by Kenneth Jackson. *Celtica* IX (1971), pp. 316–29.

Magoun, Francis P. "Oral-Formulaic Character of Anglo-Saxon Narrative Poetry", *Speculum* 28 (1953), pp. 446–67.

Malone, Kemp, ed. *The Nowell Codex: British Museum Cotton Vitellius A.XV Second Manuscript*. No. 12, Early English Manuscripts in Facsimile. Copenhagen: Rosenkilde and Bagger, 1963.

Malone, Kemp, ed. *The Thorkelin Transcripts*. No. 1, Early English Manuscripts in Facsimile. Copenhagen: Rosenkilde and Bagger, 1951.

Matonis, Ann. "Traditions of Panegyric in Welsh Poetry: The Heroic and the Chivalric", *Speculum* 53 (1978), pp. 667–87.

McC. Gatch, Milton. *Loyalties and Traditions: Man and His World in Old English Literature*. New York: Pegasus Press, 1973.

Miller, Molly. "Bede's Use of Gildas", *English Historical Review* CCCLV (1975), pp. 241–61.

Miller, Molly. "Date-Guessing and Dyfed", *Studia Celtica* 12/13 (1977/78), pp. 33–61.

Miller, Molly. "Date-Guessing and Pedigrees", *Studia Celtica* 10/11 (1975/76), pp. 96–109.

Miller, Molly. "Historicity and the Pedigrees of the Northcountrymen", *Bulletin of the Board of Celtic Studies* 26 (1974–76), pp. 255–280.

Millet, M. and S. James. "Excavations at Cowdery's Down, Basingstoke, Hampshire, 1978–81", *Archaeological Journal* 140 (1983), pp. 151–279.

Mitchell, Bruce, ed. *The Battle of Maldon and Other Old English Poems*. New York: St. Martin's Press, 1965.

Moisl, H. "Anglo-Saxon Royal Genealogies and Germanic Oral Tradition", *Journal of Medieval History* 7 (1981), pp. 215–48.

Moisl, Hermann. "A Sixth-century Reference to the British *bardd*", *Bulletin of the Board of Celtic Studies* XXIX, pp. 268–73.

Morgan, Gerald. "The Book of Aneirin and Welsh Manuscript Prickings", *Bulletin of the Board of Celtic Studies* XX (1963), pp. 12–17.

Morris, John, ed. *Nennius: British History and the Welsh Annals*. London: Phillimore, 1980.

Morris, John. *The Age of Arthur: A History of the British Isles from 350–650*. New York: Charles Scribner's Sons, 1973.

Murray, Alexander C. "*Beowulf*, the Danish Invasions, and Royal Genealogy", in *The Dating of Beowulf*, edited by Colin Chase, pp. 101–11. Toronto: University of Toronto Press, 1981.

Murray, Alexander C. *Germanic Kinship Structure: Studies in Law and Society in Antiquity and the Early Middle Ages.* Toronto: Pontifical Institute of Medieval Studies, 1983.

Newton, Sam. *The Origins of Beowulf and the Pre-Viking Kingdom of East Anglia.* Cambridge: D.S. Brewer, 1993.

Niles, John D. *Beowulf: The Poem and Its Traditions.* Cambridge, Mass.: Harvard University Press, 1983.

Niles, John D., ed. *Old English Literature in Context: Ten Essays.* Cambridge: D.S. Brewer, 1980.

Niles, John D. Review of *Beowulf and the Beowulf Manuscript*, by Kevin S. Kiernan. *Speculum* 58 (1983), pp. 76–77.

O'Hehir, Brendan, Kathryn Klar, and Eve Sweester. "The Components of Cardiff MS Welsh I, *Llyfr Aneirin*", *Bulletin of the Board of Celtic Studies* XXXII (1985), pp. 38–49.

O'Hehir, Brendan. "What is the *Gododdin?*", in *Early Welsh Poetry: Studies in the Book of Aneirin*, edited by Brynley F. Roberts, pp. 57–95. Aberystwyth: National Library of Wales, 1988.

O'Keefe, Katherine O'Brien. *Visible Song: Transitional Literacy in Old English Verse.* Cambridge Studies in Anglo-Saxon England, Vol. 4. Cambridge: Cambridge University Press, 1990.

Opland, Jeff. *Anglo-Saxon Oral Poetry: A Study of the Traditions.* New Haven: Yale University Press, 1980.

Opland, Jeff. "From Horseback to Monastic Cell: The Impact on English Literature of the Introduction of Writing", in *Old English Literature in Context: Ten Essays*, edited by John D. Niles, pp. 30–43. Cambridge: D.S. Brewer, 1980.

O'Sullivan, Thomas E. *The De Excidio of Gildas: Its Authenticity and Date.* Volume VIII, Columbia Studies in the Classical Tradition. Leiden: E.J. Brill, 1978.

Owen, Morfydd E. *"Hwn Yw E Gododdin. Aneirin ae Cant"*, in *Astudiaethau Ar Yr Hengerdd: Studies in Old Welsh Poetry*, edited by Rachel Bromwich and R. Brinley Jones, pp. 123–50. Cardiff: University of Wales Press, 1978.

Parkes, Malcolm. "Palaeographical Commentary", in *The Epinal, Erfurt, Werden, and Corups Glossaries*, edited by B. Bischoff *et al.* Copenhagen: Rosenkilde and Bagger, 1988.

Parry, Adam, ed. *The Making of Homeric Verse: The Collected Papers of Milman Parry.* New York: Oxford University Press, 1971.

Pearse, Susan M. *The Kingdom of Dumnonia: Studies in History and Traditions in South Western Britain AD 350–1150.* Padstow: Lodenek Press, 1978.

Radnor, Joan N., ed. *Fragmentary Annals of Ireland.* Dublin: Dublin Institute for Advanced Studies, 1978.

Rahtz, P., T. Dickenson, and L. Watts, edd. *Anglo-Saxon Cemeteries*, British Archaeological Reports, No. 82. Oxford: BAR Publications, 1980.

Riain, P.O. "The *Crech Rig* or Royal Prey", *Eigse* XV (1973), pp. 24–30.

Renfrew, A.C. and S. Shennan, edd. *Ranking, Resource, and Exchange.* Cambridge: Cambridge University Press, 1982.

Richards, M. *The Laws of Hywel Dda*. Cambridge: Cambridge University Press, 1954.

Roberts, Brynley F., ed. *Early Welsh Poetry: Studies in the Book of Aneirin*. Aberystwyth: National Library of Wales, 1988.

Sawyer, P.H., and I.N. Wood, edd. *Early Medieval Kingship*. 1979 reprint. Leeds: University of Leeds, 1977.

Sewell, William H. Jr. "Marc Bloch and the Logic of Comparative History", *History and Theory* VI (1967), pp. 208–18.

Short, Douglas D. *Beowulf Scholarship: An Annotated Bibliography*. Vol. 193, Garland Reference Library of the Humanities. New York: Garland Publishing, 1980.

Sims-Williams, Patrick. "Gildas and the Anglo-Saxons", *Cambridge Medieval Celtic Studies* 6 (Winter 1983), pp. 1–30.

Sims-Williams, Patrick. "Gildas and Venacular Poetry", in *Gildas: New Approaches*, edited by David Dumville and Michael Lapidge, pp. 169–92. Woodbridge, England: The Boydell Press, 1985.

Sims-Williams, Patrick. "The Emergence of Old Welsh, Cornish, and Breton Orthography, 600–800: The Evidence of Archaic Old Welsh", *Bulletin of the Board of Celtic Studies* XXXVIII (1991), pp. 20–86.

Sims-Williams, Patrick. "The Settlement of England in Bede and the *Chronicle*", *Anglo-Saxon England* 12 (1983), pp. 1–41.

Sisam, Kenneth. *Anglo-Saxon Royal Genealogies*. London: The Royal Academy, 1953.

Skocpol, Theda, and Margaret Somers. "The Uses of Comparative History in Macrosocial Inquiry", *Comparative Studies in Society and History* (April 1980), pp. 174–97.

Smyth, Alfred P. *Warlords and Holy Men: Scotland AD 80–1000*. Edinburgh: Edinburgh University Press, 1984.

Stanley, E.G. "The Date of *Beowulf*: Some Doubts and No Conclusions", in *The Dating of Beowulf*, edited by Colin Chase, pp. 197–211. Toronto: University of Toronto Press, 1981.

Stevick, Robert D. "Christian Elements and the Genesis of *Beowulf*", *Modern Philology* LXI (1963), pp. 79–89.

Stokes, Whitley, tr. *The Annals of Tigernach: A Facsimile Reprint. Volume I*. Reprinted from *Revue Celtique*, 1895/96. Felinfach, Wales: Llanerch Publishers, 1993.

Swanton, M.J. *A Corpus of Pagan Anglo-Saxon Spear-Types*, British Archaeological Reports, No. 7. Oxford: BAR Publications, 1974.

Swanton, M.J. *Crisis and Development in Germanic Society 700–800: Beowulf and the Burden of Kingship*. No. 333, Goppingen Arbeiten zur Germanistik. Goppingen: Kummerle Verlag, 1982.

Swanton, M.J. *The Spearheads of the Anglo-Saxon Settlements*. London: The Royal Archaeological Institute, 1973.

Sweester, Eve. "Line-Structure and *Rhan*-Structure: The Metrical Units of the *Gododdin* Corpus", in *Early Welsh Poetry: Studies in the Book of Aneirin*, edited by Brynley F. Roberts, pp. 139–54. Aberystwyth: National Library of Wales, 1988.

Taylor, Simon, ed. *The Anglo-Saxon Chronicle, MS B*. Vol. 4, The Anglo-Saxon Chronicle: A Collaborative Edition. Cambridge: D.S. Brewer, 1983.

Thomas, Graham C.G. "A Verse Attributed to Cadwallon fab Cadfan", *Bulletin of the Board of Celtic Studies* XXXIV (1987), pp. 67–69.

Thompson, E.A. "Gildas and the History of Britain", *Britannia* 10 (1978), pp. 203–26.

Thorpe, L., ed. and tr. *The History of the Franks*, by Gregory of Tours. Harmondsworth, N.J.: Penguin Books, 1974.

Tierney, J.J. "The Celtic Ethnography of Posidonius", *Proceedings of the Royal Irish Academy* LX (1959–60), sec. C, pp. 189–275.

Tolkien, J.R.R. "*Beowulf*: The Monsters and the Critics", in *An Anthology of Beowulf Criticism*, edited by Lewis E. Nicholson, pp. 51–103. Notre Dame, Indiana: University of Notre Dame Press, 1963. Originally published in *Proceedings of the British Academy*, XXII, pp. 245–95.

Vallier, Ivan, ed. *Comparative Methods in Sociology: Essays on Trends and Applications*. Los Angeles: University of California Press, 1971.

Vansina, Jan. *Oral Tradition as History*. London: James Currey, 1985.

Vansina, Jan. *Oral Tradition: A Study in Historical Methodology*. Oxford: Oxford University Press, 1965.

Wallace-Hadrill, J.M. *Bede's Ecclesiastical History of the English People: A Historical Commentary*. Oxford: Oxford University Press, 1988.

Watkins, T. Arwyn. "The Accent in Old Welsh – Its Quality and Development", *Bulletin of the Board of Celtic Studies* XXV (1972), pp. 1–11.

Welch, Martin G. *Early Anglo-Saxon Sussex*, British Archaeological Reports, No. 112. Oxford: BAR Publications, 1983.

Welch, Martin. "The Kingdom of the South Saxons: The Origins", in *The Origin of the Anglo-Saxon Kingdoms*, edited by Steven Bassett, pp. 75–83. Leicester: Leicester University Press, 1989.

Wenham, S.J. "Anatomical Interpretations of Anglo-Saxon Weapon Injuries", in *Weapons and Warfare in Anglo-Saxon England*, edited by Sonia Chadwick Hawkes, pp. 123–40. Oxford: Oxford University Committee for Archaeology, 1989.

Whitelock, Dorothy. *The Audience of Beowulf*. Oxford: The Clarendon Press, 1951.

Whitelock, Dorothy. *English Historical Documents, Volume I*. London: Eyre and Spottiswoode, 1961.

Wiliam, Aled Rhys. *Llyfr Iorwerth: A Critical Text of the Venedotian Code of Medieval Welsh Law*. Cardiff: University of Wales Press, 1960.

Williams, Ifor, ed. *Canu Aneirin*. 4th reprinting. Cardiff: University of Wales Press, 1978.

Williams, Ifor, ed. *Canu Taliesin*. Cardiff: University of Wales Press, 1960.

Williams, Ifor, ed. *Canu Llywarch Hen*. Cardiff: University of Wales Press, 1978.

Williams, Ifor. *The Beginnings of Welsh Poetry: Studies by Sir Ifor Williams*. 2nd edn, edited, revised, and with notes by Rachel Bromwich. Cardiff: University of Wales Press, 1980.

Williams, Ifor. *The Poems of Taliesin*. Volume III, Medieval and Modern Welsh Series. English version of *Canu Taliesin* by J.E. Caerwyn Williams. Dublin: Dublin Institute for Advanced Studies, 1975.

Williams, Stephen J. *A Welsh Grammar*. Cardiff: University of Wales Press, 1980.

Winterbottom, Michael, ed. and tr. *Gildas: The Ruin of Britain and Other Works*. London: Phillimore, 1978.

Wormald, Patrick. "Bede, *Beowulf*, and the Conversion of the Anglo-Saxon Aristocracy", in *Bede and Anglo-Saxon England: Papers in Honour of the 1300th Anniversary of the Birth of Bede*. No. 46, British Archaeological Reports, pp. 32–95. Oxford: BAR Publications, 1978.

Wormald, Patrick. "Bede, the *Bretwaldas*, and the Origins of the *Gens Anglorum*", in *Ideal and Reality in Frankish and Anglo-Saxon Society*, pp. 99–129. Oxford: Oxford University Press, 1983.

Wormald, Patrick, D. Bullough, and R. Collins, edd. *Ideal and Reality in Frankish and Anglo-Saxon Society: Studies Presented to J.M. Wallace-Hadrill*. Oxford: Oxford University Press, 1983.

Wormald, Patrick. "*Lex Scripta* and *Verbum Regis*: Legislation and Germanic Kingship From Euric to Cnut", in *Early Medieval Kingship*, edited by P.H. Sawyer and I.N. Wood, pp. 105–38. (1979 reprint). Leeds: University of Leeds, 1977.

Wrenn, C.L., ed. *Beowulf: With the Finnsburg Fragment*, 3rd edn with revisions and a preface by W.F. Bolton. London: Harrap Ltd., 1973.

Wright, Louise E. "*Merewioingas* and the Dating of *Beowulf*: A Reconsideration", *Nottingham Medieval Studies* 24 (1980), pp. 1–6.

Yorke, Barbara. *Kings and Kingdoms of Early Anglo-Saxon England*. London: B.A. Seaby, 1990.

Zupita, Julius, ed. and tr. *Beowulf: Reproduced in Facsimile From the Unique Manuscript British Museum MS. Cotton Vitellius A.XV*. 2nd edn, edited and with preface by Norman Davis. No. 245, Early English Texts Society Series. Oxford: Oxford University Press, 1959.

INDEX